THE ILLUSTRATED HISTORY ENCYCLOPEDIA
GREAT EMPIRES
& DISCOVERIES

THE ILLUSTRATED HISTORY ENCYCLOPEDIA
GREAT EMPIRES
& DISCOVERIES

Consultant Editor: Dr John Haywood

HERMES HOUSE

CONTENTS
The March of Progress...6

TRIBES, EMPIRES & CIVILIZATIONS
A World of Difference...12

POLITICS, SOCIETY & LEADERSHIP
Keeping Control...72

TRAVEL, CONQUEST & WARFARE
Breaking New Frontiers...132

SCIENCE, CRAFTS & TECHNOLOGY
Making Life Easier...192

The March of Progress

Throughout history, stories abound that chart the rise and fall of great civilizations – their mighty battles, remarkable leaders and outstanding achievements. This book explores the ways in which the most important ancient empires came into being, and how they made their mark on the world. It charts their evolution – from the first small clans, or family groups, to the long-lasting dynasties of such peoples as the ancient Egyptians and Chinese.

Civilizations had to organize their social life and govern themselves, which led them to develop a complex society. They were breeding grounds for new ideas. Discoveries in science and technology helped people understand their world, live a better quality of life and sometimes make war with their neighbours. In times of peace and prosperity, people developed fine crafts to enrich their lives and display their wealth and power.

Which empire lasted longer, Rome or Egypt? When did Viking pirates first attack Ireland and Britain? When was the horse brought over to North America, and how did it change the way Native Americans lived? By looking at the time lines, you can compare the important dates of civilizations, to see how they were alike or different from each other.

MIGHTY PHARAOHS
The Egyptian empire lasted 3,000 years. Thutmose III was a pharaoh in one of its long-lived dynasties, or ruling families.

CONQUERING THE WAVES
The Vikings were expert shipbuilders. They used oak, ash and pine to build swift boats that helped them raid and settle in new lands. Because Viking homelands were mountainous and roads were impractical, they relied on ships as their main method of travel.

The Rise of Civilizations

The first section, *Tribes, Empires & Civilizations*, traces the roots of the world's major societies. In the beginning, humans lived in small family groups called clans. They hunted wild animals, fished the rivers, lakes and seas, and gathered wild plants for food.

Gradually, some people began to settle in one place, farming to raise animals and grow crops. Farmers grew more food than they needed to feed their own families, so they could sell their surplus to other families. With more food to go around, populations grew faster and faster. People began to live in larger

HUNTING FOR SURVIVAL
The first humans lived as hunter-gatherers. They moved from place to place to find supplies of animals to hunt and plants to gather for food.

ALONG THE SILK ROAD
Trading posts like this one in India sprang up along the Silk Road, an ancient 7,000-km trade route that ran across Asia from China to Turkey. Eventually, the trading posts attracted more people, and grew into towns and city-states.

groups, and more organized societies were established.

Tribes and states developed when many people gathered in one place. Sometimes states consisted of just one city; sometimes they were made up of many towns and villages and the areas around them. Ancient Greece had hundreds of city-states – the most famous were Athens and Sparta. The ancient kingdom of Egypt consisted of an entire people or nation.

When a state grows to a vast size by conquering many different peoples and nations, it becomes an empire. The world's first empire was created in *c.*2300BC by Sargon, the ruler of the city of Akkad in Mesopotamia (present-day Iraq). Around 2,000 years ago, Rome grew from a small city-state to a large empire after conquering many areas in Europe and Africa.

In many parts of the world, tribal groups developed from clans.

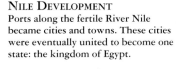

NILE DEVELOPMENT
Ports along the fertile River Nile became cities and towns. These cities were eventually united to become one state: the kingdom of Egypt.

For instance, the Celts were a group of tribes scattered over Europe. The area that is now the United States and Canada was home to many groups such as the Inuit, Cherokee and Hopi. In the 1500s, European countries sent expeditions to the Americas. They set out to conquer native peoples and make them part of their empires.

CAPTURING THE AZTECS
In 1521, Spanish invaders captured the Aztec city of Tenochtitlan in Central America by trickery. From across the ocean in Europe, Spain ruled the Aztec empire.

Getting Organized

With the rise of large communities, people needed to develop rules so that jobs would get done and everyone would know how to behave. In smaller groups, it had been easy for each person to have a say. But now leaders were needed to represent the needs of each group or society. In the section, *Politics, Society & Leadership*, you will learn about the ways that people organized themselves and how their leaders were chosen.

In places where the soil was especially fertile, large communities with thousands of people arose. This was too much work for one person

KEEPING RECORDS
The Assyrians of Mesopotamia were among the first people to use a writing system to keep business records. Here, one scribe writes on a clay tablet; the other, on a leather roll.

to rule alone. So governments were created, with administrators, advisors and record keepers. Mesopotamia was one of the first places where this happened, over 5,000 years ago. Sometimes governments worked under the direction of kings who claimed they were appointed by the gods. Indeed, the pharaohs of Egypt actually believed they became gods when they died. In tribal groups, such as the Celts, leaders called chiefs held great power over their people. At first, the most wealthy and powerful people ended up being the leaders, and ordinary people had little say in what they did. Later, a system called democracy was introduced by the Athenian Greeks. This allowed members of the community to vote on important issues. Today, most Western governments are based on this system.

RESOURCEFUL RULER
The first emperor of ancient China was Qin Shi Huangdi. He united China's seven states into one kingdom in 221BC.

BUILDING A CIVIL SERVICE
In the Han dynasty in China, the emperor Gaozu began a civil service – a group of scholars who ran his political and business affairs.

Travel and Conflict

When people began to search for new land to farm, the need for travel arose. Sometimes people wanted to live in places that were already settled, so they would wage war against the inhabitants. *Travel, Conquest & Warfare* explores the methods of transport and warfare that developed either through need or greed.

Early farmers discovered that large animals could help them plough and work the land, so they trained horses and oxen to do this. These animals could also carry goods great distances, and they became the first method of transport. Later, carts and chariots were developed by the Mesopotamians, who also developed sail boats about 6,000 years ago. Phoenician and Greek sailors spread their shipbuilding skills to the Mediterranean and beyond.

Many civilizations used ships and land transport to conquer new lands. Organized warfare began only after farming became established. People now had possessions, fields and livestock to defend, and they sometimes wanted to seize

CHARIOT WARFARE
The Assyrians and Hittites used chariots in battle, which made it easy for them to conquer enemies who fought on foot.

SAILING THE OPEN SEAS
The Portuguese developed a boat called the caravel, which was sturdy enough to sail on the open seas. They used caravels to explore the African coast in the 1400s.

their neighbours' property. Tribal peoples such as the Celts and the Vikings often raided each other to steal cattle. Chiefs and kings who were good war leaders could become wealthy and powerful.

Defeated peoples were rarely killed. It made more sense to make them into slaves to work for free. Or, they could be left to work on their farms and be made to pay taxes to their new rulers. Ancient empires, such as Rome, China and that of the Incas, worked on these principles.

BOLD AND BRAVE
Boudicca was the wife of the chieftain of the Iceni, a British tribe. She was a fierce warrior who battled against the invading Romans in AD60-1.

Ingenuity and Innovation

In the final section, *Science, Crafts & Technology,* you will see how travel and warfare led to the spread of new inventions and ideas around the world. Both were strongly influenced by technology. In China, fine silk-making became an art, and papermaking and book-printing thrived. With an abundance of gold and silver to hand, the Inca became excellent metalworkers.

POTTERY MAKERS
People of the Indus Valley in India made pottery and other clay objects. This clay model shows a cart transporting heavy pots.

Some inventions completely changed the way people lived – the wheel was one of the biggest breakthroughs. Wheeled vehicles could be used to carry heavy loads over land more efficiently, and later, to move soldiers on the battlefield. The materials used were also important. Metal was tougher and more versatile than stone. The Aztec and Inca peoples of Central and southern America relied on stone and wooden tools. But they were quickly conquered by the Spanish, who used more advanced iron tools and weapons.

PORCELAIN BEAUTY
The Chinese created a fine, delicate type of pottery called porcelain. They decorated the porcelain, such as this urn, with beautiful patterns and glazes.

In the ancient world, science was seen as part of religion and philosophy. Babylonian and Egyptian scientists studied the stars and other natural events to try and understand what the gods wanted them to do. The Maya people of Central America developed a calendar so that they could pay seasonal homage to their gods with sacrifices and offerings. Ancient Greece had more scientists than any other ancient culture. Its great thinkers, such as Pythagoras and Plato, laid the groundwork for science, mathematics and philosophy for centuries to come.

Ancient civilizations are most often remembered for their great achievements. Often, these benefited only the rich and powerful minority. For ordinary people, it was the everyday inventions, such as useful tools with which to work, that made the most difference to their lives.

GOLDEN OPPORTUNITY
The Inca people of South America were expert goldsmiths. This golden funeral mask shows the skill and beauty of their art.

Tribes, Empires & Civilizations

Find out how the great civilizations
and cultures of the past evolved
through time

A World of Difference

Today, we know a lot about people who live in different countries all over the world. We see them on television and read about them in books. But for many groups of people in the past, their tribe was their world. Everyone knew everyone else within the community. The earliest groups probably had no idea of the true extent of the world and what everyday life was like for people outside their tribe.

The members of a Stone Age community go about their everyday life. Groups of families joined forces so that they could protect themselves better. They could also pool their resources and skills to hunt more successfully and improve their way of life. Several communities like this might be part of a tribal culture that shared a similar language, beliefs, traditions and way of living.

Tribal people develop a particular way of doing things – of dressing, cooking and living, of traditions and crafts – based on the raw materials they have. If there is no need to change, or no ideas come from outside to inspire change, tribal societies often continue living in the same way, with the same language and traditions, for centuries.

There's a world of difference in a civilized society. People no longer travel from place to place to hunt for food, as the early tribal societies did, but settle in villages, towns and cities. There are more people, with many different occupations and activities. They have more wealth and an endless catalogue of needs – for homes and other buildings, roads and transport, goods and services. Law and social organization became necessary to help things run smoothly and people

Early settlements grew up near rivers, lakes or the sea. The land had to be fertile to grow crops for food. Fish was a good alternative source of food, and water provided transport as well as irrigation for crops. These communities were the first step towards civilization.

The hanging gardens of Babylon were King Nebuchadnezzar's gift to his wife. They were to make her feel more at home in the desert, as she came from a country of green hills. One mark of a civilization is an upper class with plenty of wealth to spend. Rulers usually liked to create something by which they would be remembered for eternity, such as splendid temples and palaces.

Travellers from the West are received at court in China. During the 1200s, they carried stories of splendid palaces, fabulous wealth and strange customs back to Europe. China was cut off from the rest of the world by mountains, deserts and oceans, and built up its own unique civilization. The Chinese progressed in many areas of technology long before the West, and had quite different ways of behaving.

to live together peacefully. Life in a civilized society is very complicated – this is what makes it so different from tribal life. Solving the problems of such large and complicated communities are a constant spur to human ingenuity and inventiveness. New inventions and ways of making life easier are tested out all the time and the pace of progress and change is fast.

The people of the very first civilizations, such as Mesopotamia and Egypt, had to learn how to solve these problems for themselves. No one else had ever had to face them before. Later civilizations, such as Rome, learned from the older ones as new ideas came in from the outside – from traders, travellers and soldiers. Civilizations became exciting melting pots of many different people, ideas and lifestyles.

In every civilization and culture, there are rulers, thinkers and inventors who have shaped the course of history. King Ashurbanipal (669-631BC) contributed the world's first library to civilization. He was also a ruthless empire-builder. Throughout history, there have been leaders like him, who have wanted to increase their power and conquer other lands. They forced the conquered countries to give them a share of their wealth and resources. Some empire-builders, such as Alexander the Great, allowed conquered nations to keep their national identities. Others, such as the Spanish in Mesoamerica, wiped out the native religion, language, laws and lifestyle almost completely.

The world is very different today. There are fewer subject peoples and no great empires. Countries have their own national identities, but may be made up of many different races and tribes, religions and ways of life. This book presents some of the building blocks of today's world.

The Romans marked the northern limit of their empire in Britain by building Hadrian's Wall from coast to coast. Beyond it lived the barbarians! It was hard work and very expensive for an empire to keep control of the territories it had won.

Life in the Stone Age

THE STONE AGE is the longest period of human history. It began two million years ago, when the ancestors of modern humans started to use stone tools. Gradually, using their tools and their intelligence, they learned how to adapt to different environments. Humans began to move out of Africa, where they had first evolved, and by 10,000BC they had settled on every continent except Antarctica. The Stone Age came to an end when people began to work metals on a large scale.

Stone Age people lived in groups called clans, that were made up of several families, probably closely related to each other. It was safer to live in a clan than as a single family unit, and groups of people could work as a team when hunting or gathering food. As generations passed, the clans grew into bigger, tribal communities. Close family relationships diluted through the generations, but everyone shared the same ancestor. Some communities grew bigger still and split into different tribes that moved to other areas. They kept the same language, beliefs and traditions – they were still part of the same tribal culture. In some tribal cultures, different tribes gathered at certain times of the year, for festivals or meetings. Their lifestyle remained much the same for the rest of the year, though, as hunter-gatherers or simple farmers.

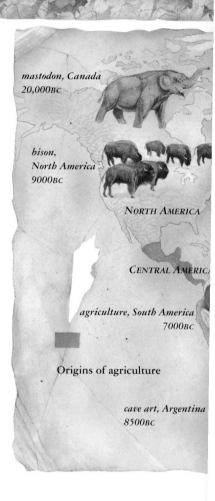

mastodon, Canada
20,000BC

bison,
North America
9000BC

NORTH AMERICA

CENTRAL AMERICA

agriculture, South America
7000BC

Origins of agriculture

cave art, Argentina
8500BC

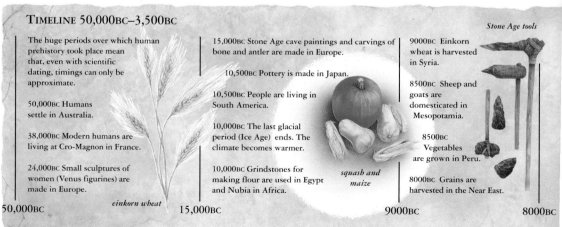

TIMELINE 50,000BC–3,500BC

Stone Age tools

The huge periods over which human prehistory took place mean that, even with scientific dating, timings can only be approximate.

50,000BC Humans settle in Australia.

38,000BC Modern humans are living at Cro-Magnon in France.

24,000BC Small sculptures of women (Venus figurines) are made in Europe.

einkorn wheat

15,000BC Stone Age cave paintings and carvings of bone and antler are made in Europe.

10,500BC Pottery is made in Japan.

10,500BC People are living in South America.

10,000BC The last glacial period (Ice Age) ends. The climate becomes warmer.

10,000BC Grindstones for making flour are used in Egypt and Nubia in Africa.

squash and maize

9000BC Einkorn wheat is harvested in Syria.

8500BC Sheep and goats are domesticated in Mesopotamia.

8500BC Vegetables are grown in Peru.

8000BC Grains are harvested in the Near East.

50,000BC   15,000BC   9000BC   8000BC

EUROPE

ASIA

AFRICA

SOUTH AMERICA

N

AUSTRALIA

migrating reindeer, Russia
15,000BC

clay figurine,
Czech Republic
24,000BC

cave art, France
15,000BC

pottery, Japan
10,500BC

rock art,
Sahara
6000BC

settlement,
Turkey
6,500BC

Peking Man, China
460,0000BC

Homo erectus *skull*,
Java, 120,000BC

Homo habilis *skull, Kenya*
2.5 million years ago

cave art, Namibia
8000BC

indigenous peoples,
Australia
50,000BC

THE STONE AGE WORLD
This map shows places of
importance during the Stone Age.

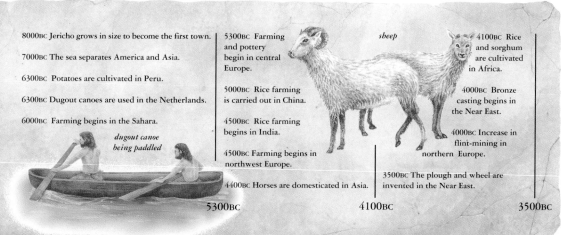

8000BC Jericho grows in size to become the first town.

7000BC The sea separates America and Asia.

6300BC Potatoes are cultivated in Peru.

6300BC Dugout canoes are used in the Netherlands.

6000BC Farming begins in the Sahara.

*dugout canoe
being paddled*

5300BC Farming
and pottery
begin in central
Europe.

5000BC Rice farming
is carried out in China.

4500BC Rice farming
begins in India.

4500BC Farming begins in
northwest Europe.

4400BC Horses are domesticated in Asia.

sheep

4100BC Rice
and sorghum
are cultivated
in Africa.

4000BC Bronze
casting begins in
the Near East.

4000BC Increase in
flint-mining in
northern Europe.

3500BC The plough and wheel are
invented in the Near East.

5300BC

4100BC

3500BC

Mesopotamia's First Empires

SUMERIAN WORSHIPPERS
Statues of a man and woman from Sumer are shown in an act of worship. The Sumerians were some of the earliest people to live in the south of Mesopotamia. They lived in small, independent cities. At the centre of each city was a temple built as the home for the local god. These two Sumerians had statues made of themselves and put in a temple, so that the god could bless them.

MESOPOTAMIA IS THE NAME of an ancient region where some of the world's first cities and empires grew up. Mesopotamia means 'the land between the rivers' – for the country lay between the Tigris and the Euphrates, two mighty rivers that flowed from the highlands of Turkey in the north down to the Gulf. Today, most of it lies in modern Iraq.

The first farmers settled in the low, rolling hills of the north about 9,000 years ago. Here, there was enough rainfall to grow crops and provide pasture for animals. The land in north Mesopotamia became known as Assyria.

The first cities developed about 3,500 years later, mostly in the fertile plains of the south. This area had rivers and marshes which provided water to irrigate crops and reeds to build houses and boats. Fish, dates and other food were easy to find. At first the south was called Sumer. Later it was known as Babylonia.

THE WORK OF GIANTS
Most of what we know about the ancient civilizations of Mesopotamia has come from excavations by archaeologists over the last 150 years. In 1845, the British archaeologist Henry Layard unearthed the remains of a once-magnificent palace in the ancient Assyrian city of Nimrud. He found walls decorated with scenes of battles and hunting, and a statue of a human-headed, winged lion so huge that local people were astonished and thought it had been made by giants.

TIMELINE 7000BC–2100BC

Humans have lived in northern Iraq since the Old Stone Age, when hunter-gatherers lived in caves and rock shelters and made stone tools. Mesopotamian civilization began when people began to settle in villages. They learned how to grow crops and keep animals. Later, city-states grew up, and people developed writing. They became good at building, working metal and making fine jewellery.

painted pottery

7000BC The first villages are established. Edible plants and animals are domesticated, and farming develops. Pottery is made and mud-bricks used for building.

6000BC Use of copper. First mural paintings, temples and seals. Irrigation is used in agriculture to bring water to the fields. Decorated pottery, clay and alabaster figurines. Wide use of brick.

clay figurine

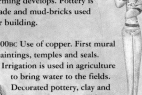

4000BC Larger houses and temples are built. Terracotta sickles and pestles are developed.

3500BC Growth of towns. Development of *writing tablet* the potter's wheel, the plough, the first cylinder seals and writing. Bronze, silver and gold worked. Sculptures are made. Trading systems develop.

3000BC Sumerian civilization begins. City-states and writing develop.

7000BC   4000BC   2700BC

TEMPLES OF THE GODS

The ziggurat of Nanna, the Moon god, rises above the dusty plains of modern Iraq. It was once part of the massive temple complex in the city of Ur. Ziggurats showed how clever the Mesopotamians were at building. They were designed as a link between heaven and earth.

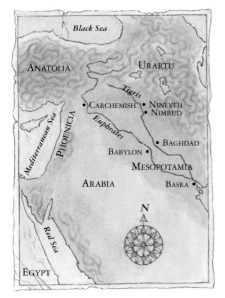

WRITING TABLET

A clay tablet shows an example of some of the earliest writing in the world. The symbols were pressed into a damp clay tablet using a reed pen. The Sumerians originally used writing to keep accounts of goods bought and sold including grain and cattle. Later on, kings used clay tablets as a record of their victories and building activities. Scribes wrote letters, poems and stories about heroes.

POWERFUL NEIGHBOURS

By about 2000BC the Assyrians were trading with Anatolia in the north-west of Mesopotamia. The Assyrians later conquered Phoenician cities in the west and fought Urartu in the north.

Sumerian chariot

2700BC Early Dynastic period. Kings and city administrations rule.

2600BC Royal Standard of Ur made, probably as the sounding box of a lyre.

2500BC Royal Graves of Ur made. Queen Pu-abi and other wealthy individuals buried in tombs with soldiers, musicians and court ladies.

2440BC Inter-state warfare. Kings of Lagash go to war with Umma.

2334BC Sargon of Agade becomes king. He creates the world's first empire, which is maintained by his grandson Naram-sin.

Pu-abi

2200BC The Agade Empire comes to an end. The Gutians, a mountain people, move into Mesopotamia and take some cities.

ziggurat of Ur-nammu

2141BC Gudea takes the throne of Lagash. Ambitious temple-building programme at Girsu.

2112BC Ur-nammu of Ur tries to re-create the Agade Empire. He builds the famous ziggurat of Ur.

2500BC   2200BC   2100BC

MESOPOTAMIA'S FIRST EMPIRES   17

City-states of Mesopotamia

MANY OF THE GREAT EMPIRES in Mesopotamia grew up around small city-states. Each state consisted of a city and the surrounding countryside, and had its own ruler and god. Uruk, in the south, was the first state to become important, in 2,700BC. Its leader was called Gilgamesh and many legends grew up around him.

Around 2300BC, a leader called Sargon conquered all the cities of Mesopotamia and several in neighbouring lands. In doing so, he created the world's first empire. After his dynasty died out in about 2150BC, the kings of Ur, a city further south, tried to re-create Sargon's empire, but with limited success. Ur fell to the Elamites, invaders from a region in the east. About 100 years later, a nomadic people called the Amorites settled in Mesopotamia. They took over the old Sumerian cities, including Babylon, and several of their chiefs became kings.

Meanwhile, in the north, the Assyrian Empire had grown from its beginnings in the city-state of Ashur. It developed slowly over 2,000 years and reached a glorious peak around 645BC. The Empire crumbled when the Babylonians conquered their key cities in 612BC. Babylonia became the most powerful empire in the known world until it was conquered by the Persian king, Cyrus, in 539BC.

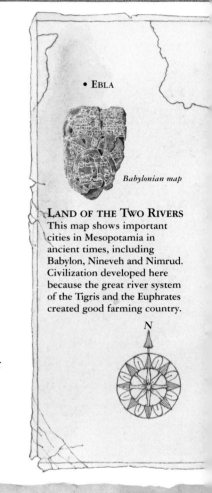

• EBLA

Babylonian map

LAND OF THE TWO RIVERS
This map shows important cities in Mesopotamia in ancient times, including Babylon, Nineveh and Nimrud. Civilization developed here because the great river system of the Tigris and the Euphrates created good farming country.

N

TIMELINE 2100BC–1000BC

2004BC Ibbi-Sin, last king of Ur, is captured by Elamites and taken to Susa.

2000BC Fall of the Sumerian Empire. Amorites interrupt trade routes. Ur attacked by Elamites and falls. Assyria becomes independent and establishes trading network in Anatolia.

1900BC Amorite chiefs take over some cities as rulers.

1792BC Hammurabi, an Amorite ruler, becomes King of Babylon.

1787BC King Hammurabi conquers the major southern city of Isin.

1763BC Hammurabi conquers the city of Larsa.

1761BC Hammurabi conquers Mari and Eshnunna and may have conquered the city of Ashur.

1740BC Expansion of the Hittite kingdom in Anatolia, based on the city of Hattusas.

Hammurabi

scorpion man

1595BC The Hittite king, Mursulis, conquers North Syria. Marching further south, he destroys Babylon but does not take over the city.

1570BC The Kassites, a foreign dynasty, begin a 400-year rule of peace and prosperity. King Kurigalzu builds a new capital city, naming it after himself. Babylon becomes a world power on an equal level with the kingdom of Egypt.

2100BC   1790BC   1600BC   1500BC

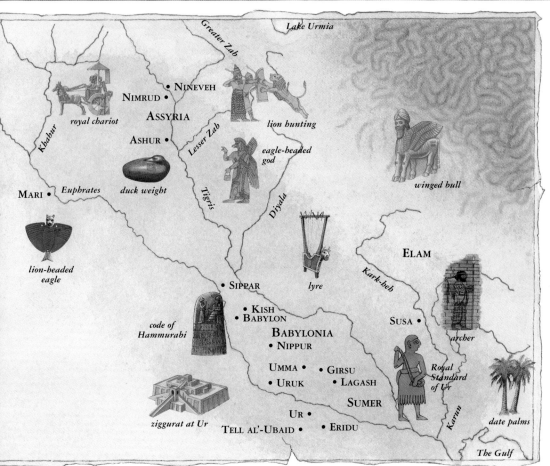

Lake Urmia

Greater Zab

NINEVEH

NIMRUD

royal chariot

ASSYRIA

lion hunting

ASHUR

Lesser Zab

eagle-headed
god

Khabur

MARI

Euphrates

duck weight

Tigris

Diyala

winged bull

lion-headed
eagle

SIPPAR

lyre

ELAM

Kark-heh

code of
Hammurabi

KISH
BABYLON

BABYLONIA

NIPPUR

SUSA

archer

UMMA

GIRSU

URUK

LAGASH

Royal
Standard
of Ur

SUMER

UR

ziggurat at Ur

TELL AL'-UBAID

ERIDU

Karun

date palms

The Gulf

1500BC Mitanni, a new state, develops
to the north of Mesopotamia. The people
speak Hurrian and fight in
two-wheeled horse-drawn chariots.
They conquer land from the
Mediterranean to the Zagros Mountains,
including Assyria.

1365BC Ashur-uballit becomes King
of Assyria and gains Assyria's
independence from Mitanni.

1150BC The Elamites conquer Babylon,
ending Kassite rule.

copper peg

1124BC Nebuchadnezzar I, a later
king of Babylon, successfully
attacks Elam, bringing back
large amounts of booty,
including the statue of Marduk, the
Babylonian god the Elamites had
captured some years earlier.

1115BC Tiglath-pileser I becomes
king. He expands Assyrian territory
and captures Babylon and other
southern cities. First written
account of the royal hunt in
Mesopotamia. Egyptian king sends
him a crocodile as a present.

1076BC Death of Tiglath-pileser I.

1050BC Ashurnasirpal I becomes king.

1000BC Assyria is attacked by
many enemies, including the
nomadic Aramaeans,who
move into Mesopotamia
and take over large
areas. Their language,
Aramaic, and its
alphabetic script gradually
replace Akkadian and
cuneiform.

Humbaba the giant

1130BC

1100BC

1000BC

Mesopotamian Leaders

THE NAMES OF Mesopotamian kings are known because their victories and other achievements were recorded on clay tablets and palace wall decorations. The kings wanted to be sure that the gods knew that they had ruled well, and that their names would be remembered for ever. The names of ordinary soldiers and temple builders, the craftsmen who created the beautiful painted wall reliefs and the authors of the sagas and histories were not written down. Some astrologers, army commanders and state officials are known by name because they wrote letters to the king.

EANNATUM OF LAGASH (C. 2440BC)
Eannatum was king of Lagash, a city in southern Sumer. He was a great warrior and temple-builder. His victory over the nearby state of Umma was recorded on the Vulture Stela, a limestone carving that showed vultures pecking at the bodies of dead soldiers.

SARGON OF AGADE (2334–2279BC)
King Sargon created the world's first empire by conquering all the cities of Sumer, Mari and Ebla. He founded the city of Agade, no trace of which has yet been found. A legend tells that when Sargon was a baby, his mother put him in a reed basket and set him afloat on a river. The man who found him trained him to be a gardener. When Sargon grew up, it was believed that he had been favoured by the goddess Ishtar, and he became cup-bearer to the king of Kish (a city north of Babylon).

ENHEDUANNA(C. 2250BC)
The daughter of King Sargon of Agade is one of the few women in Mesopotamian history whose name is known. She held the important post of high priestess to the Moon-god at Ur. Her hymn to the god made her the first known woman author.

TIMELINE 1000BC–500BC

911BC Adad-nirari becomes king. Assyria recovers some of her lost possessions and defeats the Aramaeans and Babylon.

879BC Ashurnasirpal II holds a banquet to celebrate the opening of his new palace at Nimrud.

858BC Shalmaneser III, son of Ashurnasirpal II, spends most of his 34-year reign at war, campaigning in Syria, Phoenicia, Urartu and the Zagros Mountains.

stela of Ashurnasirpal II

c. 845BC Palace of Balawat built.

744BC Tiglath-pileser III brings more territory under direct Assyrian control. Deportation of conquered peoples begins.

721BC Sargon II decorates his palace at Khorsabad with carved reliefs showing his battle victories.

black obelisk of Shalmaneser III

705BC Sennacherib becomes king of Assyria.

701BC Sennacherib attacks Hezekiah in Jerusalem.

694BC Ashur-nadin-shumi rules Babylon on behalf of his father Sennacherib. He is captured by the Elamites and taken to Susa. In revenge, Sennacherib burns Babylon to the ground.

Balawat Gates

1000BC   850BC   710BC   690BC

ASHURBANIPAL OF ASSYRIA (669–631BC)

A great warrior king, Ashurbanipal reigned at the peak of the Assyrian Empire. He fought successfully against the Elamites, Babylonians and Arabs, and even made Egypt part of his empire for a time. But his greatest gift to civilization was the vast library in his palaces at Nineveh. Here, over 25,000 clay tablets were collected, including letters, legends and astronomical, mathematical and medical works.

HAMMURABI (1792–1750BC)

King Hammurabi of Babylon collected 282 laws concerning family, town and business life and had them recorded on a black stela, a large stone. Other rulers had made laws, but his is the largest collection to survive. The picture shows Shamash, god of justice, giving Hammurabi the symbols of kingship. Towards the end of his reign, he went to war and created an empire, but it did not last long after his death.

NEBUCHADNEZZAR II (604–562BC)

As crown prince, Nebuchadnezzar fought at the side of his father, the king of Babylon, and brought the Assyrian Empire to an end. Under his own rule, the Babylonians conquered neighbouring countries, such as Palestine, and became one of the world powers of the time. Nebuchadnezzar built great fortifying walls around the city of Babylon and a magnificent ziggurat. He features in the Bible, as the king who captured Jerusalem and sent the people of Judah into captivity.

681BC Sennacherib killed by his eldest son. His youngest son Esarhaddon becomes king.

671BC Esarhaddon invades Egypt and captures the Egyptian capital of Memphis.

668BC Ashurbanipal becomes king of Assyria. His brother Shamash-shum-ukin becomes king of Babylon.

Tiglath-pileser III

664BC Ashurbanipal invades Egypt and destroys the southern city of Thebes.

663 or 653BC Ashurbanipal begins a series of wars with Elam.

652BC Rebellion of Shamash-shum-ukin. Ashurbanipal invades Babylonia.

648BC Ashurbanipal lays siege to Babylon, which suffers starvation.

631BC Death of Ashurbanipal. Assyrian Empire begins to collapse.

Nimrud

612BC Babylonians attack and burn the Assyrian cities of Nimrud and Nineveh.

605BC Assyrians defeated by the Babylonians at the battle of Carchemish.

Ashurbanipal on horseback

604BC Nebuchadnezzar II becomes King of Babylon, and Babylon becomes a world power.

562BC Nebuchadnezzar II dies.

539BC Cyrus of Persia takes Babylon.

663BC

620BC

500BC

Egyptian Civilization

EGYPT IS A COUNTRY at the crossroads of Africa, Europe and Asia. If you could step back in time 5,000 years, you would discover an amazing civilization – the kingdom of the ancient Egyptians.

Most of Egypt is made up of baking hot, sandy deserts. These are crossed by the river Nile as it snakes its way north to the Mediterranean Sea. Every year, floods cover the banks of the Nile with mud.

HORUS' EYE
This symbol can be seen on many Egyptian artefacts. It is the eye of the god Horus.

Plants grow well in this rich soil, and 8,000 years ago farmers were planting crops here. Wealth from farming led to trade and to the building of towns. By 3100BC a great kingdom had grown up in Egypt, ruled by royal families.

Ancient Egypt existed for over 3,000 years. Pyramids, temples and artefacts survive from this period to show us what life was like in the land of the pharaohs.

AMAZING DISCOVERIES
In 1922, the English archaeologist Howard Carter made an amazing discovery. He found the tomb of the young pharaoh Tutankhamun. No single find in Egypt has ever provided as much evidence as the discovery of this well-preserved tomb.

LIFE BY THE NILE
Tomb paintings show us how people lived in ancient Egypt. Here people water and harvest their crops, using water from the river Nile.

TIMELINE 6000BC–2100BC

The kingdom of ancient Egypt existed for over 3,000 years. The most successful periods of Egyptian power are known as the Old Kingdom, the Middle Kingdom and the New Kingdom.

boat with sail

sheep

wheat

c.6000BC
Early people settle in the fertile Nile valley. They grow wheat and barley.

c.5020–4500BC
Craftsmen make clay figures and fine pottery vessels. They also carve objects from ivory.

c.4800BC
Farmers keep sheep, cattle and other animals.

c.4000BC
Sails are used on Egyptian ships for the first time.

| 6000BC | 5500BC | 5000BC | 4500BC | 4000BC |

THE KINGDOM OF EGYPT

This map of Egypt today shows where there were important cities and sites in ancient times. The ancient Egyptians lived mostly along the banks of the river Nile and in the green, fertile lands of the delta. Through the ages, the Egyptians built many imposing temples in honour of their gods and mysterious tombs to house their dead. Most of these temples and tombs were built close to the major cities of Memphis and Thebes.

SURVIVORS OF THE DESERT

The face of the great pharaoh Ramesses II stares out at us. Huge statues of Ramesses were part of a temple cut from the rock face at Abu Simbel in 1269BC. During the 1960s the statues had to be raised because a new dam at Aswan turned this part of the Nile into a lake. Temples, tombs and statues such as those at Abu Simbel have survived for thousands of years in the dry desert heat. More recently, many monuments have started to disintegrate because of the polluted air around modern cities such as Luxor.

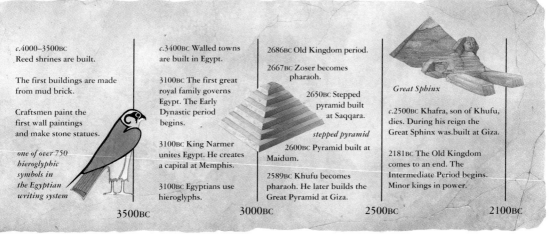

c.4000–3500BC Reed shrines are built.

The first buildings are made from mud brick.

Craftsmen paint the first wall paintings and make stone statues.

one of over 750 hieroglyphic symbols in the Egyptian writing system

c.3400BC Walled towns are built in Egypt.

3100BC The first great royal family governs Egypt. The Early Dynastic period begins.

3100BC King Narmer unites Egypt. He creates a capital at Memphis.

3100BC Egyptians use hieroglyphs.

2686BC Old Kingdom period.

2667BC Zoser becomes pharaoh.

2650BC Stepped pyramid built at Saqqara.

stepped pyramid

2600BC Pyramid built at Maidum.

2589BC Khufu becomes pharaoh. He later builds the Great Pyramid at Giza.

Great Sphinx

c.2500BC Khafra, son of Khufu, dies. During his reign the Great Sphinx was built at Giza.

2181BC The Old Kingdom comes to an end. The Intermediate Period begins. Minor kings in power.

3500BC   3000BC   2500BC   2100BC

The Kingdom on the Nile

AFRICA

THE STORY OF ANCIENT EGYPT began about 8,000 years ago when farmers started to plant crops and raise animals in the Nile Valley. By about 3400BC the Egyptians were building walled towns. Soon after that the northern part of the country (Lower Egypt) was united with the lands upstream (Upper Egypt) to form one country under a single king. The capital of this new kingdom was established at Memphis.

The first great period of Egyptian civilization is called the Old Kingdom. It lasted from 2686BC to 2181BC. This was when the pharaohs built great pyramids, the massive tombs that still stand in the desert today.

During the Middle Kingdom (2050–1786BC), the capital was moved south, to the city of Thebes. The Egyptians gained control of Nubia and extended the area of land being farmed. Despite this period of success, the rule of the royal families of ancient Egypt was sometimes interrupted by disorder. In 1663BC, control of the country fell into foreign hands. The Hyksos, a group of Asian settlers, ruled Egypt for almost 100 years.

In 1567BC the Hyksos were overthrown by the princes of Thebes. The Thebans established the New Kingdom. This was the highest point of Egyptian civilization. Traders and soldiers travelled into Africa, Asia and the lands of the Mediterranean. However, by 525BC, the might of the Egyptians was coming to an end and Egypt became part of the Persian Empire. In 332BC rule passed to the Greeks. Finally, in 30BC, conquest was complete as Egypt fell under the control of the Roman Empire.

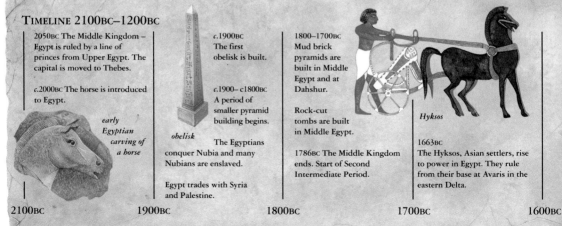

TIMELINE 2100BC–1200BC

2050BC The Middle Kingdom – Egypt is ruled by a line of princes from Upper Egypt. The capital is moved to Thebes.

c.2000BC The horse is introduced to Egypt.

early Egyptian carving of a horse

obelisk

c.1900BC The first obelisk is built.

c.1900– c1800BC A period of smaller pyramid building begins.

The Egyptians conquer Nubia and many Nubians are enslaved.

Egypt trades with Syria and Palestine.

1800–1700BC Mud brick pyramids are built in Middle Egypt and at Dahshur.

Rock-cut tombs are built in Middle Egypt.

1786BC The Middle Kingdom ends. Start of Second Intermediate Period.

Hyksos

1663BC The Hyksos, Asian settlers, rise to power in Egypt. They rule from their base at Avaris in the eastern Delta.

2100BC   1900BC   1800BC   1700BC   1600BC

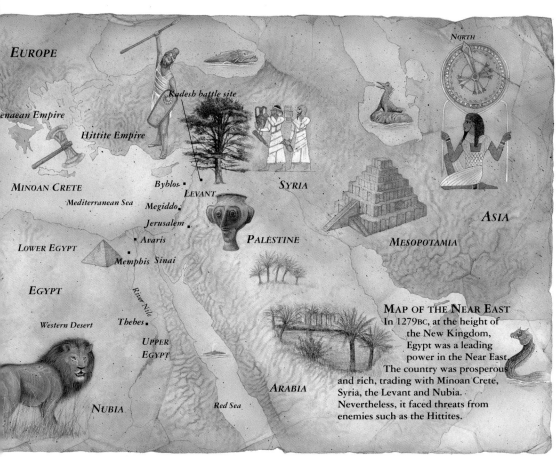

EUROPE

NORTH

enaean Empire

Hittite Empire

Kadesh battle site

SYRIA

ASIA

MINOAN CRETE

Byblos

LEVANT

Mediterranean Sea

Megiddo

Jerusalem

LOWER EGYPT

Avaris

PALESTINE

MESOPOTAMIA

Memphis Sinai

EGYPT

River Nile

Western Desert

Thebes

UPPER
EGYPT

ARABIA

Red Sea

NUBIA

MAP OF THE NEAR EAST

In 1279BC, at the height of
the New Kingdom,
Egypt was a leading
power in the Near East.
The country was prosperous
and rich, trading with Minoan Crete,
Syria, the Levant and Nubia.
Nevertheless, it faced threats from
enemies such as the Hittites.

Akhenaten

c1567BC The Hyksos are
defeated by Egyptians from the
southern city of Thebes.

1550BC The New Kingdom
is founded. Royal
tombs are built in the
Valley of the Kings.

1525BC Amenhotep
becomes pharaoh.

1500BC A village is
founded at Deir el-
Medina, near the
Valley of the Kings.

Thutmose III

1498BC Queen Hatshepsut
rules as co-regent with the
child king Thutmose III.

1483BC Hatshepsut dies.

1478BC The rebellious
prince of Kadesh is
defeated by
Thutmose III at the
Battle of Megiddo
in the Near East.
*the cartouche of
Tutankhamun*

1379BC
Akhenaten
introduces
worship of the
Sun god, Aten, as
the only religion.
A new capital is
established at el-Amarna.

c1334BC Smenkhkare,
Akhenaten's successor, moves
the capital back to Memphis.

1325BC Tutankhamun is
buried in the Valley of
the Kings.

1291BC Seti I comes to power.
He builds the Hypostyle Hall
at Karnak.

1279BC
Ramesses
II becomes
pharaoh.

Ramesses II

1274BC Ramesses II fights
the Hittites at the battle
of Kadesh.

1500BC   1400BC   1300BC   1200BC

Famous Pharaohs

KHAFRA
(reigned 2558–2532BC)
Khafra is the son of the pharaoh Khufu. He is remembered for his splendid tomb, the Second Pyramid at Giza and the Great Sphinx that guards it.

AMENHOTEP I
(reigned 1525–1504BC)
The pharaoh Amenhotep led the Egyptian army to battle in Nubia. He also founded a village for workmen at Deir el-Medina.

FOR THOUSANDS OF YEARS ancient Egypt was ruled by royal families. We know much about the pharaohs (kings) and queens from these great dynasties because of their magnificent tombs and the public monuments raised in their honour.

Egypt's first ruler was King Narmer, who united the country in about 3100BC. Later pharaohs such as Zoser and Khufu are remembered for the great pyramids they had built as their tombs.

Pharaohs usually succeeded to the throne through royal birth. However, in some cases military commanders such as Horemheb came to power. Although Egypt's rulers were traditionally men, a few powerful women were made pharaoh. The most famous of these is the Greek queen Cleopatra, who ruled Egypt in 51BC.

HATSHEPSUT
(reigned 1498–1483BC)
Hatshepsut was the half-sister and wife of Thutmose II. When her husband died, she was appointed to rule Egypt until her young stepson Thutmose III was old enough. However Queen Hatshepsut was ambitious and had herself crowned pharaoh. Hatshepsut is famous for her trading expeditions to the land of Punt. The walls of her temple at Deir el-Bahri show these exotic trips.

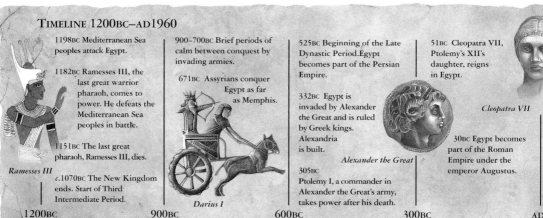

TIMELINE 1200BC–AD1960

1198BC Mediterranean Sea peoples attack Egypt.

1182BC Ramesses III, the last great warrior pharaoh, comes to power. He defeats the Mediterranean Sea peoples in battle.

1151BC The last great pharaoh, Ramesses III, dies.

Ramesses III

c.1070BC The New Kingdom ends. Start of Third Intermediate Period.

900–700BC Brief periods of calm between conquest by invading armies.

671BC Assyrians conquer Egypt as far as Memphis.

Darius I

525BC Beginning of the Late Dynastic Period.Egypt becomes part of the Persian Empire.

332BC Egypt is invaded by Alexander the Great and is ruled by Greek kings. Alexandria is built.

Alexander the Great

305BC Ptolemy I, a commander in Alexander the Great's army, takes power after his death.

51BC Cleopatra VII, Ptolemy's XII's daughter, reigns in Egypt.

Cleopatra VII

30BC Egypt becomes part of the Roman Empire under the emperor Augustus.

1200BC   900BC   600BC   300BC   AD0

TUTANKHAMUN
(reigned 1334–1325BC)
This pharaoh came to the throne when he was only nine years old. He died at the age of 18. Tutankhamun is remembered for his tomb in the Valley of the Kings, which was packed with amazing treasure.

THUTMOSE III
(reigned 1479–1425BC)
Thutmose III is remembered as a brave warrior king. He launched many military campaigns against the Syrians in the Near East. Records from the time tell of Thutmose marching fearlessly into battle at the head of his army, unconcerned about his own safety. He won a famous victory at Megiddo and then later at Kadesh. Thutmose III was buried in the Valley of the Kings.

AKHENATEN
(reigned 1379–1334BC)
The Egyptians believed in many gods. However, when Akhenaten came to power, he introduced worship of one god, the Sun disc Aten. He moved the capital from Memphis to Akhetaten (now known as el-Amarna). His chief wife was the beautiful Queen Nefertiti.

RAMESSES II
(reigned 1279–1212BC)
One of the most famous pharaohs of all, Ramesses II, was the son of Seti I. He built many fine temples and defeated the Hittites at the Battle of Kadesh in 1274BC. The chief queen of Ramesses was Nefertari. Carvings of this graceful queen can be seen on Ramesses II's temple at Abu Simbel. Ramesses lived a long life and died at the age of 92. He was buried in the Valley of the Kings.

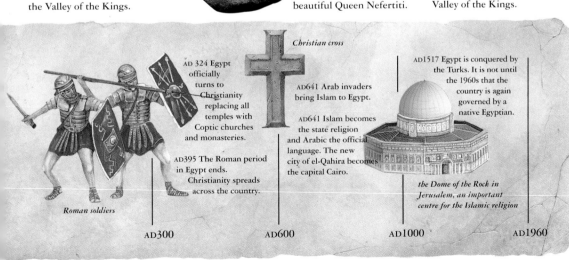

Christian cross

AD 324 Egypt officially turns to Christianity replacing all temples with Coptic churches and monasteries.

AD641 Arab invaders bring Islam to Egypt.

AD641 Islam becomes the state religion and Arabic the official language. The new city of el-Qahira becomes the capital Cairo.

AD1517 Egypt is conquered by the Turks. It is not until the 1960s that the country is again governed by a native Egyptian.

AD395 The Roman period in Egypt ends. Christianity spreads across the country.

the Dome of the Rock in Jerusalem, an important centre for the Islamic religion

Roman soldiers

AD300   AD600   AD1000   AD1960

India's Glorious Heritage

THE INDIAN SUBCONTINENT IS HOME to one of the world's most varied civilizations because many different groups of people have travelled over the Himalayan mountains and settled there. From the arrival of Aryan tribes about 3,000 years ago until the invasion of the Mughals in the 1500s, each new wave of people brought fresh ideas and ways of life. As a result, India's religious and artistic life became very rich and mixed.

Two major world religions – Hinduism and Buddhism – developed in India, and for hundreds of years, India was also at the heart of Muslim life in Asia. These three religions shaped the course of India's history, and led to the building of magnificent monuments, many of which still stand.

With its Hindu and Buddhist temples and sculptures, and the sumptuous palaces of the Muslim rulers, India is full of amazing treasures from the past.

DAWN OF INDIAN CIVILIZATION
Ancient stone buildings, such as the Great Bath at Mohenjo-Daro in the Indus Valley, tell archaeologists a great deal about the dawn of civilization in India. Fewer buildings of later times have been excavated, partly because later houses were made of mud, thatch and wood, none of which has survived.

BEAUTY IN STONE
A beautiful carving of a Yakshi (tree spirit) from Bharhut in central India. It is made of red sandstone and dates from 100BC. This Buddhist sculpture has a distinctive Indian style that you can see in sculptures from much later periods. Buddhism was the first religion in India to inspire people to build monuments and make sculptures.

TIMELINE 6000BC–AD400

From early times until the coming of the British in 1757, India was divided into many kingdoms. It was never a single state. The regions of Ancient India were linked by a common culture, rather than by politics, religion or language.

*c.*6000BC Neolithic settlements in Baluchistan.

*c.*2800–2600BC Beginnings of settlements in the Indus Valley region.

statue of priest king from Indus valley

rice cultivation

*c.*2300–1700BC The great cities of the Indus Valley (Mohenjo-Daro and Harappa), the Punjab (Kalibangan) and Gujarat (Lothal) flourished.

*c.*1700BC Sudden and mysterious decline of the Indus Valley civilization.

*c.*1500–1200BC Immigration of Vedic Aryans into north-western India.

*c.*1200–600BC The Vedic texts are composed.

*c.*800BC Use of iron for weapons and the spread of Aryan culture into the Gangetic plains (the area near the River Ganges).

*c.*500–300BC Rice cultivation and the introduction of iron agricultural tools in the eastern Gangetic plains lead to the formation of more complex societies, cities and states.

fragment of pot with brahmi inscription

6000BC   2500BC   1200BC   500BC

LIFE STORY

A limestone frieze dating from AD100 shows a good deed carried out by the spiritual leader, Buddha. The frieze comes from Amaravati, in south-eastern India, which was an important Buddhist site from 300BC. Stories of the Buddha's past lives, called jatakas, were popular in ancient India.

TEMPLE OF THE SUN

A huge carved stone wheel forms a panel on the wall of the Sun Temple at Konarak on India's east coast. This part of the temple is carved in the shape of a gigantic twelve-wheeled chariot, drawn by seven stone horses. It dates from the 1200s, when medieval Hindu kings built magnificent temples to their gods.

GRAND ENTRANCE

The Alamgiri Gate is one of three magnificent entrances built by the Mughal emperor Aurangzeb to the Shahadra fort at Lahore (in modern-day Pakistan). The fort doubled as a luxurious palace.

A COUNTRY OF MOUNTAINS AND PLAINS

India is bounded to the north by the Himalayan mountains. The central Deccan plateau is framed by mountain ranges known as the Eastern and Western Ghats. The first settlements grew up near rivers on the fertile plains in the north.

*c.*500–400BC Inscribed fragments of pots from Sri Lanka discovered.

*c.*478–400BC Life of the Buddha. He is born a prince but leaves his family and lives in poverty.

327–325BC Alexander the Great arrives in north-western India.

coin of Alexander the Great

320BC The rise of the Magadhan Empire under the Maurya family, founded by King Chandragupta I.

268–233BC King Ashoka, the grandson of Chandragupta I, issues the first royal edicts on pillars and rocks throughout the subcontinent.

c. 50BC–AD100 Intensive trade connections with the Roman Empire.

AD50–AD200 Kushanas and Shakas (tribes from Central Asia) set up kingdoms and adopt Indian religions. Indian dynasty of Satavahanas arises in southern India.

Ashokan pillar

c. AD150 Kushana and Shaka kings in the north and west adopt Sanskrit as the courtly language.

c. AD200–400 *Ramayana,* *Mahabharata* and the *Bhagavad-Gita* Hindu epic poems are composed in their final form.

AD400 Nearly all courts are using Sanskrit.

gateway to Buddhist stupa

300BC   AD100   AD400

The Land of Ancient India

INDIA IS ISOLATED FROM THE main continent of Asia by the world's highest mountains, the Himalayas. The mountains made it difficult for people to invade. The easiest overland route, taken by the earliest settlers from Asia, is from the north-west (present-day Afghanistan) through the Karakoram mountains. However, it was still a difficult journey. Once people had arrived in India, they tended to stay.

The first people settled in the bare mountain foothills, and survived by keeping herds of animals such as sheep and goats. People gradually moved south of the Himalayas, to areas where mighty rivers run through huge, fertile plains. Here, the climate enabled them to grow various crops.

India's climate is dominated by the monsoon, a wind that brings alternating seasons of hot, dry weather and heavy rain and flooding. In the drier west and north, wheat was the main crop from very early times, while higher rainfall in the east and south was ideal for growing rice. Rice cultivation was so successful in the plains around the Ganges river that many people settled there. This led to the growth of cities from around 300BC. Later, cities developed along rivers farther south.

From the 1st century AD, people no longer needed to make the overland journey into India. They came by ship from as far away as the Mediterranean Sea to ports on the west coast, in search of trade.

TRADING NATION
From 200BC, ancient India traded with the outside world by sea. They also bought and sold goods by land along the Silk Road – a route that cut across the Himalayas and through Central Asia to Samarkand and beyond.

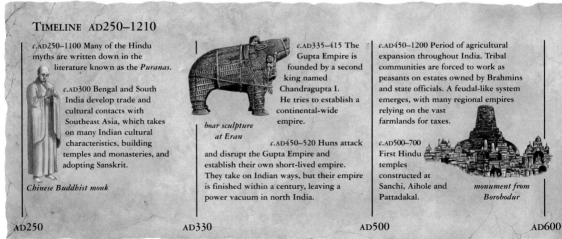

TIMELINE AD250–1210

*c.*AD250–1100 Many of the Hindu myths are written down in the literature known as the *Puranas*.

*c.*AD300 Bengal and South India develop trade and cultural contacts with Southeast Asia, which takes on many Indian cultural characteristics, building temples and monasteries, and adopting Sanskrit.

Chinese Buddhist monk

boar sculpture at Eran

*c.*AD335–415 The Gupta Empire is founded by a second king named Chandragupta I. He tries to establish a continental-wide empire.

*c.*AD450–520 Huns attack and disrupt the Gupta Empire and establish their own short-lived empire. They take on Indian ways, but their empire is finished within a century, leaving a power vacuum in north India.

*c.*AD450–1200 Period of agricultural expansion throughout India. Tribal communities are forced to work as peasants on estates owned by Brahmins and state officials. A feudal-like system emerges, with many regional empires relying on the vast farmlands for taxes.

*c.*AD500–700 First Hindu temples constructed at Sanchi, Aihole and Pattadakal.

monument from Borobodur

AD250   AD330   AD500   AD600

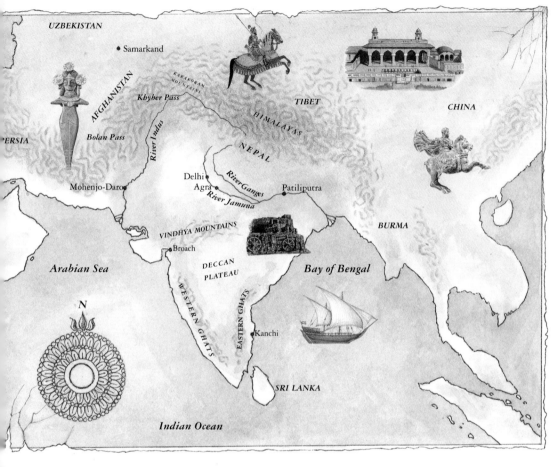

UZBEKISTAN

• Samarkand

AFGHANISTAN

KARAKORAM MOUNTAINS

Khyber Pass

TIBET

HIMALAYAS

CHINA

PERSIA

Bolan Pass

River Indus

NEPAL

Delhi •
Agra •

River Ganges

Patiliputra

BURMA

Mohenjo-Daro •

River Jamuna

VINDHYA MOUNTAINS

• Broach

Arabian Sea

DECCAN PLATEAU

Bay of Bengal

N

WESTERN GHATS

EASTERN GHATS

• Kanchi

SRI LANKA

Indian Ocean

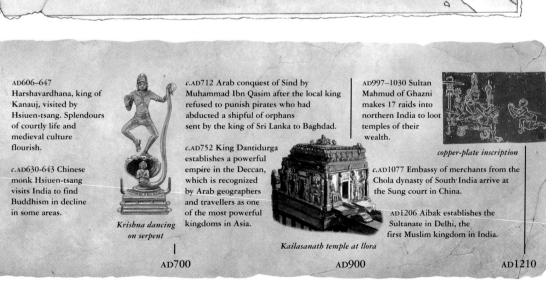

AD606–647 Harshavardhana, king of Kanauj, visited by Hsiuen-tsang. Splendours of courtly life and medieval culture flourish.

c.AD630-643 Chinese monk Hsiuen-tsang visits India to find Buddhism in decline in some areas.

Krishna dancing on serpent

c.AD712 Arab conquest of Sind by Muhammad Ibn Qasim after the local king refused to punish pirates who had abducted a shipful of orphans sent by the king of Sri Lanka to Baghdad.

c.AD752 King Dantidurga establishes a powerful empire in the Deccan, which is recognized by Arab geographers and travellers as one of the most powerful kingdoms in Asia.

Kailasanath temple at Ilora

AD997–1030 Sultan Mahmud of Ghazni makes 17 raids into northern India to loot temples of their wealth.

copper-plate inscription

c.AD1077 Embassy of merchants from the Chola dynasty of South India arrive at the Sung court in China.

AD1206 Aibak establishes the Sultanate in Delhi, the first Muslim kingdom in India.

AD700

AD900

AD1210

India's History Makers

MANY OF THE REMARKABLE FIGURES of Indian history who shaped the country's destiny were great leaders. Ashoka was a powerful ruler 2,500 years ago who encouraged the spread of Buddhism. Many centuries later, Babur, a warlord from Samarkand in Central Asia, founded the Mughal Empire in India in the early 1500s. His grandson, Akbar, was a gifted politician and soldier who ruled for 49 years. The Mughal period was a time of huge development in the arts. Some Mughal rulers built magnificent cities, and many of their fine monuments and royal tombs can still be seen today.

From the time of the ancient civilization of the Aryans in the Indus Valley, religious teachers and scholars were respected. This may be because poverty and suffering have always been problems in India, which led people to think about why life was so difficult, and to seek ways of coping. Two of the most famous religious leaders are Gautama Buddha, who established the Buddhist way of life, and Guru Nanak, who founded the Sikh religion.

AN INFLUENTIAL LEADER
A statue of Gautama Buddha seated on a lotus flower. He founded Buddhism, which shaped life in India for thousands of years. Buddhism eventually died out in India, but it spread through many other parts of Asia. This created a link between India and many different eastern peoples and cultures.

TIMELINE AD1290–1870

1293 Marco Polo visits south India. A flourishing trade is conducted throughout the Indian Ocean in silks, fabrics, spices and other luxuries.

1334–1370 The sultanate of Madurai, the southernmost Muslim kingdom, established briefly in south India before being defeated by southern kingdoms.

stone chariot from Vijayanagar

c.1346–1565 The last great Hindu empire of Vijayanagar founded in south India.

c.1360 Vedic and Hindu revival by the brothers Sayana and Madhava at the Vijayanagar court.

1398 The Mongol Timur devastates Delhi.

c.1440 Death of the Bhakti saint Kabir at Gorakhpur, where both Hindus and Muslims claim him as a great teacher.

tomb from the Sultanate period

1469–1539 Life of Guru Nanak, founder of Sikhism.

1498 Portuguese explorer Vasco da Gama visits Calicut.

1510 The Portuguese conquer Goa.

1526 Babur, the Mongol, defeats the Sultan of Delhi and founds the Mughal empire.

Quth Minar marble fountain

AD1290   AD1340   AD1400   AD1520

ROYAL HANDWRITING

This signature of Emperor Harsha (AD606–647) is carved in copper. Harsha was a patron (supporter) of arts and literature, and during his reign, the richness and elegance of the court reached new heights.

A SAINTLY LIFE

A statuette of Karaikal Ammaiyar, a woman who lived in southern India around AD600. She was so devoted to the god Shiva that she left her home and family, and gave her life entirely to him. She fasted as a symbol of her faith and became incredibly thin. Karaikal Ammaiyar is revered as a saint even today in southern India.

ART LOVER

Shah Jahan was one of the greatest statesmen of the Mughal Empire. He extended Mughal power south into the Deccan plateau and north into Afghanistan. However, he did not fulfil the Mughal dream of capturing the trading city of Samarkand, the 'blue pearl of the Orient', in Central Asia. Shah Jahan was a great patron of architecture.

ASHOKA'S PILLAR

An edict (order) of Ashoka, the ruler of India's first empire, is inscribed on this pillar. He published his edicts on pillars and rockfaces throughout the land. Ashoka was a Buddhist. He claimed to have improved the lives of humans and animals, and had helped to spread justice.

1556–1605 Reign of Akbar, the most enlightened Mughal emperor.

1739 Nadir Shah sacks Delhi and carries off the Peacock Throne.

Mongol horseman

palace at Phata Pursi

1757 Nawab of Bengal defeated by the British at Plassey.

1758 The Mughal rulers in Bengal give the British East India Company the right to collect land taxes.

1857–8 The British government imposes direct rule and the East India Company is dissolved.

1870 Construction of Red Sea telegraph brings direct link with Britain.

farman (order) of Mughal emperor to East India Company

AD1750   AD1850   AD1870

The Chinese Empire

IMAGINE YOU COULD travel back in time 5,000 years and visit the lands of the Far East. In northern China you would come across smoky settlements of small thatched huts. You might see villagers fishing in rivers, sowing millet or baking pottery. From these small beginnings, China developed into an amazing civilization. Its towns grew into huge cities, with palaces and temples. Many Chinese became great writers, thinkers, artists, builders and inventors. China was first united under the rule of a single emperor in 221BC, and continued to be ruled by emperors until 1912.

China today is a modern country. Its ancient past has to be pieced together by archaeologists and historians. They dig up ancient tombs and settlements, and study textiles, ancient books and pottery. Their job is made easier because historical records were kept. These provide much information about the long history of Chinese civilization.

REST IN PEACE
A demon is trodden into defeat by a guardian spirit. Statues like this were commonly put in tombs to protect the dead against evil spirits.

ALL THE EMPEROR'S MEN
A vast model army marches again. It was dug up by archaeologists in 1974, and is now on display near Xian. The lifesize figures are made of terracotta (baked clay). They were buried in 210BC near the tomb of Qin Shi Huangdi, the first emperor of all China. He believed that they would protect him from evil spirits after he died.

TIMELINE 7000BC–110BC

Prehistoric remains of human ancestors dating back to 600,000BC have been found in China's Shaanxi province. The beginnings of Chinese civilization may be seen in the farming villages of the late Stone Age (8000BC–2500BC). As organized states grew up, the Chinese became skilled at warfare, working metals and making elaborate pottery and fine silk.

Banpo hut

c.7000BC Bands of hunters and fishers roam freely around the river valleys of China. They use simple stone tools and weapons.

c.3200BC Farming villages such as Banpo produce pottery in kilns. This way of life is called the Yangshao culture.

c.2100BC The start of a legendary 500-year period of rule, known as the Xia dynasty.

c.2000BC Black pottery is made by the people of the so-called Longshan culture.

Shang bronze vessel

c.1600BC Beginning of the Shang dynasty. Bronze worked and silk produced. The first picture-writing is used (on bones for telling fortunes).

1122BC Zhou ruler Wu defeats Shang emperor. Wu becomes emperor of the Western Zhou dynasty.

Zhou spearheads

7000BC   2100BC   1600BC   780BC

A HEAVENLY HALL

The Hall of Prayer for Good Harvests (*shown right*) is part of Tiantan, the Temple of Heavenly Peace in Beijing. It was originally built in 1420, but had to be rebuilt in the 1890s after it was destroyed by lightning. Buildings like these tell us about traditional technology and design, as well as about Chinese religious beliefs.

THE HAN EMPIRE (206BC–AD220)

China grew rapidly during the Han dynasty. By AD2 it had expanded to take in North Korea, the south-east coast, the south-west as far as Vietnam and large areas of Central Asia. Northern borders were defended by the Great Wall, which was extended during Han rule.

THE JADE PRINCE

In 1968, Chinese archaeologists excavated the tomb of Prince Liu Sheng. His remains were encased in a jade suit when he died in about 100BC. Over 2,400 pieces of this precious stone were joined with gold wire. It was believed that jade would preserve the body.

Zhou soldier

771BC Capital city moves from Anyang to Luoyang. Beginning of Eastern Zhou dynasty.

*c.*604BC Birth of the legendary Laozi, founder of Daoism.

551BC Teacher and philosopher Kong Fuzi (Confucius) born.

513BC Iron-working develops.

453BC Break-up of central rule. Small states fight each other for 200 years. Work begins on Grand Canal and Great Wall.

221BC China unites as a centralized empire under Zheng (Qin Shi Huangdi). Great Wall is extended.

213BC Qin Shi Huangdi burns all books that are not 'practical'.

Chinese writing

210BC Death of Qin Shi Huangdi. Terracotta army guards his tomb, near Chang'an (modern Xian).

206BC Qin dynasty overthrown. Beginnings of Han dynasty as Xiang Yu and Liu Bang fight for control of the Han kingdom.

202BC The Western Han dynasty formally begins. It is led by the former official Liu Bang, who becomes emperor Gaozu.

200BC Chang'an becomes the capital of the Chinese Empire.

terracotta warrior and horse

112BC Trade with the peoples of Western Asia and Europe begins to flourish along the Silk Road.

550BC	210BC	140BC	110BC

The Centre of Civilization

CHINA IS A VAST COUNTRY, about the size of Europe. Its fertile plains and river valleys are ringed by many deserts, mountains and oceans. The ancient Chinese named their land Zhongguo, the Middle Kingdom, and believed that it was at the centre of the civilized world. Most Chinese belong to a people called the Han, but the country is also inhabited by 50 or more different peoples, some of whom have played an important part in Chinese history. These groups include the Hui, Zhuang, Dai, Yao, Miao, Tibetans, Manchus and Mongols.

The very first Chinese civilizations grew up around the Huang He (Yellow River), where the fertile soil supported farming villages and then towns and cities. These became the centres of rival kingdoms. Between 1700BC and 256BC Chinese rule spread southwards to the Chang Jiang (Yangzi River), the great river of Central China. All of eastern China was united within a single empire for the first time during Qin rule (221–206BC).

The rulers of the Han dynasty (206BC–AD220) then expanded the Empire southwards as far as Vietnam. The Chinese Empire was now even larger than the Roman Empire, dominating Central and South-east Asia. The Mongols, from lands to the north of China, ruled the Empire from 1279 to 1368. They were succeeded by the Ming dynasty, which was in turn overthown by the Manchu in 1644. In later centuries, China became inward-looking and unable to resist interference from Europe. The Empire finally collapsed, with China declaring itself a republic in 1912.

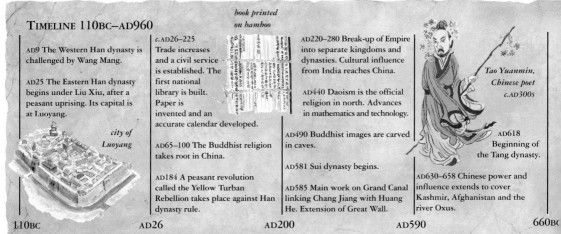

TIMELINE 110BC–AD960

book printed on bamboo

AD9 The Western Han dynasty is challenged by Wang Mang.

AD25 The Eastern Han dynasty begins under Liu Xiu, after a peasant uprising. Its capital is at Luoyang.

city of Luoyang

*c.*AD26–225 Trade increases and a civil service is established. The first national library is built. Paper is invented and an accurate calendar developed.

AD65–100 The Buddhist religion takes root in China.

AD184 A peasant revolution called the Yellow Turban Rebellion takes place against Han dynasty rule.

AD220–280 Break-up of Empire into separate kingdoms and dynasties. Cultural influence from India reaches China.

AD440 Daoism is the official religion in north. Advances in mathematics and technology.

AD490 Buddhist images are carved in caves.

AD581 Sui dynasty begins.

AD585 Main work on Grand Canal linking Chang Jiang with Huang He. Extension of Great Wall.

*Tao Yuanmin, Chinese poet c.*AD300s

AD618 Beginning of the Tang dynasty.

AD630–658 Chinese power and influence extends to cover Kashmir, Afghanistan and the river Oxus.

110BC   AD26   AD200   AD590   660BC

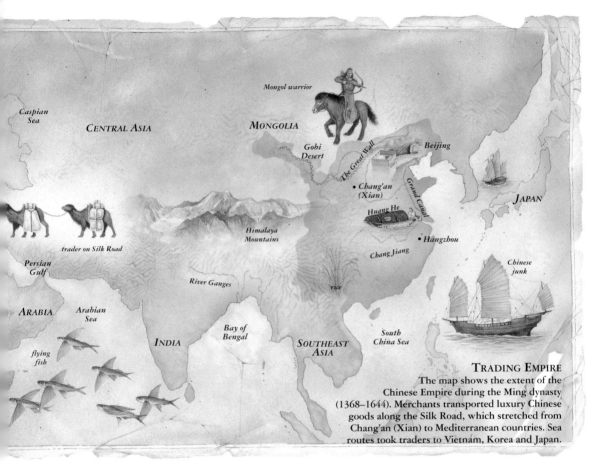

Mongol warrior

Caspian
Sea

CENTRAL ASIA

MONGOLIA

Gobi
Desert

The Great Wall

Beijing

Chang'an
(Xian)

Grand Canal

Huang He

JAPAN

trader on Silk Road

Himalaya
Mountains

Hangzhou

Chang Jiang

Chinese
junk

Persian
Gulf

River Ganges

rice

ARABIA

Arabian
Sea

INDIA

Bay of
Bengal

South
China Sea

SOUTHEAST
ASIA

flying
fish

TRADING EMPIRE
The map shows the extent of the
Chinese Empire during the Ming dynasty
(1368–1644). Merchants transported luxury Chinese
goods along the Silk Road, which stretched from
Chang'an (Xian) to Mediterranean countries. Sea
routes took traders to Vietnam, Korea and Japan.

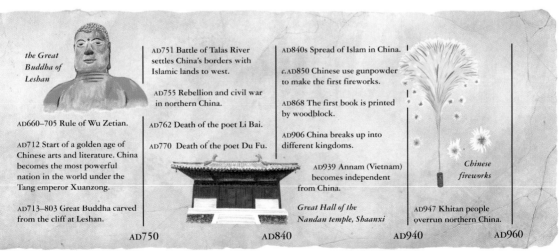

*the Great
Buddha of
Leshan*

AD751 Battle of Talas River
settles China's borders with
Islamic lands to west.

AD840s Spread of Islam in China.

c. AD850 Chinese use gunpowder
to make the first fireworks.

AD755 Rebellion and civil war
in northern China.

AD868 The first book is printed
by woodblock.

AD660–705 Rule of Wu Zetian.

AD762 Death of the poet Li Bai.

AD712 Start of a golden age of
Chinese arts and literature. China
becomes the most powerful
nation in the world under the
Tang emperor Xuanzong.

AD770 Death of the poet Du Fu.

AD906 China breaks up into
different kingdoms.

AD939 Annam (Vietnam)
becomes independent
from China.

*Chinese
fireworks*

AD713–803 Great Buddha carved
from the cliff at Leshan.

*Great Hall of the
Nandan temple, Shaanxi*

AD947 Khitan people
overrun northern China.

AD750

AD840

AD940

AD960

People of the Chinese Empire

GREAT EMPIRES ARE made by ordinary people as much as by their rulers. The Chinese Empire could not have been built without the millions of peasants who planted crops, built defensive walls and dug canals. The names of these people are largely forgotten, except for those who led uprisings and revolts against their rulers. The inventors, thinkers, artists, poets and writers of imperial China are better known. They had a great effect on the society they lived in, and left behind ideas, works of art and inventions that still influence people today.

The royal court was made up of thousands of officials, artists, craftsmen and servants. Some had great political power. China's rulers came from many different backgrounds and peoples.

Many emperors were ruthless former warlords who were hungry for power. Others are remembered as scholars or artists. Some women also achieved great political influence, openly or from behind the scenes.

LAOZI (born *c.*604BC)
The legendary Laozi is said to have been a scholar who worked as a court librarian. It is thought that he wrote the book known as the *Daodejing*. He believed people should live in harmony with nature, and his ideas later formed the basis of Daoism.

KONG FUZI (551–479BC)
Kong Fuzi is better known in the West by the Latin version of his name, Confucius. He was a public official who became an influential teacher and thinker. His views on family life, society and the treatment of others greatly influenced later generations.

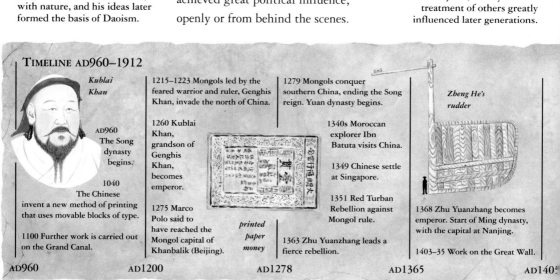

TIMELINE AD960–1912

Kublai Khan

AD960
The Song dynasty begins.

1040
The Chinese invent a new method of printing that uses movable blocks of type.

1100 Further work is carried out on the Grand Canal.

1215–1223 Mongols led by the feared warrior and ruler, Genghis Khan, invade the north of China.

1260 Kublai Khan, grandson of Genghis Khan, becomes emperor.

1275 Marco Polo said to have reached the Mongol capital of Khanbalik (Beijing).

printed paper money

1279 Mongols conquer southern China, ending the Song reign. Yuan dynasty begins.

1340s Moroccan explorer Ibn Batuta visits China.

1349 Chinese settle at Singapore.

1351 Red Turban Rebellion against Mongol rule.

1363 Zhu Yuanzhang leads a fierce rebellion.

Zheng He's rudder

1368 Zhu Yuanzhang becomes emperor. Start of Ming dynasty, with the capital at Nanjing.

1403–35 Work on the Great Wall.

AD960   AD1200   AD1278   AD1365   AD1405

QIN SHI HUANGDI (256–210BC)
Scholars plead for their lives before the first emperor. Zheng came to the throne of a state called Qin at the age of nine. He went on to rule all China and was given his full title, meaning First Emperor of Qin. His brutal methods included burying his opponents alive.

HAN GAOZU (256–195BC)
In the Qin dynasty (221–206BC) Liu Bang was a minor public official in charge of a relay station for royal messengers. He watched as the centralized Qin Empire fell apart. In 206BC he declared himself ruler of the Han kingdom. In 202BC he defeated his opponent, Xiang Yu, and founded the Han dynasty. As emperor Gaozu, he tried to unite China without using Qin's harsh methods.

EMPRESS WU ZETIAN (AD624–705)
The emperor Tang Gaozong enraged officials when he replaced his legal wife with Wu, his concubine (secondary wife). After the emperor suffered a stroke in AD660, Wu took control of the country. In AD690 she became the only woman in history to declare herself empress of China.

KUBLAI KHAN (AD1214–1294)
The explorer Marco Polo was said to have visited emperor Kublai Khan at Khanbalik (Beijing). Kublai Khan was a Mongol who conquered northern, and later southern, China.

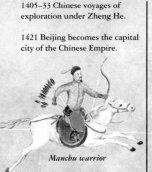

1405–33 Chinese voyages of exploration under Zheng He.

1421 Beijing becomes the capital city of the Chinese Empire.

Manchu warrior

1428 The Chinese are expelled from Annam (Vietnam).

1550 Japanese pirates mount raids on China. Mongols invade north again.

1644 Li Zicheng leads a rebellion against Ming rule. Manchu invasion. Qing dynasty founded.

Boxer rebels

1673 Rebellions against Qing rule in south.

1839–42 First Opium War. Britain forces China to accept opium imports from India.

1842 Treaty of Nanjing. Britain gains Hong Kong.

1850–64 Taiping rebellion.

1858 Treaty of Tianjin. Chinese ports taken over by foreign powers.

1862 The Empress Dowager Cixi becomes regent.

1894–5 War with Japan. Loss of Taiwan.

1899–1900 Boxer Rebellion against Qing and foreign governments.

1908 Last emperor, Puyi, ascends to throne as a small boy.

1912 Declaration of republic by Sun Yatsen. Emperor Puyi abdicates.

Puyi, the last emperor

AD1425   AD1650   AD1880   AD1912

A Golden Age in Greece

O N THE SHORES of the eastern Mediterranean, 3,000 years ago, one of the most enduring and influential civilizations of the Western world emerged. Ancient Greece was made up of a number of self-supporting city states, each of which developed a strong, individual identity. They developed from an agricultural society that wrote in simple pictograms into a sophisticated culture. Centuries on, the Greek legacy survives in parts of modern society. The origins of democracy, mathematics, medicine and philosophy can be traced back to this time in history. Even some of our modern words are made up from ancient Greek. 'Telephone' comes from the ancient Greek words 'tele' meaning far and 'phonos' meaning sound.

A FEAT OF PERFECTION
The Parthenon is regarded as the supreme achievement of Greek architecture. It was the most important building in Athens, where it still sits on top of the Acropolis. The temple took 15 years to build and was dedicated to Athena, guardian goddess of Athens. Around 22,000 tonnes of marble, transported from over 15km away, were used in its construction.

TIMELINE 40,000BC–1100BC

The first people lived in Greece about 40,000 years ago. They lived in a tribal, hunter-gatherer society. Settlements and the beginning of farming did not occur until 6,000BC. The first great Greek civilization, and also the first in Europe, flourished on the island of Crete around 2000BC. This was the mighty Minoan civilization whose decline heralded in the glorious age of the Mycenaeans. After this a period known as the Dark Ages began. It was followed by the golden age of Classical Greece which lasted from about 500BC to 336BC.

a drinking vessel (rhyton) in the shape of a bull's head from Knossos

*c.*6000BC The first settlers arrive on the island of Crete and the Greek mainland.

*c.*2900–1000BC The Bronze Age in Greece. People discover how to mix copper and tin to make bronze.

disc from Crete with unique pictographic script

*c.*2000BC Minoan civilization flourishes on Crete. The Minoans use a script called Linear A, which has not yet been deciphered.

*c.*1600BC The Mycenaeans dominate mainland Greece.

statuette of worshipping woman from Mycenae

40,000BC   6000BC   2000BC   145

CENTRE STONE

The omphalos was a carved stone kept at the shrine at Delphi. The ancient Greeks thought that this holy sanctuary was the centre of the world. The omphalos stone was placed there to mark the centre. It was said to have been put there by Zeus, ruler of the gods. It may have also served as an altar on which sacrifices were made.

THE PAST REVEALED

Archaeological evidence in the shape of pottery such as this vase help us to piece together the history of Greece. This vase is typical of the superior craftsmanship for which the Greeks were admired. It was common for vases to be decorated with pictures showing historical events. In this one, we see a scene from the siege of Troy in which the king is being murdered. The siege was an important event in Greek folklore. These decorative vases were used as containers for liquids such as oil, water and wine. The export of such pottery contributed an enormous amount of wealth to the Greeks.

THE ANCIENT GREEK WORLD

The map above shows the main ports and cities through which the Greeks traded. The ancient Greek world centred on the Aegean Sea, but the Greeks were adventurous seafarers. Trade took them from the Aegean Sea to the Atlantic Ocean and the shores of the Black Sea, where they formed many settlements. These colonies helped Greece to spread its influence beyond the mainland and its offshore islands.

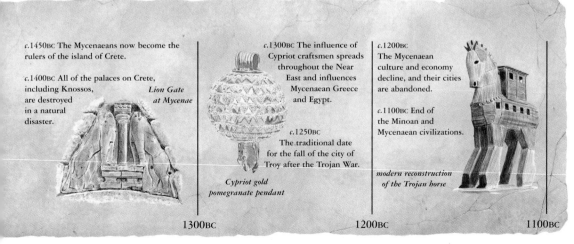

*c.*1450BC The Mycenaeans now become the rulers of the island of Crete.

*c.*1400BC All of the palaces on Crete, including Knossos, are destroyed in a natural disaster.

Lion Gate at Mycenae

*c.*1300BC The influence of Cypriot craftsmen spreads throughout the Near East and influences Mycenaean Greece and Egypt.

*c.*1250BC The traditional date for the fall of the city of Troy after the Trojan War.

Cypriot gold pomegranate pendant

*c.*1200BC The Mycenaean culture and economy decline, and their cities are abandoned.

*c.*1100BC End of the Minoan and Mycenaean civilizations.

modern reconstruction of the Trojan horse

1300BC   1200BC   1100BC

Greek Civilizations

THE HISTORY OF ANCIENT GREECE spans 20 centuries. It starts with the Minoan civilization on the island of Crete, which reached its height between 1900 and 1450BC. This culture was also the first to develop in Europe. The Minoans were a lively and artistic people who built palaces and towns and were also great seafarers. Their achievements greatly influenced the Mycenaeans, who built their own civilization on the Greek mainland from around 1600BC. Both the Minoan and Mycenaean cultures collapsed, probably under the impact of natural disasters and warfare, and were followed by centuries of poverty.

Revival was under way by 750BC, and the Greek world reached its economic peak during the 5th century BC. This period is known as the Classical Age, when Athens was at the height of its power and prosperity. During this century, Athens led the Greeks into many victorious battles against Persia. However, Athens itself later suffered an economic decline because of a series of wars fought against its rival, Sparta. Then, in the 4th century BC, Greece was conquered by Macedonia. The Macedonian ruler, Alexander the Great, spread Greek culture throughout his empire. Finally, between 168 and 146BC Macedonia and Greece were absorbed into the Roman Empire, and Greek civilization became part of the heritage that Rome passed on to the rest of Europe.

TRADE AND EXPANSION

The Classical Age in Greek history dates from around 500 to 336BC. This period was marked by an increase in the wealth of most Greek city states. Greek trade ships were sailing throughout the Mediterranean and Black Sea. Colonies were also being set up on the shorelines of these two seas.

ITALY

• *Locri*

SICILY
• *Naxos*

• *Syracuse*

N

W   E

S

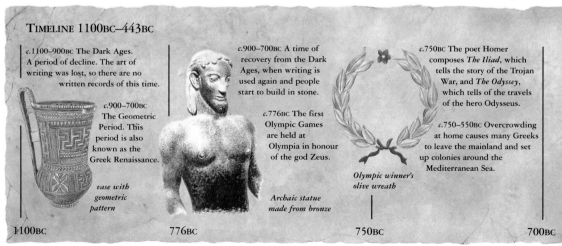

TIMELINE 1100BC–443BC

*c.*1100–900BC The Dark Ages. A period of decline. The art of writing was lost, so there are no written records of this time.

*c.*900–700BC The Geometric Period. This period is also known as the Greek Renaissance.

vase with geometric pattern

*c.*900–700BC A time of recovery from the Dark Ages, when writing is used again and people start to build in stone.

*c.*776BC The first Olympic Games are held at Olympia in honour of the god Zeus.

Archaic statue made from bronze

Olympic winner's olive wreath

*c.*750BC The poet Homer composes *The Iliad*, which tells the story of the Trojan War, and *The Odyssey*, which tells of the travels of the hero Odysseus.

*c.*750–550BC Overcrowding at home causes many Greeks to leave the mainland and set up colonies around the Mediterranean Sea.

1100BC   776BC   750BC   700BC

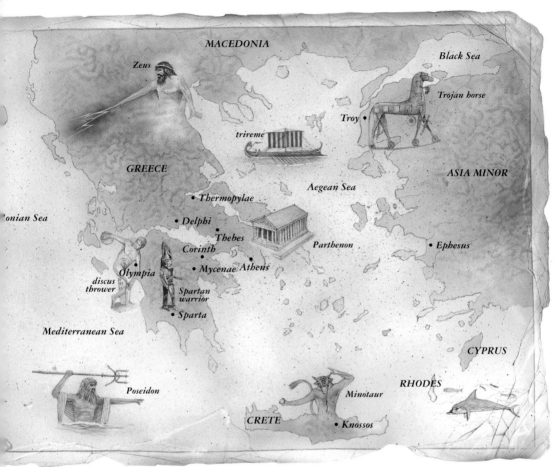

MACEDONIA

Zeus

Black Sea

Trojan horse

Troy •

GREECE

trireme

ASIA MINOR

Aegean Sea

Ionian Sea

• Thermopylae

• Delphi

• Thebes

Corinth

• Mycenae Athens

Parthenon

• Ephesus

discus
thrower

Olympia

Spartan
warrior

• Sparta

Mediterranean Sea

CYPRUS

Poseidon

RHODES

Minotaur

CRETE

• Knossos

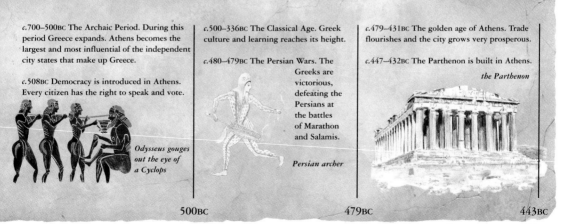

*c.*700–500BC The Archaic Period. During this period Greece expands. Athens becomes the largest and most influential of the independent city states that make up Greece.

*c.*508BC Democracy is introduced in Athens. Every citizen has the right to speak and vote.

Odysseus gouges out the eye of a Cyclops

*c.*500–336BC The Classical Age. Greek culture and learning reaches its height.

*c.*480–479BC The Persian Wars. The Greeks are victorious, defeating the Persians at the battles of Marathon and Salamis.

Persian archer

*c.*479–431BC The golden age of Athens. Trade flourishes and the city grows very prosperous.

*c.*447–432BC The Parthenon is built in Athens.

the Parthenon

500BC

479BC

443BC

Heroes of Greek Society

THE GREEKS TREASURED THEIR rich store of myths and legends about the gods, but they also took a keen interest in human history. They valued fame and glory far more than riches. Their ultimate aim in life was to make a name for themselves that would live on long after death. Statues were put up in prominent places to honour Greeks who had won fame in different ways – as generals on the battlefield, as poets, teachers, philosophers, mathematicians, orators or sportsmen. These heroes represented the human qualities the Greeks most admired – physical courage, endurance and strength, and the intelligence to create, invent, explain and persuade.

HOMER (c700BC)
The blind poet Homer (above) was honoured for writing two epic tales. The first is *The Iliad,* a story about the siege of Troy. The other is *The Odyssey* which follows the adventures of Odysseus in his travels after the battle of Troy. Scholars now believe that the tales may have been written by two poets or even groups of several poets.

SAPPHO (c600BC)
The poet Sappho was born on the island of Lesbos. She wrote nine books of poetry, but only one complete poem survives. Beauty and love were the subjects of her poetry. Her work inspired other artists of the time and influenced many writers and poets in later centuries.

SOPHOCLES (496–406BC)
Only seven of Sophocles' plays have survived. He is thought to have written 123 altogether. Besides being a playwright, Sophocles was also a respected general and politician. His name means 'famed for wisdom'.

TIMELINE 443BC–146BC

443–429BC The great statesman, Pericles, dominates politics in Athens.

431–404BC The Peloponnesian Wars take place between Athens and its great rival, Sparta. The Spartans defeat the Athenians.

399BC The Athenian philosopher, Socrates is condemned to death because his views prove unpopular.

marble bust of the philosopher, Socrates

371BC Sparta is defeated by Thebes. Thebes becomes the leading power in Greece.

362BC Sparta and Athens combine forces to defeat the Thebans at the battle of Mantinea.

338BC The Greeks are defeated by the Macedonians at the battle of Chaeronea. Philip II of Macedonia becomes ruler of Greece.

iron corselet, which is thought to have belonged to Philip II of Macedonia

336BC Philip II of Macedonia dies and is succeeded by his son, Alexander the Great. Alexander builds a huge empire, stretching from Greece as far east as India.

bronze statuette of Alexander the Great

443BC   371BC   336BC   334BC

PERICLES (495–429BC)

A popular figure and brilliant public speaker, Pericles was elected as a general 20 times. While in office, he built up a powerful navy and organized the building of strong defences, beautiful temples and fine monuments. He also gave ordinary citizens more say in government. Pericles' career ended after he led Athens into a disastrous war against Sparta. He was ostracized (expelled) as punishment for his misjudgement.

ALEXANDER THE GREAT (356–323BC)

Alexander was the son of Philip II of Macedonia. His life was spent in conquest of new territory, and his empire stretched across the Middle East, Persia and Afghanistan as far as the river Indus. His empire was swiftly divided when he died after suspected poisoning.

ARCHIMEDES (287–211BC)

The mathematician, scientist, astronomer and inventor, Archimedes came from Syracuse. When his city was besieged by the Romans, he designed a huge lens that focused sunlight on the Roman ships and set them on fire. He also devised a screw for raising water out of the ground and studied the concepts of floating and balance.

SOCRATES (469–399BC)

A renowned teacher and philosopher, Socrates encouraged people to think about how to live a good life. The Athenians sentenced him to die by drinking hemlock (a poison). Plato, Socrates' most brilliant pupil and himself a great philosopher, recorded his teacher's last days.

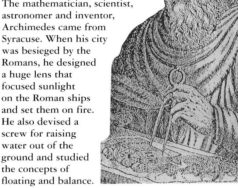

334BC Alexander the Great invades Persia to include it in his empire.

333BC The Persian army, led by King Darius, is defeated by Alexander the Great at the battle of Issus.

331BC Alexander the Great becomes king of Persia after defeating the Persians at the battle of Gaugamela.

King Darius of Persia

Romulus and Remus, legendary founders of Rome

323BC Alexander the Great dies, and his successors fight over the throne.

275BC Greek colonies are taken over by the Romans.

168BC Rome defeats the Macedonian rulers of Greece.

147–146BC The Achaean War. The Romans take control of Greece and Macedonia.

Roman soldier in full armour

323BC   168BC   146BC

Rome: From City to Empire

THE CITY OF ROME today is a bustling place, full of traffic and crowds. But if you could travel back in time to around 800BC, you would find only a few small villages on peaceful, wooded hillsides along the banks of the river Tiber. According to legend, Rome was founded here in 753BC. In the centuries that followed, the Romans came to dominate Italy and the Mediterranean. They farmed and traded and fought for new lands. Rome grew to become the centre of a vast empire that stretched across Europe into Africa and Asia. The Empire lasted for centuries and brought a sophisticated way of life to vast numbers of people. Many Roman buildings and artefacts still survive to show us what life was like in the Roman Empire.

ROMAN ITALY
As the city of Rome prospered, the Romans gradually conquered neighbouring tribes. By 250BC they controlled most of Italy. This map shows some of the important towns and cities of that time.

ANCIENT AND MODERN
In Rome today, people live alongside the temples, marketplaces and public buildings of the past. This is the Colosseum, a huge arena called an amphitheatre. It was used for staging games and fights, and first opened to the public in AD80.

TIMELINE 750BC–300BC

Rome's rise to power was sudden and spectacular. Its eventful history includes bloody battles, eccentric emperors, amazing inventions and remarkable feats of engineering. The Roman Empire prospered for almost 500 years, and still influences the way we live today.

Romulus, the first king of Rome

c.753BC The city of Rome is founded by Romulus, according to legend.

673–641BC Tullus Hostilius, Rome's third king, expands the city's territory by conquering a neighbouring settlement. Rome's population doubles as a result.

641–616BC Pons Sublicius, the first bridge across the river Tiber, is constructed. The harbour town of Ostia is founded at the mouth of the Tiber.

600BC The Latin language is first written in a script that is still used today.

inscription in Latin, carved in stone

750BC   753BC   600BC   550B

CLUES TO THE PAST
The coin on this necklace dates from the reign of the Emperor Domitian, AD81–96. Gold does not rot like wood and other materials, so jewellery like this can give us clues about Roman craft methods, changing fashions, trade and even warfare.

SECRETS BENEATH THE SEA
Divers have discovered Roman shipwrecks deep under the waters of the Mediterranean Sea. Many have their cargo still intact. These jars were being transported over 2,000 years ago. By examining shipwrecks, archaeologists can learn how Roman boats were built, what they carried and where they traded.

ARCHAEOLOGISTS AT WORK
These archaeologists are excavating sections of wall plaster from the site of a Roman house in Britain. Many remains of Roman buildings and artefacts, as well as books and documents, have survived from that time. These all help us build up a picture of what life was like in the Roman Empire.

Jupiter, one of the most important Roman gods

509BC The Temple of Jupiter in Rome is completed.

509BC Rome becomes a republic, throwing out the last king.

493BC The office of Tribune is created to protect the rights of the plebeians, the common people.

390BC Celtic warriors ransack Rome.

Servius Tullius, the king who gave his name to the Servian Wall

380BC The Servian Wall is built to defend Rome from any future attacks.

Celtic warrior

312BC The construction of the Via Appia, Rome's first great road, begins.

312BC The Aqua Appia, Rome's first aqueduct, is built.

an aqueduct

380BC   312BC   300BC

The Vast Roman Empire

BY THE YEAR AD117, the Roman Empire was at its height. It was possible to travel 4,000km from east to west and still hear the trumpets of the Roman legions. As a Roman soldier you might have had to shiver in the snowy winters of northern Britain, or sweat and toil in the heat of the Egyptian desert.

The peoples of the Empire were very different. There were Greeks, Egyptians, Syrians, Jews, Africans, Germans and Celts. Many of them belonged to civilizations that were already ancient when Rome was still a group of villages. Many revolted against Roman rule, but uprisings were quickly put down. Gradually, conquered peoples came to accept being part of the Empire. From AD212 onwards, any free person living under Roman rule had the right to claim "I am a Roman citizen". Slaves, however, had very few rights.

In AD284, after a series of violent civil wars, this vast empire was divided into several parts. Despite being reunited by the Emperor Constantine in AD324, the Empire was doomed. A hundred years later, the western part was invaded by fierce warriors from the north, with disastrous consequences. Although the Western Empire came to an end in AD476, the eastern part continued until 1453. The Latin language survived, used by the Roman Catholic Church and by scientists and scholars in Europe. It is still learned today, and is the basis of languages such as Italian, Spanish, French and Romanian.

TIMELINE 300BC–1 BC

264BC First record of a gladiatorial contest.

264–241BC The first of three wars between Rome and Carthage, which came to be known as the Punic Wars.

250BC Rome controls most of Italy.

a gladiator

one of Hannibal's war elephants

240BC The first Roman dramas are performed on stage.

218–201BC Second war between Rome and Carthage. Hannibal, a Carthaginian general, crosses the Alps by elephant.

c.211BC The first Roman silver coin, *denarius*, is minted at Rome.

206BC Rome conquers Iberia (present-day Spain).

200BC The Romans are using concrete in buildings.

196BC Rome defeats the Macedonian rulers of Greece. Triumphal arches are built in Rome.

a triumphal arch, built to celebrate a victory

300BC   240BC   206BC   196

N

Caspian Sea

GERMANY

Black Sea

ITALY
Tiber

CORSICA   *Rome*

SARDINIA

Mediterranean Sea
Carthage

SICILY

GREECE

CRETE

TURKEY

CYPRUS

SYRIA

Mediterranean Sea

EGYPT

Nile

Red Sea

NORTH AFRICA

The extent of the Roman Empire in AD117

THE HUGE EMPIRE

The Roman Empire reached its greatest size in AD117. This map shows its extent, stretching thousands of kilometres to the east, west, north and south. Present-day names are used on the map to help compare the Empire to Europe and the Middle East today.

Roman soldiers armed for battle

149–146BC Third and final war between Rome and Carthage in which Carthage is destroyed.

146BC Greece and North Africa come under Roman rule.

73BC Spartacus leads a slave revolt in southern Italy.

58–50BC Roman armies, led by Julius Caesar, conquer Gaul after a series of wars.

55BC Pompey's Theatre, the first stone-built theatre in Rome, is completed.

slaves in chains

55–54BC Roman attacks on Britain begin.

44BC Julius Caesar is murdered in the Senate.

a Roman open-air theatre

31BC Battle of Actium – Octavian defeats Cleopatra of Egypt and Mark Antony, bringing an end to civil war.

29BC Egypt becomes part of the Roman Empire.

27BC Octavian becomes Rome's first emperor and is given the title Augustus.

60BC   40BC   1BC

THE VAST ROMAN EMPIRE 49

History Makers of Rome

THE PEOPLE who made Roman history came from many different backgrounds. The names of the famous survive on monuments and in books. There were consuls and emperors, successful generals and powerful politicians, great writers and historians. However, it was thousands of ordinary people who really kept the Roman Empire going – merchants, soldiers of the legions, tax collectors, servants, farmers, potters, and others like them.

Many of the most famous names of that time were not Romans at all. There was the Carthaginian general, Hannibal, Rome's deadliest enemy. There were also Celtic chieftains and queens, such as Vercingetorix, Caractacus and Boudicca.

ROMULUS AND REMUS
According to legend, Romulus was the founder and first king of Rome. The legend tells how he and his twin brother Remus were abandoned as babies. They were saved by a she-wolf, who looked after them until they were found by a shepherd.

AUGUSTUS (63BC–AD14)
Augustus, born Octavian, was the great-nephew and adopted son of Julius Caesar. After Caesar's death, he took control of the army. He became ruler of the Roman world after defeating Mark Antony at the Battle of Actium in 31BC. In 27BC, he became Rome's first emperor and was given the title Augustus.

CICERO (106–43BC)
Cicero is remembered as Rome's greatest orator, or speaker. Many of his letters and speeches still survive. He was a writer, poet, politican, lawyer and philosopher. He was elected consul of Rome in 63BC, but he had many enemies and was murdered in 43BC.

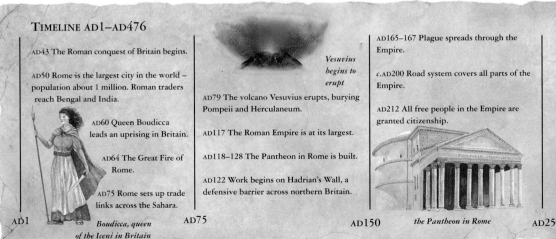

TIMELINE AD1–AD476

AD43 The Roman conquest of Britain begins.

AD50 Rome is the largest city in the world – population about 1 million. Roman traders reach Bengal and India.

AD60 Queen Boudicca leads an uprising in Britain.

AD64 The Great Fire of Rome.

AD75 Rome sets up trade links across the Sahara.

Boudicca, queen of the Iceni in Britain

Vesuvius begins to erupt

AD79 The volcano Vesuvius erupts, burying Pompeii and Herculaneum.

AD117 The Roman Empire is at its largest.

AD118–128 The Pantheon in Rome is built.

AD122 Work begins on Hadrian's Wall, a defensive barrier across northern Britain.

AD165–167 Plague spreads through the Empire.

c.AD200 Road system covers all parts of the Empire.

AD212 All free people in the Empire are granted citizenship.

the Pantheon in Rome

AD1   AD75   AD150   AD25

HADRIAN (AD76–138)

Hadrian became emperor in AD117 and spent many years travelling around the Empire. He had many splendid buildings constructed, as well as a defensive barrier across northern Britain, now known as Hadrian's Wall.

NERO (AD37–68) AND AGRIPPINA

In AD54 Nero became emperor after the death of his adoptive father Claudius. A cruel ruler, he was blamed for a great fire that destroyed much of Rome in AD64. Agrippina, his mother, was a powerful influence on him. She was suspected of poisoning two of her three husbands, and was eventually killed on her son's orders.

CLEOPATRA (68–30BC)

An Egyptian queen of Greek descent, Cleopatra had a son by Julius Caesar. She then fell in love with Mark Antony, a close follower of Caesar. They joined forces against Rome, but after a crushing defeat at Actium in 31BC, they both committed suicide. Egypt then became part of the Roman Empire.

JULIUS CAESAR (100–44BC)

Caesar was a talented and popular general and politician. He led Roman armies in an eight-year campaign to conquer Gaul (present-day France) in 50BC. In 49BC, he used his victorious troops to seize power and declare himself dictator for life. Five years later he was stabbed to death in the Senate by fellow politicians.

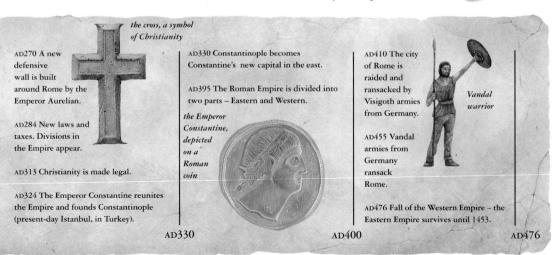

the cross, a symbol of Christianity

AD270 A new defensive wall is built around Rome by the Emperor Aurelian.

AD284 New laws and taxes. Divisions in the Empire appear.

AD313 Christianity is made legal.

AD324 The Emperor Constantine reunites the Empire and founds Constantinople (present-day Istanbul, in Turkey).

AD330 Constantinople becomes Constantine's new capital in the east.

AD395 The Roman Empire is divided into two parts – Eastern and Western.

the Emperor Constantine, depicted on a Roman coin

AD410 The city of Rome is raided and ransacked by Visigoth armies from Germany.

Vandal warrior

AD455 Vandal armies from Germany ransack Rome.

AD476 Fall of the Western Empire – the Eastern Empire survives until 1453.

AD330   AD400   AD476

The Coming of the Vikings

THE YEAR IS AD795. Imagine you are an Irish monk, gathering herbs to make medicines. Walking along the river bank you hear the sound of creaking oars and curses in a strange language. Through the reeds you see a long wooden ship slipping upstream. It has a prow carved like a dragon. Inside it are fierce-looking men – battle-scarred warriors, armed with swords and axes.

Incidents like this happened time after time around the coasts of Europe in the years that followed. In the West, these invaders were called Northmen, Norsemen or Danes. In the East, they were known as Rus or Varangians. They have gone down in history as Vikings. This name comes from a word in the Old Norse language meaning sea raiding. Who were they? The Vikings were Scandinavians from the lands known today as Denmark, Norway and Sweden. Archaeologists have found their farms and houses, the goods they traded, the treasure they stole and their fine wooden ships.

BATTLE ART
The Vikings were skilled artists, as well as fierce warriors. This Danish battle axe is made of iron inlaid with silver. It has been decorated with beautiful swirling patterns.

INTO THE PAST
Archaeologists have excavated Viking towns and found ships, weapons and hoards of treasure. This excavation is in York, in northern England.

SEAFARERS
The outline of the Viking ship, with its high prow and square sail, became widely feared. This carving is from the Swedish island of Gotland.

TIMELINE AD750-875

The Vikings were descended from German tribes who moved northwards into Scandinavia. They were restless, energetic people. By the AD780s, they were raiding other lands. Soon they were exploring, settling and trading far from home, from North America to Baghdad. By 1100 the Vikings had become Christian and their lands had become more like the other countries in western Europe.

Viking sword

AD750 Trade opens up between northern Europe and the East. Trading routes are established.

c.AD750 Small trading and manufacturing towns flourish, such as Ribe in Denmark, Paviken on Gotland and Helgo in Sweden.

treasure hoard

AD789 Vikings raid southern England.

AD793 Vikings raid Lindisfarne, an island off the north-east coast of England.

massacre at Lindisfarne

AD795 Vikings raid Scotland and Ireland.

AD750   AD775   AD80●

THE VIKING HOMELANDS
The Vikings came from Scandinavia. This map shows some of the most important Viking sites. Most of these were in present-day Denmark, southern Sweden and along Norway's coastal fjords.

INVASION FLEET
The Vikings invaded England in AD866. They went on to defeat and murder Edmund, King of the East Angles. Much of our knowledge of the Vikings comes from accounts written by their enemies. Many of these, such as this one about the life of St Edmund, were written later.

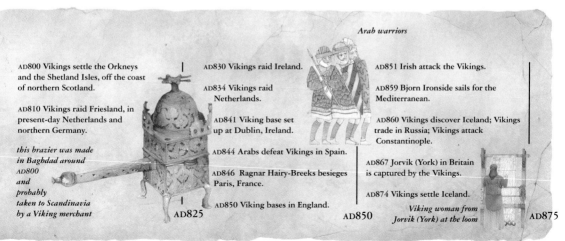

Arab warriors

AD800 Vikings settle the Orkneys and the Shetland Isles, off the coast of northern Scotland.

AD810 Vikings raid Friesland, in present-day Netherlands and northern Germany.

this brazier was made in Baghdad around AD800 and probably taken to Scandinavia by a Viking merchant

AD825

AD830 Vikings raid Ireland.

AD834 Vikings raid Netherlands.

AD841 Viking base set up at Dublin, Ireland.

AD844 Arabs defeat Vikings in Spain.

AD846 Ragnar Hairy-Breeks besieges Paris, France.

AD850 Viking bases in England.

AD850

AD851 Irish attack the Vikings.

AD859 Bjorn Ironside sails for the Mediterranean.

AD860 Vikings discover Iceland; Vikings trade in Russia; Vikings attack Constantinople.

AD867 Jorvik (York) in Britain is captured by the Vikings.

AD874 Vikings settle Iceland.

Viking woman from Jorvik (York) at the loom

AD875

The Viking World

T HE VIKINGS took to the sea in search of wealth, fortune and better land for farming. At that time, Denmark was mostly rough heath or woodland. The other Viking homelands of Norway and Sweden were harsh landscapes, with mountains and dense forests, which were difficult to farm.

From the AD780s onwards, bands of Vikings launched savage attacks on England, Scotland, Ireland and Wales. They later settled large areas of the British Isles, including the Orkneys, Shetlands and the Isle of Man. Viking raiders also attacked settlements along the coasts and rivers of Germany, the Netherlands and France. The area they settled in France became known as Normandy, meaning land of the Northmen.

Viking warriors sailed as far as Spain, where they clashed with the Arabs who then ruled it. They also travelled west across the Atlantic Ocean, settling in Iceland, Greenland and even North America.

Viking traders founded states in the Ukraine and Russia and sailed down the rivers of eastern Europe. They hired themselves out as the emperor's bodyguards in the city they called Miklagard – also known as Constantinople (modern Istanbul).

By the 1100s, the descendants of the Vikings lived in powerful Christian kingdoms. The wild days of piracy were over.

N

L'Anse aux
Meadows

NEWFOUNDLAN
(VINLANI

CANADA

TIMELINE AD875–1000

carved prow

Viking longship

*proclamation
of Althing*

AD878 In England, Alfred (whom the Victorians called The Great) of Wessex defeats the Vikings.

AD885 Viking army attacks Paris.

AD886 Danelaw treaty in England.

AD900 Harald Finehair becomes first king of a united Norway.

AD910 Anglo-Saxon king, Edward the Elder, recaptures large areas of England from the Danes.

AD911 French give Normandy to the Vikings under King Rollo (Hrolf).

AD930 One of many meetings of the Iceland Althing. The settlement of Iceland is largely completed.

AD937 At the Battle of Brunanburh, Athelstan of Wessex defeats an alliance of Danes, Scots and Welsh.

AD940 Edmund of Wessex makes peace with Olaf of Jorvik.

AD875   AD900   AD925   AD950

Greenland Sea

GREENLAND

Norwegian Sea

Thingvellir
ICELAND

NORWAY

SWEDEN

Brattahlid

HEBRIDES

Kaupang

Birka

North Atlantic Ocean

SCOTLAND

Lindisfarne
priory is
burned

DENMARK

Ribe

Dublin

York
(Jorvik)

Hedeby

IRELAND

WALES

ENGLAND

FRANCE

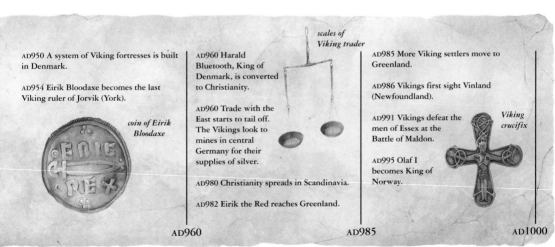

AD950 A system of Viking fortresses is built in Denmark.

AD954 Eirik Bloodaxe becomes the last Viking ruler of Jorvik (York).

coin of Eirik Bloodaxe

scales of Viking trader

AD960 Harald Bluetooth, King of Denmark, is converted to Christianity.

AD960 Trade with the East starts to tail off. The Vikings look to mines in central Germany for their supplies of silver.

AD980 Christianity spreads in Scandinavia.

AD982 Eirik the Red reaches Greenland.

AD985 More Viking settlers move to Greenland.

AD986 Vikings first sight Vinland (Newfoundland).

AD991 Vikings defeat the men of Essex at the Battle of Maldon.

AD995 Olaf I becomes King of Norway.

Viking crucifix

AD960

AD985

AD1000

Viking Heroes

BRAVERY AND A SPIRIT OF ADVENTURE were greatly admired by the Vikings. The names and nicknames of their heroes – explorers, ruthless pirates and brave warriors – have gone down in history. Two of the most famous were Ragnar Hairy-Breeks, who terrorized the city of Paris in AD846, and a red-bearded Norwegian, called Eirik the Red, who named and settled Greenland in AD985.

The Vikings we know most about were powerful kings. Harald Hardradi (meaning stern in counsel) saw his brother, King Olaf of Norway, killed in battle. He then fled to Russia and went on to join the emperor's bodyguard in Constantinople. After quarrelling with the Empress Zoë, he returned to Russia before becoming ruler of Norway.

BLOODAXE
This coin is from Eirik Bloodaxe's reign. He was the son of Norway's first king and ruled Jorvik (York).

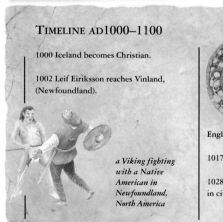

Viking women could be just as tough and stubborn as their men. They were well respected, too. Archaeologists found two women buried in a splendid ship at Oseberg in Norway. One was a queen, the other her servant. They were buried with beautiful treasures.

MEMORIAL IN STONE
This memorial was raised at Jelling in Denmark by King Harald Bluetooth. An inscription on it says that King Harald 'won all of Denmark and Norway and made all the Danes Christians'.

FROM WARRIOR TO SAINT
Olaf Tryggvasön was Harald Finehair's grandson. He seized the throne of Norway in AD995. King Olaf became a Christian and was made a saint after his death in AD1000.

TIMELINE AD1000–1100

1000 Iceland becomes Christian.

1002 Leif Eiriksson reaches Vinland, (Newfoundland).

a Viking fighting with a Native American in Newfoundland, North America

Anglo-Saxon brooch in Scandinavian style

1014 Irish defeat Vikings at Clontarf.

1016 Svein Forkbeard, King of England, is succeeded by Cnut.

1017 King Cnut rules Denmark.

1028 King Olaf II of Norway is overthrown in civil war.

1030 King Olaf II dies in battle at Stiklestad.

King Olaf II, who was later made a saint

1030 King Cnut comes to the throne in Norway.

1035 King Cnut dies. The Anglo-Saxons rule all of England.

AD1000   AD1010   AD1030   AD1040

THE NORMANS

Hrolf, or Rollo, was a Viking chief. In AD911 he and his followers were granted part of northern France by the French king. The region became known as Normandy, and the Normans went on to conquer Britain and parts of Italy.

THE WISE RULER

Cnut was the son of Svein Forkbeard, King of Denmark. He led extremely savage raids on England, becoming its king in 1016. He proved to be a kinder and wiser king than he had been a warrior. By 1018 he was King of Denmark and by 1030 he had become King of Norway as well. He died at Shaftesbury, England in 1035.

LEIF THE LUCKY

Leif the Lucky was Eirik the Red's son. He sailed even further west than his famous father. In about AD1000 he reached Canada, sailing to a land he named Vinland. This was probably Newfoundland. Other Vikings, including Leif's brother Thorwald, tried to settle these North American lands, but with little success.

Elizabeth, Russian wife of Harald Hardradi

1047 Harald Hardradi is made King of Norway.

1050 Oslo founded by Harald Hardradi.

1053 The Norman Empire begins in southern Italy.

1066 Harald Hardradi invades England. He is defeated by Harold I at the Battle of Stamford Bridge. An exhausted Harold I is in turn defeated by William of Normandy at the Battle of Hastings.

Norwegian foot soldier with axe

1070 The English pay Danegeld (a ransom) to persuade the Viking raiders to leave them alone.

1080 Cnut IV becomes King of Denmark.

1084 The Normans sack (raid) Rome.

1086 Cnut IV is assassinated.

1087 William of Normandy dies.

1098 King Magnus III of Norway asserts his authority over the Orkneys, the Hebrides and the Isle of Man. Although these were Viking settlements, there was dissent in these places.

1100 End of Viking era.

AD1070   AD1080   AD1100

Mesoamerican Civilizations

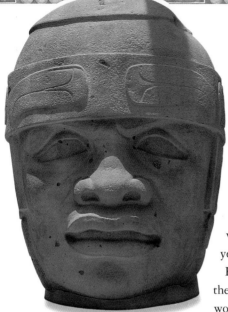

THE AZTECS LIVED IN MESOAMERICA — the region where North and South America meet. It includes the countries of Mexico, Guatemala, Honduras, El Salvador and Belize. During the past 3,000 years, Mesoamerica has been home to many great civilizations, including the Olmecs, the Maya, the Toltecs and the Aztecs. The Aztecs were the last of these to arrive, coming from the north in around AD1200. In about 1420 they began to conquer a mighty empire. But in 1521 they were themselves conquered by Spanish soldiers, who came to America in search of gold. Over the next hundred years, the rest of Mesoamerica also fell to the Spaniards.

Even so, the descendants of these cultures still live in the area today. Many ancient Mesoamerican words, customs and beliefs survive, as do beautiful hand-painted books, mysterious ruins and amazing treasures.

OLMEC POWER
This giant stone head was carved by the Olmecs, the earliest of many great civilizations that flourished in Mesoamerica. Like the Maya and Aztecs, the Olmecs were skilled stone workers and built great cities.

UNCOVERING THE PAST
This temple is in Belize. Remains of such great buildings give archaeologists important clues about the people who built them.

TIMELINE 5000BC–AD800

Various civilizations were powerful in Mesoamerica at different times. The Maya were most successful between AD600–900. The Aztecs were at the height of their power from AD1428–AD1520.

Olmec figure

5000BC The Maya settle along the Pacific and Caribbean coasts of Mesoamerica.

2000BC People begin to farm in Belize, Guatemala and south-east Mexico.

2000BC The beginning of the period known as the Preclassic era.

1200BC Olmec people are powerful in Mesoamerica. They remain an important power until 400BC.

1000BC Maya craftworkers begin to copy Olmec pottery and jade carvings.

900BC Maya farmers design and use irrigation systems.

600BC The Zapotec civilization begins to flourish at Monte Alban.

Maya codex

300BC The Maya population starts to grow rapidly. Cities are built.

292BC The first-known Maya writing is produced.

150BC–AD500 The people living in the city of Teotihuacan grow powerful.

AD250 The beginning of the greatest period of Maya power, known as the Classic Maya era. This lasts until AD900.

mask from Teotihuacan

| 5000BC | 2000BC | 300BC | AD500 |

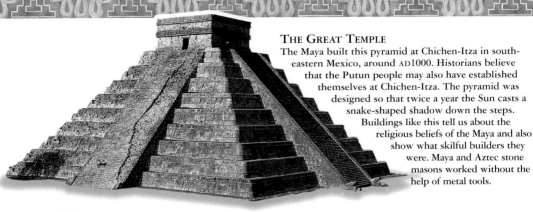

THE GREAT TEMPLE

The Maya built this pyramid at Chichen-Itza in south-eastern Mexico, around AD1000. Historians believe that the Putun people may also have established themselves at Chichen-Itza. The pyramid was designed so that twice a year the Sun casts a snake-shaped shadow down the steps. Buildings like this tell us about the religious beliefs of the Maya and also show what skilful builders they were. Maya and Aztec stone masons worked without the help of metal tools.

THE FACE OF A GOD

This mask represents the god Tezcatlipoca. It is made of pieces of semi-precious stone fixed to a real human skull. Masks like this were worn during religious ceremonies, or displayed in temples as offerings to the gods.

■ Home of the Mesoamerican civilizations

MESSAGES IN CODE

These are Aztec picture-symbols for days, written in a folding book called a codex. Mesoamerican civilizations kept records of important people, places and events in picture-writing.

MESOAMERICA IN THE WORLD

For centuries, Mesoamerica was home to many different civilizations, but there were links between them, especially in farming, technology and religious beliefs. Until around AD1500, these Mesoamerican civilizations had very little contact with the rest of the world.

AD550 This is the time of the Maya's greatest artistic achievements. Fine temples and palaces in cities such as Kabah, Copan, Palenque, Uxmal and Tikal are built. These great regional city-states are ruled by lords who claim to be descended from the gods. This period of Maya success continues until AD900.

temple at Tikal

AD615 The great Maya leader Lord Pacal rules in the city of Palenque.

AD650 The city of Teotihuacan begins to decline. It is looted and burned by unknown invaders around AD700.

AD684 Lord Pacal's rule ends. He is buried in a tomb within the Temple of the Inscriptions in Palenque.

jade death mask of Lord Pacal

Bonampak mural

AD790 Splendid Maya wall-paintings are created in the royal palace in the city of Bonampak.

AD600   AD700   AD800

The Rise and Fall of Empires

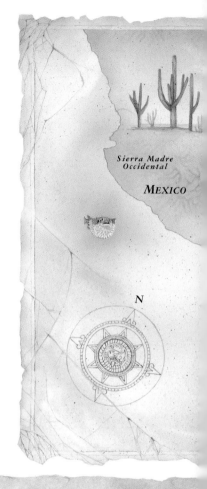

Sierra Madre Occidental

MEXICO

N

MESOAMERICA IS A LAND of contrasts. There are high, jagged mountains, harsh deserts and swampy lakes. In the north, volcanoes rumble. In the south, dense, steamy forests have constant rain for half the year. These features made travelling around difficult, and also restricted contact between the regions.

Mesoamerica was never ruled as a single, united country. For centuries it was divided into separate states, each based on a city that ruled the surrounding countryside. Different groups of people and their cities became rich and strong in turn, before their civilizations weakened and faded away.

Historians divide the Mesoamerican past into three main periods. In Preclassic times (2000BC–AD250), the Olmecs were most powerful. The Classic era (AD250–900) saw the rise of the Maya and the people living in the city of Teotihuacan. During the Postclassic era (AD900–1500), the Toltecs, followed by the Aztecs, controlled the strongest states.

Each civilization had its own language, laws, traditions and skills, but there were also many links between the separate states. They all built big cities and organized long-distance trade. They all practised human sacrifice and worshipped the same family of gods. And, unlike all other ancient American people, they all measured time using their own holy calendar of 260 days.

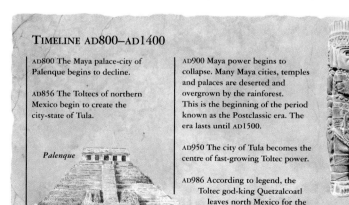

TIMELINE AD800–AD1400

AD800 The Maya palace-city of Palenque begins to decline.

AD856 The Toltecs of northern Mexico begin to create the city-state of Tula.

Palenque

AD900 Maya power begins to collapse. Many Maya cities, temples and palaces are deserted and overgrown by the rainforest. This is the beginning of the period known as the Postclassic era. The era lasts until AD1500.

AD950 The city of Tula becomes the centre of fast-growing Toltec power.

AD986 According to legend, the Toltec god-king Quetzalcoatl leaves north Mexico for the Maya lands of Yucatan.

Toltec warrior

1000 The Maya city of Chichen-Itza becomes powerful. Historians believe that the Maya may have been helped by Putun warriors from the Gulf coast of Mexico.

1000 Toltec merchants do business along long-distance trade routes around the coast. They are helped by Maya craftworkers. Long-distance trade has already been taking place in Mesoamerica for hundreds of years.

1011–1063 The Mixtecs are ruled by the leader Eight Deer, in the area of Oaxaca. The Mixtecs are master goldsmiths.

AD800   AD900   AD1000   AD1100

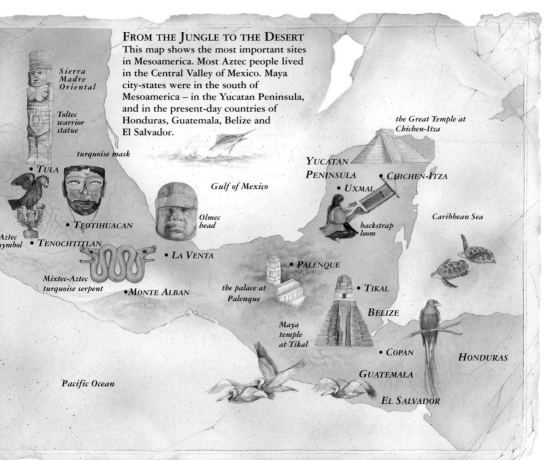

FROM THE JUNGLE TO THE DESERT

This map shows the most important sites in Mesoamerica. Most Aztec people lived in the Central Valley of Mexico. Maya city-states were in the south of Mesoamerica – in the Yucatan Peninsula, and in the present-day countries of Honduras, Guatemala, Belize and El Salvador.

Sierra Madre Oriental

Toltec warrior statue

turquoise mask

the Great Temple at Chichen-Itza

• TULA

Aztec symbol

• TEOTIHUACAN

• TENOCHTITLAN

Mixtec-Aztec turquoise serpent

• MONTE ALBAN

Gulf of Mexico

Olmec head

• LA VENTA

the palace at Palenque

• PALENQUE

Maya temple at Tikal

Pacific Ocean

YUCATAN PENINSULA

• UXMAL

• CHICHEN-ITZA

backstrap loom

Caribbean Sea

• TIKAL

BELIZE

• COPAN

GUATEMALA

EL SALVADOR

HONDURAS

1100 Aztecs leave their homeland in the dry, semi-desert land to the north of Mexico and travel southwards in search of a new place to live.

Aztec settlers

1168 The Chichimec people from central Mexico destroy the city of Tula and end Toltec power.

Aztec warrior

c.1200 Aztecs arrive in central Mexico. They find Tepanecs, Culhuas and Acolhuacans living there. At first, the Aztecs work as soldiers and slaves for these people, but they grow strong and fight against their masters.

c.1220 A new Maya city is founded at Mayapan.

1300 The Mixtec civilization begins to thrive in Oaxaca, southern Mexico.

1325 Aztecs found the city of Tenochtitlan on an island in the centre of Lake Texcoco, central Mexico.

1350 Aztecs begin to build *chinampas* (gardens) around Lake Texcoco.

1372–91 The first-known Aztec ruler, Acamapichtli, reigns.

eagle on cactus, the symbol of Tenochtitlan

AD1200

AD1300

AD1400

THE RISE AND FALL OF EMPIRES 61

Mesoamerican History Makers

Fame in Maya and Aztec times usually came with power. We know the names of powerful Aztec and Maya rulers, and sometimes of their wives. However, very few ordinary people's names have been discovered.

Rulers' names were written in a codex (book) or carved on a monument to record success in battle or other great achievements. Scribes also compiled family histories, in which rulers often claimed to be descended from gods. This gave them extra religious power. Aztec and Maya rulers made sure their names lived on by building huge palaces, amazing temples and tombs.

Some of the most well-known Mesoamerican rulers lived at a time when their civilization was under threat from outsiders. Explorers from Europe have left us detailed accounts and descriptions of the rulers they met.

ROYAL TOMB
This pyramid-shaped temple was built to house the tomb of Lord Pacal. He ruled the Maya city-state of Palenque from AD615 to 684. Its walls are decorated with scenes from Pacal's life.

MAYA RULER
This statue shows a ruler from the Maya city of Kabah, in Mexico. Most Maya statues were designed as symbols of power, rather than as life-like portraits.

TIMELINE AD1400–AD1600

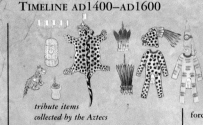

tribute items collected by the Aztecs

1400–25 The Aztec city of Tenochtitlan continues to thrive and grow.

1415–1426 The Aztec leader Chimalpopoca reigns.

1428 Aztecs defeat the Tepanecs and begin to conquer neighbouring lands and collect tribute from them.

1428 Aztecs set up the Triple Alliance. This was an agreement with neighbouring city-states Texcoco and Tlacopan that made them the strongest force in Mexico.

1440 Moctezuma Ilhuicamina, the greatest Aztec ruler, begins his reign. He reigns until 1468.

1441 The Maya city of Mayapan is destroyed by civil war.

1468 Aztec ruler Axayacatl reigns.

1473 The Aztecs conquer the rich market-city of Tlatelolco in central Mexico.

market traders in the market-city of Tlatelolco

AD1400   AD1425   AD1450   AD1475

GOLD-SEEKER

Soldier and explorer Hernando Cortés (1485–1547) came from a poor but noble Spanish family. After Columbus' voyages, many Spanish adventurers travelled to Mesoamerica and the Caribbean hoping to make their fortunes. Cortes sailed to Cuba and then, in 1519, went on to explore Mexico. His example inspired many treasure-seekers. One such man, Pizarro, went on to conquer the Incas of Peru.

BETWEEN TWO WORLDS

Malintzin (far right above) was from a Mesoamerican state hostile to the Aztecs. She was of vital help to the Spanish conquerors because she spoke the Aztec language and quickly learned Spanish. The Spanish called her Doña Marina.

THE LAST EMPEROR

Aztec emperor Moctezuma II (above right) ruled from 1502 to 1520. He was the last emperor to control the Aztec lands. Moctezuma II was a powerful warrior and a good administrator, but he was tormented by gloomy prophecies and visions of disaster. He was captured when Cortés and his soldiers invaded the capital city of Tenochtitlan in 1519. The following year he was stoned in a riot whilst trying to plead with his own people.

1481–1486 Aztec ruler Tizoc reigns.

1486 Aztec ruler Ahuitzotl begins his reign.

1487 The Aztecs' Great Temple in Tenochtitlan is finished. Twenty thousand captives are sacrificed at a special ceremony to consecrate it (make it holy).

1492 The European explorer Christopher Columbus sails across the Atlantic Ocean to America.

Columbus lands

1502 Columbus sails along the coast of Mesoamerica and meets Maya people.

a comet appears in the sky

1502–1520 Moctezuma II reigns. During his reign, a comet appears in the sky. Aztec astronomers fear that this, and other strange signs, mean the end of the world.

1519 Hernando Cortés, a Spanish soldier, arrives in Mexico. A year later, Cortés and his soldiers attack Tenochtitlan. Moctezuma II is killed.

1521 The Spanish destroy Tenochtitlan.

1525 Spain takes control of Aztec lands.

1527 Maya lands are invaded by the Spanish.

1535 Mexico becomes a Spanish colony.

1600 War and European diseases wipe out 10 million Aztecs, leaving fewer than a million, but the Aztec language and many customs live on. By 1600, between 75% and 90% of Maya people are also dead, but Maya skills, beliefs and traditions survive.

Spanish soldier

AD1500   AD1525   AD1600

The First North Americans

DESCENDANTS OF THE ANASAZIS, who were among the earliest known North American Indians, have colourful tales of their origins. One story tells how their ancestors climbed into the world through a hole. Another describes how all of the tribes were created from a fierce monster who was ripped apart by a brave coyote. The early history of the many nations or tribes is not clear, though archaeological finds have helped to build a picture of their way of life. If you could step back to before 1500, you would find that the United States and Canada were home to hundreds of different Indian tribes. Each had its own leader(s) and a distinctive language and culture. Some tribes were nomadic, some settled permanently in large communities. Remains of pottery, woodcarvings and jewellery show how many of the North American peoples developed expert craft skills.

KEEPING THE PAST ALIVE
Descendants of the different tribes survive throughout North America, passing down stories and traditions to new generations. This boy in Wyoming is dressed in ceremonial costume for a modern powwow. He is helping to preserve his tribe's cultural history.

BRIDGING THE GAP
Archaeological evidence suggests that the first American Indians travelled from Asia. They crossed ice and land bridges formed at the Bering Strait around 13,000BC or earlier. From here, they moved south, some settling along the coasts.

TIMELINE 32,000BC–AD1400

Most historians believe that hunters walked to North America from Siberia. Evidence suggests there may have been two migrations – one around 32,000BC, the second between 28,000BC and 13,000BC. Some historians think there may have been earlier ancient populations already living there. More research is needed to support this theory. The hunters spread out, each group, or tribe, adapting their way of life to suit their environment. Later, some gave up the nomadic hunting life and began to settle as farmers.

3000BC Inuit of the Arctic are probably the last settlers to come from Asia.

1000BC Early cultures are mound builders such as the Adena and later, the Hopewell people. The Hopewell are named after the farmer on whose Ohio land their main site was found.

serpent mound of the Hopewell culture

1000BC Farming cultures develop in the South-west with agricultural skills brought in from Mexico.

black and yellow maize

300BC–AD1450 Cultures, such as the Hohokam, use shells as currency.

AD200 (or before) There is evidence of maize being grown by the mound-building people, probably introduced from Mexico.

AD700–900 Pueblo people bury their dead with black and white painted pots.

burial pot

3000BC   300BC

BUCKSKIN RECORD
Tales of events were painted on animal skins, such as this one, created by an Apache. The skins serve as a form of history book. North American Indians had no real written alphabet, so much of the evidence about their way of life comes from pictures.

FALSE FACE
Dramatic, carved masks were worn by several tribes to ward off evil spirits thought to cause illnesses. This one is from the Iroquois people. It was known as a False Face mask because it shows an imaginary face. False Face ceremonies are still performed in North America today.

DIGGING UP EVIDENCE
Hopewell Indians made this bird from hammered copper. It dates back to around 300BC and was uncovered in a burial mound in Ohio. The mounds were full of intricate trinkets buried alongside the dead. Finds like this tell us about the crafts, materials and customs of the time.

ANCIENT TOWN
Acoma (right) is one of the oldest continuously inhabited traditional Pueblo settlements in the South-west. It is still partly inhabited by Pueblo descendants. The Pueblo people were given their name by Spaniards who arrived in the area in 1540. *Pueblo* is a Spanish word meaning village. It was used to describe the kind of tribe that lived in a cluster of houses built from mud and stone. Flat-roofed homes were built in terraces, two or three storeys high.

AD700 Mound-building cultures build temples at Cahokia near the Mississippi. The city holds the largest population in North America before the 1800s.

AD900 Earliest Anasazis (ancient people) on the Colorado Plateau live in sunken pit homes. Later they build their homes above the ground but keep pit dwellings as kivas, which are their religious buildings.

kiva (underground temple) of the Anasazis

AD982 First Europeans reach Greenland (north-east of Canada) under the Viking, Eirik the Red.

1002 Leif Eiriksson lands in Newfoundland, Canada, and creates the first European settlements.

Vikings arrive

1100 The Anasazi people move into the mountains, building settlements in cliffs.

Mesa Verde, a cliff palace

1200 The Calusa in Florida are skilful carvers and craftsmen who trade extensively.

1270s–1300 Anasazis abandon many of their prehistoric sites and stone cities – many move eastwards.

1300 Beginnings of the Pueblo tribes (Hopi and Zuni) in the South-west. Many of these are descendants of the Anasazis.

AD1400

Inhabiting a Vast Land

orca
(killer whale)

THE FIRST NORTH AMERICANS were hunters who followed musk oxen, bison and other animals to the grassland interior of the huge continent. Early settlements grew up in the rugged, hostile terrain of the South-west where three dominant cultures evolved. The Mogollon (Mountain People) are thought to be the first South-west dwellers to build houses, make pottery and grow their own food from around 300BC. The Hohokam (Vanished Ones) devised an extensive canal system to irrigate the desert as early as 100BC, while the Anasazi (Ancient Ones) were basket makers who built their homes high among the cliffs and canyons.

In contrast, the eastern and midwestern lands abounded with plant and animal life. Here, tribes such as the Adena (1000BC to AD200) and the Hopewell (300BC to AD700), created huge earth mounds to bury their dead. The central Great Plains was home to over 30 different tribes, who lived by hunting bison. In the far north, the Inuit had a similar existence, relying on caribou and seals for their food and clothes. Europeans began to arrive around AD982 with the Vikings. Then in the 1500s, Spanish explorers came looking for gold, land and slaves. Over the next 400 years, many other foreign powers laid claim to different parts of the land. By 1910, the native population was at its lowest, about 400,000, and many tribes had been forced from their homelands on to reservations.

TRIBAL HOMELANDS
In the 1400s, there were more than 300 tribes, or nations, spread across North America (between two and three million people). These are often divided into ten cultural areas based on the local environment:
1 Arctic
2 Subarctic
3 Woodlands
4 South-east
5 Great Plains
6 South-west
7 Great Basin
8 Plateau
9 North-west Coast
10 California

TIMELINE AD1400–1780

Columbus

1400 Apaches arrive in the South-west, probably by two routes – one from the Plains after following migrating buffalo, the other via the Rockies.

1492 Christopher Columbus sails from Spain to the Bahamas where he meets the peaceful, farming Arawaks.

1510 The powerful Calusas of Florida abandon their ancient centre, Key Marco, possibly after hearing of foreign invaders.

1513 Calusas drive off Ponce de León, a Spanish explorer.

1541 Zuni people get a first glimpse of horses when Spain's Francisco Vasquez de Coronado travels to the South-west.

1541 Caddo people of the Plains oppose Spanish Hernando de Soto's soldiers.

1542 The large Arawak population that Columbus first encountered has been reduced to just 200 people. Ten years later the Arawaks die out through mistreatment.

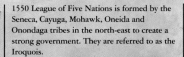

shell wampum belt celebrates the League of Five Nations

1550 League of Five Nations is formed by the Seneca, Cayuga, Mohawk, Oneida and Onondaga tribes in the north-east to create a strong government. They are referred to as the Iroquois.

1585 Sir Walter Raleigh reaches the north-east coast and, ignoring the rights of the Secotan natives, claims the land for the English, calling it Virginia.

1590 Raleigh and John White return to Virginia, but the colony has disappeared. White draws pictures documenting Secotan life.

AD1400   AD1540   AD1550   AD1595

BAFFIN ISLAND

seal

NEWFOUNDLAND

1

Hudson Bay

2

Inuit with igloo

Inuit fisherman

QUEBEC

Chipewyan canoe

Cree

Cree

2

Tsimshian

Plains Cree

Blackfoot

Hidatsa

Ojibwa

Algonquin

Huron

beaver

9

Plains Ojibwa

Mandan

salmon

8

Chippewa

Menominee

3

New York

Noolka

Crow

maize

Iroquois

Nez Perce

Western Sioux

Sioux

Algonquian groups

Shoshone

Pawnee

Shawnee

Washington

Salish

Ute

Arapaho

N

Powhatan

Washoe

Cayuse

Cheyenne warrior hunting bison

Hopewell mound

Secotan village

Yurok

Osage

10

Paiute basket-maker

Hopi katchina doll

Kiowa camp

Cherokee village of Echota

Chumash

Navajo hogans

NEW MEXICO

5

Wichita

Chickasaw

Choctaw

Creek

Seminole

eagle

Los Angeles

Mohave

Comanche

4

Natchez

Apache

TEXAS

Calusa

Miami

6

Pueblo village

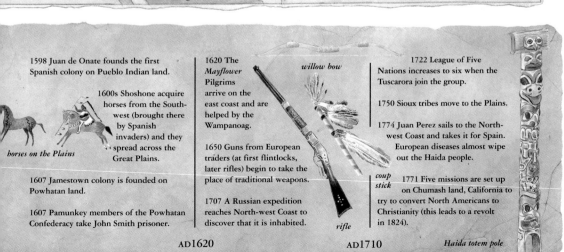

1598 Juan de Onate founds the first Spanish colony on Pueblo Indian land.

1600s Shoshone acquire horses from the South-west (brought there by Spanish invaders) and they spread across the Great Plains.

horses on the Plains

1607 Jamestown colony is founded on Powhatan land.

1607 Pamunkey members of the Powhatan Confederacy take John Smith prisoner.

1620 The Mayflower Pilgrims arrive on the east coast and are helped by the Wampanoag.

willow bow

1650 Guns from European traders (at first flintlocks, later rifles) begin to take the place of traditional weapons.

1707 A Russian expedition reaches North-west Coast to discover that it is inhabited.

coup stick

rifle

1722 League of Five Nations increases to six when the Tuscarora join the group.

1750 Sioux tribes move to the Plains.

1774 Juan Perez sails to the North-west Coast and takes it for Spain. European diseases almost wipe out the Haida people.

1771 Five missions are set up on Chumash land, California to try to convert North Americans to Christianity (this leads to a revolt in 1824).

AD1620

AD1710

Haida totem pole

Shapers of History

MANY NORTH AMERICAN Indians who have earned a place in history lived around the time that Europeans reached North America. They became famous for their dealings with explorers and with the white settlers who were trying to reorganize the lives of Indian nations. Some tribes welcomed the new settlers. Others tried to negotiate peacefully for rights to their own land. Those who led their people in battles, against the settlers, became the most legendary. One of these was Geronimo, who led the last defiant group of Chiricahua Apaches in their fight to preserve the tribe's homeland and culture.

POCAHONTAS (1595–1617)
The princess became a legend, and the topic of a Disney film, for protecting English Captain John Smith against her father, Chief Powhatan. The English took Pocahontas captive to force Powhatan's people to agree to their demands. She married John Rolfe, an English soldier, and in 1616 left for England with their baby. She never returned, as she died of smallpox, in Gravesend, Kent, aged 22.

CORNPLANTER (died 1796)
In the 1700s, Cornplanter was a chief of the Iroquois. He was a friend to the Americans and fought on their side in the Revolution of 1776–85. The land of Cornplanter's tribe was spoiled but his people were given a reservation for their help. Many Iroquois people fought on the side of the British which split the group.

Opechancanough, Powhatan

Black Hawk, Sauk

Geronimo, Apache

Pontiac, Ottawa

Lapowinsa, Lenape

TIMELINE AD1780–1924

1783 The colonists (settlers) sign a treaty with Britian which recognizes their independence and calls them Americans. The tribes are never regarded as American.

1788 The Chinook in the North-west have their first encounter with Europeans when they meet Englishman John Mears.

1789 Explorers encounter Kutchin and other Subarctic tribes, who later set up trade with the Hudson's Bay Company (formed in 1831).

1795 Tecumseh refuses to sign the Treaty of Greenville giving up Shawnee land.

William Clark and Meriwether Lewis

1803 The US federal government buys Mississippi land from the French, squeezing out the Indians even more.

1804 Sacawagea guides Lewis and Clark on the first overland journey from Mississippi to the Pacific Coast.

1830–40s Painters such as Frederic Remington, George Catlin and Karl Bodmer, document lifestyles of the Plains Indians.

1832 Sauk chief, Black Hawk, leads a final revolt against the US and is defeated.

1848 Discovery of gold in California. *coming on the train*

1848–58 Palouse tribe of the Plateau resist white domination, refusing to join a reservation.

George Catlin painting a Mandan chief

AD1780

AD1803

AD1848

SARAH WINNEMUCCA (1844–1891)

Sarah was from the Paviotso Paiutes of northern Nevada. Her grandfather escorted British Captain John Fremont in his exploration of the West in the 1840s. But in 1860 her mother, sister and brother were all killed in the Paiute War against white settlers. Sarah acted as a mediator between her people and the settlers to help improve conditions. She later wrote a book, Life Among the Paiutes, telling of the suffering of the tribe and her own life.

SITTING BULL (1831–1890)

The Hunkpapa Sioux had a spiritual leader, a medicine man known as Sitting Bull. He brought together sub-tribes of the Sioux and refused to sign treaties giving up the sacred Black Hills in South Dakota. He helped to defeat General Custer at Little Bighorn.

TECUMSEH (died 1813)

A great chief of the Shawnees, Tecumseh, tried to unite tribes of the Mississippi valley, Old North-west and South against the United States. He even fought for the British against the US in the 1812–14 war. The picture shows his death.

PROTECTING THEIR TRIBES

These eight North American chiefs are some of the most famous. Not all fought. Lapowinsa of Delaware, was cheated out of land when he signed a contract allowing settlers as much land as they could cover in a day and a half. Pontiac traded with the French but despised English intrusion. Chief Joseph tried to negotiate peacefully for land for the Nez Perce tribe but died in exile. Red Cloud successfully fought to stop gold seekers invading Sioux hunting grounds.

Oscelo, Seminole

Red Cloud, Sioux

Chief Joseph

1850 The Navajo sign their third treaty with the US but hostilities continue.

1850s–80s Railways open up the West to settlers.

1864 The Long Walk – Navajo people and animals are massacred by US troops, their homes burned. Survivors are forced to walk 500km to Fort Sumner.

1864 Sand Creek Massacre – 300 Cheyenne women and children are killed by US soldiers.

Sand Creek Massacre

1876 General Custer is killed by Sioux warriors in the Battle of Little Bighorn.

1886 Surrender of Geronimo to the US. He is a prisoner for many years.

1890 Ghost dance springs up as Sioux tribes mourn their dead – it worries the white settlers who see it as provocation.

1890 Sitting Bull is killed at Standing Rock (a Sioux reservation) by Indian police hired by the US.

1890 Sioux chief Big Foot and many of his tribe are killed in the Massacre of Wounded Knee. This ends the Sioux's struggle for their homelands.

buffalo coin

1924 US citizenship granted to American Indians and marked by a coin bearing a buffalo.

ghost dance shirt

AD1870

AD1924

Politics, Society & Leadership

Learn about the development of
power and control, and the evolvement
of cities, laws and governments in
different civilizations

Keeping Control

IMAGINE WHAT it would be like if there were no rules at school, or no one had ever told you how to behave or what to do! When human beings live or work together, they work out basic rules about how to behave. This saves arguing all the time, and makes sure that jobs for the good of everyone, such as cleaning, get done. Often, we can work out for ourselves how to be sociable – to behave with other people. But rules may also be made by leaders and teachers. Throughout history, there have been leaders who used their experience and wisdom to guide, teach and organize – or govern – others in the best possible way. There have also been many cruel and greedy tyrants whose interest lay in increasing their own power and wealth rather than the good of the people.

The first humans lived very simply, in small family groups. There were no chiefs or rulers. The leaders were the strongest and fittest. Each group was only concerned with survival.

People live or work together at all sorts of different levels – from little groups such as your family or your class at school to the school itself and the community in which it lives. At each new level, there are additional sets of rules, and more leaders –

The warrior kings of Mycenae in ancient Greece ruled from 1500BC. They lived in palaces enclosed by massive walls, called citadels. Administrators and the rest of the population lived outside the walls.

TIMELINE 8000BC–40BC

8000BC The farming way of life begins in the Middle East. People begin to settle down and live in villages.

Cuneiform writing from Mesopotamia

Differences in wealth and status emerge.

3500BC The first cities develop in Mesopotamia. Each is an independent state with its own ruler.

One of over 750 hieroglyphic symbols in the Egyptian writing system

3000BC The kingdom of Egypt is founded. Its rulers, or pharaohs, are believed to be living gods.

2600BC City-states develop in northern India.

2350BC King Urukagina of Lagash in Mesopotamia issues the oldest known law code.

Chinese soldier of the Zhou Dynasty

2000BC Ancesters of the modern Inuit arrive in Alaska from Siberia.

*c.*1792–1750BC Hammurabi of Babylon issues a law code about property and marriage.

1112BC Beginning of Zhou dynasty in China, during which emperors become known as 'Sons of Heaven'.

The Greek philosopher, Socrates

8000BC   3000BC   2000BC   750B

from the grown-ups in a family and the teachers and head teacher in a school, to the prime minister or president of a country. A number of people organized in this way is called society. Throughout history, society has become more and more complex as populations have grown. In this book you will be able to see how society evolved in different ways around the world, and how the leaders in various cultures and civilizations, controlled or governed their peoples.

In the beginning, it was all very simple. In prehistoric times, people hunted animals and picked plants for food. There was rarely any food to spare. A few related families lived together in small bands called clans. Everyone knew one another, and looked to the oldest and most experienced people in the clan for advice and decisions. Where there was water and fertile land, though, people learned how to farm and began to settle in permanent

Viking communities were at first small and tribal, hemmed in by high mountains. Land for big settlements to develop was limited. Some Viking chieftains conquered other tribes and built up kingdoms.

Among tribal peoples, such as the Celts and Vikings, fighting for new land was a way of life and survival. Their warriors were important and respected members of tribal society. Those who were good at leading people often became chieftans.

homes. Some farmers were more successful than others. They could use their wealth to control or persuade others. In this way, differences of status or rank developed. The Celts, for example, were made up of many tribes, each of which

750BC Celtic chiefdoms develop in central Europe.

680–627BC The Assyrian Empire is at its greatest extent.

594BC Athenian statesman Solon reforms the laws of Athens.

509–507BC Democratic government is introduced in Athens.

509BC The Romans overthrow their king and create a republic.

A triumphal arch, built to celebrate a Roman victory

c.300BC Maya city-states develop in Mesoamerica.

221BC Qin Shi Huangdi becomes the first emperor of China.

58–52BC The Roman commander Julius Caesar conquers the Celts of Gaul (modern France).

44BC Julius Caesar destroys the Roman republic when he appoints himself dictator for life. He is murdered soon afterwards.

500BC　　　　　　**300BC**　　　　　　**40BC**

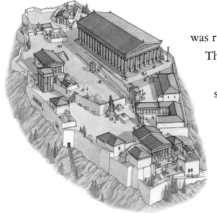

was ruled by a chief. Below the chief came warriors and then priests. Then came the farmers and last of all, the unpaid slave labour.

Although they were powerful, chiefs and kings in these simple societies had to listen to their followers or they lost their support. Like many other rulers throughout history, Celtic leaders rewarded their warriors with gifts to keep them loyal.

The Celtic tribes were scattered, and remained small and clan-based. In the fertile valleys of big rivers in the Middle East, China, India and Egypt, though, there were the resources, the climate and the space for settlements to expand.

Encouraging belief in powerful gods was one way of keeping citizens in order. In Athens, temples to the guardian goddess Athena dominated the city from the rocky Acropolis. Many public festivals were held there.

Great cities, with populations of tens of thousands, and a huge range of peoples and skills, grew up. Organizing such large communities was far too much for the ruler alone. Administrators, clerks and specialist advisers were needed to help decide how their cities and lands should be run. These groups of rulers and advisers were the first governments.

Rulers of early civilizations and cultures had to work hard at holding on to their power. The kings of city-states in Mesopotamia, the pharaohs of ancient Egypt and the Incas of South America promoted the idea that they were appointed by the gods, or even took on godly status themselves. Many leaders

In the Islamic world, it was not only scholars like these who had to study. Every Muslim had to learn the Arabic language so that they could read the laws laid down in the Koran.

Timeline 60bc–ad1912

The Maya temple at Tikal

27bc Augustus becomes the first emperor of Rome.

ad476 Fall of the Roman Empire.

ad593–622 Imperial government is introduced in Japan.

ad793 Viking pirates attack Britain and Ireland.

A Japanese samurai warrior

ad800–900 Maya city-states collapse after an environmental disaster.

ad930 Viking settlers found the Icelandic Althing (national assembly).

Doubloons, made from the gold found in the Americas

1185 The Japanese emperor falls under the domination of the shoguns (military commanders).

60bc   30bc   ad800   1200

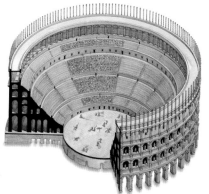

Roman emperors staged increasingly bloodthirsty gladiatorial games in the Colosseum in Rome. The events showed off the emperor's power and impressed the people. The stadium held up to 50,000 spectators.

ruled by fear, threatening dreadful punishments if they were disobeyed. Others won over those who might be useful by handing out riches, land or status.

Mesopotamian rulers were among the first to issue a formal set of rules, or laws, which the inhabitants of their city-states had to follow. The laws were inscribed on stone pillars – together with the punishments for breaking them – and erected in public places so that everyone could see them.

Those who made the rules were the few – the rich, the powerful or those who had inherited leadership from their fathers before them. The ordinary citizen did not have a say in how society was run. Then the Athenian Greeks introduced the idea of democracy, a system of government that allowed members of the community to vote. Most governments in the Western world today are democratically elected (chosen). The Romans developed a type of government called a republic. The United States and France are two countries that are run as republics today with democratically elected representatives. You can look at the different forms of government around the world today, and then see how they began and developed through history.

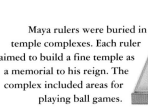

Maya rulers were buried in temple complexes. Each ruler aimed to build a fine temple as a memorial to his reign. The complex included areas for playing ball games.

Himeji castle, Japan

c.1200 The legendary emperor Manco Capac founds the Inca Empire.

1325 Foundation of the Aztec Empire.

1407 Building of the Chinese emperors' palace, the Forbidden City, in Beijing begins.

1521 The Spanish under Cortés conquer the Aztecs.

1526 The Mughals under Babur begin to conquer India.

1532 The Spanish under Pizarro conquer the Incas.

1687 Mughal empire reachest its peak under Aurangzeb.

1868 In Japan the shogunate falls and the emperors are returned to power.

1912 China becomes a republic after the last emperor is deposed.

Body of a Chinese princess in a jade suit

1400   1600   1912

Beginnings of Social Structure

IN STONE AGE TIMES, there were very few people in the world. Experts estimate that the world's population in 13,000BC was about eight million. Today it is nearly six billion – 750 *thousand* times as many. We can guess how Stone Age people lived together by looking at hunter-gatherer societies that still exist today in South America and the Pacific.

Groups of families lived together in clans. All the members of each clan were related to each other, usually through their mother's family or by marriage. Clans were large enough to protect and feed everyone, but not so large that they were unmanageable. All the members of a clan, including children, were involved in finding and gathering food for everyone. Clans were probably also part of larger tribes, which may have met up at certain times of year, such as for a summer hunt. The members of a tribe shared a language and a way of life. When people learned how to farm, populations increased and societies began to be organized in more complicated ways.

MOTHER GODDESSES
Eight thousand years ago, this clay sculpture from Turkey may have been worshipped as a goddess of motherhood. Families were often traced through the female line because mothers give birth, so everyone knew who the babies belonged to. The fathers were not always known.

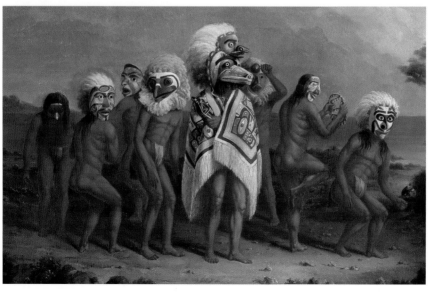

SHAMAN LEADERS
This painting from the 1800s shows Native American shamans performing a ritual dance. Shamans were the spiritual leaders of their tribes. They knew the dances, chants, prayers and ceremonies that would bring good luck and please the spirits. Shamanism is found in hunter-gatherer societies around the world today and was practised in prehistoric times.

TRIBAL CHIEF

This man is a Zulu chief from South Africa. His higher rank is shown by what he wears. In prehistoric times, tribes might have been ruled by chiefs or councils of elders. An old man buried at Sungir in Russia around 23,000BC was probably a chief. His body was found richly decorated with fox teeth and beads made of mammoth ivory.

SCENES FROM LONG AGO

Paintings on cliff walls in the Sahara Desert in Africa show hippopotamuses being hunted and herders tending cattle. Other images show a woman pounding flour, ceremonies and a family with a dog. They show that, in 6000BC, it was a fertile area with organised communities.

FINE FIGURE

Between 3000 and 2000BC, some of the finest prehistoric sculpture was made on the Cycladic Islands of Greece. This figurine is made of ground marble and shows a slender woman with her arms folded above her waist. Finely worked sculpture was a sign that a society had become more complex than a simple clan. There were more people with more specialized jobs, and more free time.

A TRADITIONAL WAY OF LIFE

The man on the right is helping a boy prepare for his coming-of-age ceremony in Papua New Guinea. Traditional ways of life are still strong in that country, where there are many remote tribes. In some villages, all the men live together, rather than with their wives and children. This allows them to organize their work, such as hunting, more easily.

Legendary Kings of Mesopotamia

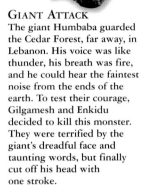

FROM AROUND 3000BC, the people of Mesopotamia lived in walled cities. Each city had its own ruler and guardian god. The rulers wanted to be remembered for ever, by the wonderful temples and palaces they had built, or by having their deeds and battle victories carved into stone pillars called stelae.

Some of the world's oldest stories are about Gilgamesh, king of one of Sumer's most important cities in around 2700BC. Stories and poems about him passed from the Sumerian people to those who lived in the Babylonian and Assyrian empires. Finally, in the 7th century BC, the Assyrians wrote down all these exciting stories on to clay tablets. The *Epic of Gilgamesh* was stored in the great libraries of King Ashurbanipal of Assyria, where it was discovered by archaeologists over 100 years ago. Gilgamesh was not a good king at first, so the gods created Enkidu, a wild, hairy man, to fight him. The king realized he had met his match, and the two then became good friends and went everywhere together.

GIANT ATTACK
The giant Humbaba guarded the Cedar Forest, far away, in Lebanon. His voice was like thunder, his breath was fire, and he could hear the faintest noise from the ends of the earth. To test their courage, Gilgamesh and Enkidu decided to kill this monster. They were terrified by the giant's dreadful face and taunting words, but finally cut off his head with one stroke.

THE BULL OF HEAVEN
Ishtar, the goddess of love and war (on the left), tries to stop Enkidu and Gilgamesh from killing the Bull of Heaven. Ishtar had fallen in love with the hero-king, and she wanted to marry him. Gilgamesh knew that the goddess was fickle, and turned her down. Ishtar was furious and asked her father, Anu the sky god, to give her the Bull of Heaven so she could take revenge on Gilgamesh. The Bull was a deadly beast who had the power to bring death and long-term misery to the city of Uruk. The two friends fought and killed the bull. Enkidu (on the right) hung on to its tail, as Gilgamesh delivered the death blow with his sword.

THE CITY OF URUK

There is very little of Uruk left today, but it was a very important city when Gilgamesh was king. The city had splendid temples dedicated to Anu, the sky god, and his daughter Ishtar who fell in love with Gilgamesh. The king also built a great wall round the city. When his friend Enkidu died, Gilgamesh was heartbroken, and also frightened because he realized he would die one day, too. He wanted to live for ever. In the end, he decided that creating a beautiful city was his best chance of immortality. He would be remembered for ever for creating the fine temples and massive walls of Uruk.

THE PLANT OF ETERNAL LIFE

This massive stone carving of a heroic figure found in the palace of King Sargon II may be of Gilgamesh. Sargon II created the world's first empire by conquering all the cities of Sumer, Mari and Ebla. Gilgamesh set out to find Utnapishtim, the ruler of another Sumerian city who was said to have found the secret of eternal life. The way was long and dangerous, and led into the mountains where lions prowled. After a terrifying walk in total darkness, Gilgamesh emerged on the other side of the mountain into the garden of the gods. Beyond the garden were the Waters of Death, but our hero found a ferryman to take him safely across. At last he met Utnapishtim, who told him he would never die if he found a plant that grew on the sea bed. Gilgamesh tied stones on his feet, dived into the sea and picked the plant. However, on the way home, he stooped down to drink at a pool. A water snake appeared and snatched the plant. With it went Gilgamesh's hope of immortality.

LASTING FAME

The figures on this stone vase from Uruk probably show Gilgamesh. The king found the lasting fame he wanted because his name lived on in stories and legends, and in statues and carvings such as this.

Kingly Duties in Mesopotamia

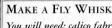

THE KINGS OF MESOPOTAMIA considered themselves to have been chosen by the gods. For example, Ur-Nanshe of Lagash (2480BC) said that he was granted kingship by Enlil, chief of the gods, and Ashurbanipal (669BC) claimed he was the son of the Assyrian god, Ashur, and his wife, Belit. The Mesopotamian kings ran the state on the god's behalf. Even in the Assyrian Empire, when the kings had grand titles such as 'King of the Universe', they still felt they were responsible to the gods for the well-being of their people. Another of their titles was 'Shepherd'. This meant they had to look after their people, just as a shepherd tends his flock.

AUTHORITY
An onyx mace was carried by the Babylonian kings of Mesopotamia as a symbol of authority. At New Year, the king laid the mace before the statue of the chief god, Marduk. When he picked it up again, it meant he would reign for another year.

SUN GOD TABLET FROM SIPPAR
Kings had to see that temples and statues of the gods were kept in good repair. This tablet shows King Nabu-apla-iddina of Babylon being led into the presence of the god Shamash. The story on the tablet tells us that the king wanted to make a new statue of the god. He was meant to repair the old one but it had been stolen by enemies. Fortunately a priest found a model of the statue that could be copied.

MAKE A FLY WHISK
You will need: calico fabric, pencil, ruler, PVA glue and brush, scissors, thick card, paints and paintbrushes, newspaper.

1 Draw long leaf shapes about 45cm long on to the calico fabric with the pencil. Paint the shapes with watered down PVA glue. Leave to dry.

2 Cut out the leaf shapes. Make a card spine for the centre of each leaf as shown, thicker at the bottom than at the top, and glue them on.

3 Paint the leaves in gold, yellow and red paints on both sides. Add fine detail by cutting carefully into the edge of each leaf using the scissors.

FIGHTING FOR THE GODS

Kings believed that they were commanded by the gods to conquer other cities and states in their name. In this relief, King Sennacherib is sitting on his throne receiving the booty and prisoners taken after the city of Lachish had fallen. The king devoted a whole room in his palace at Nineveh to the story of this siege. He also made war on Babylon and completely devastated the city. In 612BC the Babylonians had their revenge. They destroyed the city of Nineveh and hacked out Sennacherib's face on this sculpture.

EXPLORATION AND DISCOVERY

Another mark of good kingship was the expansion of knowledge. King Shalmaneser III sent an expedition to find the source of the River Tigris (pictured here). His men set up a stela (a carved monument) to record the discovery and made offerings to the gods to celebrate. Many Mesopotamian kings were learned men. They collected clay tablets to make great libraries or built up collections of exotic plants and animals.

Fly whisks made of long thin leaves or feathery reeds kept the flies away from the king. They could also be used as a fan to keep him cool.

4 Draw two identical handle shapes on to the stiff card. They should be about 22cm long and 10cm wide at the top. Cut out the shapes with the scissors.

5 Tear up newspaper strips and dip into glue. Wrap the strips around the edges of the two handles to fasten them together. Leave the top of the handle unglued.

6 Decorate the handle with gold paint. Leave to dry. Paint decorative details on to the gold with black paint using a fine paintbrush.

7 Glue the bottoms of the leaves and push them into the top of the handle, between the two pieces of cardboard. Spread the leaves well apart.

Running the Assyrian Empire

Ｆ ROM THE BEGINNING of the 800s BC, the country of Assyria
in the north of Mesopotamia began to grow into a vast
empire. The land was divided into provinces that were named
after the main city, such as Nineveh, Samaria or Damascus.
Every city had a governor who made sure that taxes were
collected, called up soldiers in times of war, and supplied
workers when a new palace or temple was to be built. The
governor made sure that merchants could travel safely, and he
was also responsible for law and order. If the king and his
army passed through the province, the governor supplied
them with food and drink. A vast system of roads connected
the king's palace with governors' residences and the important
cities of the Empire.

ENFORCED REMOVAL
Conquered people were banished from
their homelands, and forced to go and
live in Assyria. These people were from
Lachish, near Jerusalem, and were
moved to the Assyrian city of Nineveh.
The men were used as forced labour in
the limestone quarries.

THE KING'S MEN
An Assyrian king was constantly
surrounded by bodyguards,
astrologers and other members
of the court. There were also
visitors such as provincial
governors who helped the king
run the Empire. The King's
servants included scribes to
write down orders, messengers
to deliver them and an
attendant to hold a parasol. In
this picture King Ashurnasirpal
is celebrating a successful bull
hunt with priests and musicians.

MAKE A PARASOL
*You will need: pencil,
coloured card 60cm x 60cm,
scissors, masking tape,
paints in bright colours and
paintbrushes, white card,
string or twine, glue, dowel.*

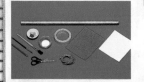

1 Draw a circle on the
coloured card measuring
roughly 60cm across. Cut
out the circle with the
scissors keeping the edge
as neat as possible.

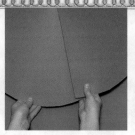

2 Cut a slit from the edge
of the circle to the
centre. Pull one edge of
the slit over the other to
make a conical shape.
Secure with masking tape.

3 Paint your parasol with
red paint. Leave to dry.
Then paint stripes in lots
of different shades of
orange and red from the
top to the bottom.

TOWARDS A NEW LIFE

Defeated people camp out en route to a new life in Assyria. The Assyrian Empire grew so big, that it could take months to travel back from a newly won territory. Conquered people were usually kept together in families and given homes in the countryside. Often they were set to work to cultivate more land.

KEEPING ACCOUNTS

Assyrian scribes at the governor's palace at Til Barsip on the River Euphrates make a note of taxes demanded by the king. Taxes were exacted not only from the local Assyrian people, but also from the conquered territories. They could be paid in produce, such as grain, horses or cattle, and wine.

Kings were accompanied by an attendant carrying a sunshade, which was probably made of fine woollen material and decorated with tassels.

USEFUL TRIBUTE

Conquered people had to give tributes such as horses to the Assyrian king, as well as food for the animals. The horses swelled the chariot and cavalry units in the Assyrian army. The best-bred and strongest horses came from the foothills of the Zagros Mountains to the east of Assyria.

4 Cut 20 oval shapes about 5cm by 4cm from the white card. Cover with a base colour of gold. Leave to dry, then paint with bright designs.

5 Use the scissors to make holes around the edge of the parasol and in the ovals. Attach the ovals to the parasol with twine, knotting it as shown.

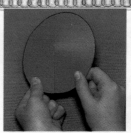

6 Cut a small circle out of coloured card measuring 10cm across. Make a slit to the centre, and pull one edge over the other as before. Paint the small cone gold.

7 Glue it to the top of the parasol. Paint the handle with gold paint and allow to dry. Attach it to the inside of the parasol using plenty of masking tape.

The Pharaohs of Egypt

THE CROOK AND FLAIL
These emblems of the god Osiris became badges of royal authority. The crook stood for kingship and the flail for the fertility of the land.

flail

crook

THE WORD PHARAOH comes from the Egyptian *per-aa*, which meant 'great house' or 'palace'. It later came to mean the man who lived in the palace, the ruler. Pictures and statues show pharaohs with special badges of royalty, such as crowns, headcloths, false beards, sceptres and a crook and flail held in each hand.

The pharaoh was the most important person in Egypt. He was the link between the people and their gods, and therefore had to be protected and cared for. The pharaoh's life was busy. He was high priest, chief law-maker, commander of the army and in charge of the country's wealth. He had to be a clever politician, too. The ancient Egyptians believed that on his death, the pharaoh became a god. Pharaohs were usually men, but women sometimes ruled Egypt as Queen Hatshepsut did, when her husband Thutmose II died and his son was still a child. A pharaoh could take several wives. Within royal families, it was common for fathers to marry daughters and for brothers to marry sisters. Sometimes pharaohs married foreign princesses in order to make an alliance with another country.

MOTHER GODDESS OF THE PHARAOHS
Hathor was worshipped as the mother goddess of each pharaoh. Here she is shown welcoming the pharaoh Horemheb to the afterlife. Horemheb was a nobleman who became a brilliant military commander. He was made pharaoh in 1323BC.

MAKE A CROWN

You will need: 2 sheets of A1 card (red and white), pencil, ruler, scissors, masking tape, cardboard roll, bandage, pva glue and brush, acrylic paint (white, gold), brush, beads, skewer, water pot and brush.

White crown of Upper Egypt

46cm

40cm

8cm

54cm

20cm

Snake

15cm

55cm

Red crown of Lower Egypt

Mark out these patterns on to your card. Cut around them with scissors.

1 Bend the shape made from the white card into a cylinder, as shown. Use lengths of masking tape to join the two edges together firmly.

Ramesses Meets the Gods

This painting shows the dead pharaoh Ramesses I meeting the gods Horus (left) and Anubis (right). Pharaohs had to pass safely through the afterlife. If they did not, the link between the gods and the world would be broken forever.

The Queen's Temple

This great temple (*below*) was built in honour of Queen Hatshepsut. It lies at the foot of towering cliffs at Deir el-Bahri, on the west bank of the Nile near the Valley of the Kings. The queen had the temple built as a place for her body to be prepared for burial. Pyramids, tombs and temples were important symbols of power in Egypt. By building this temple, Hatshepsut wanted people to remember her as a pharaoh in her own right.

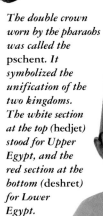

Hatshepsut

A female pharaoh was so unusual that pictures of Queen Hatshepsut show her with all the badges of a male king, including a false beard! Here she wears the pharaoh's crown. The cobra on the front of the crown is the badge of Lower Egypt.

The double crown worn by the pharaohs was called the pschent. *It symbolized the unification of the two kingdoms. The white section at the top* (hedjet) *stood for Upper Egypt, and the red section at the bottom* (deshret) *for Lower Egypt.*

2 Tape a cardboard roll into the hole at the top. Plug its end with a ball of bandage. Tape the bandage in position and glue down the edges.

3 Wrap the white section with lengths of bandage. Paint over these with an equal mixture of white paint and glue. Leave the crown in a warm place to dry.

4 Now take the shape made from the red card. Wrap it tightly around the white section, as shown, joining the edges with masking tape.

5 Now paint the snake gold, sticking on beads as eyes. When dry, score lines across its body. Bend the snake's body and glue it to the crown, as shown.

High Society in Egypt

EGYPTIAN PALACES were vast complexes. They included splendid public buildings where the pharaoh met foreign rulers and carried out important ceremonies. Members of the royal family lived in luxury in beautiful townhouses with painted walls and tiled floors near the palace.

The governors of Egypt's regions also lived like princes, and pharaohs had to be careful that they did not become too rich and powerful. The royal court included large numbers of officials and royal advisors. There were lawyers, architects, tax officials, priests and army officers. The most important court official of all was the vizier, who carried out many of the pharaoh's duties for him.

The officials and nobles were at the top of Egyptian society. But most of the hard work that kept the country running smoothly was carried out by merchants and craft workers, by farmers, labourers and slaves.

GREAT LADIES
Ahmose-Nefertari was the wife of Ahmose I. She carries a lotus flower and a flail. Kings could take many wives. It was common for them to have a harem of beautiful women.

A NOBLEMAN AND HIS WIFE
This limestone statue shows an unknown couple from Thebes. The man may have worked in a well-respected profession, as a doctor, government official or engineer. Noblewomen did not work but were quite independent. Any property that a wife brought into her marriage remained hers.

THE SPLENDOURS OF THE COURT
This is the throne room of Ramesses III's palace at Medinet Habu, on the west bank of the Nile near Thebes. Pharaohs often had many palaces, and Medinet Habu was one of Ramesses III's lesser ones. Surviving fragments of tiles and furniture give us an idea of just how splendid the royal court must have been. A chamber to one side of the throne room is even believed to be an early version of a shower cubicle!

RELAXATION
Ankherhau (above), a wealthy overseer of workmen, relaxes at home with his wife. They are listening to a harpist. Life was pleasant for those who could afford it. Kings and nobles had dancers, musicians and acrobats to entertain them. Cooks worked in their kitchens preparing sumptuous meals. By comparison, ordinary people ate simple food, rarely eating meat except for the small animals they caught themselves.

HAIR CARE
The royal family was waited on by domestic servants who attended to their every need. Here (left), the young Queen Kawit, wife of the pharaoh Mentuhotep II, has her hair dressed by her personal maid. Although many of the female servants employed in wealthy households were slaves, a large number of servants were free. This meant that they had the right to leave their employer at any time.

Rulers of India

DISPLAY OF POWER
A Mughal emperor rides through the city on top of an elephant, a symbol of royalty. Kings often processed through their cities to display their power and majesty. They were always followed by attendants and courtiers.

O VER THE CENTURIES, India has been ruled by leaders from many different lands, cultures and religions. Their titles and the symbolic objects that surrounded them are often a clue to their roles and beliefs. From the time of the emperor Ashoka, around 250BC, the ruler became known as *cakravartin* (wheel-turner). The wheel was a Buddhist symbol for the world, so this suggested that the king made the world go round. Objects that were symbols of royalty included sceptres, crowns and yak-tail fans. The most important object was the *chatra* (umbrella), which signified the king's protection of his realm. Hindu *maharajadhirajas* (kings) developed the idea that the god Vishnu lived within them. When Islam arrived in the 1300s, the sultans showed their obedience to the caliph (the head of Islam in Baghdad) by taking titles such as *nasir* (helper). Rulers in the Mughal Empire (1526-1857), took Persian titles such as *padshah* (emperor).

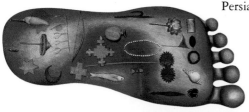

THE MARKS OF A KING
A picture of the foot of Hindu ruler Rama bears images of a lotus, conch shell, umbrella, fly whisk and other royal symbols. People believed that a world-ruling king was born with features such as these on their soles and palms. Rama was said to be a wise and good ruler. He was later deified (made into a god).

MAKE A CHAURI

You will need: strip of corrugated cardboard measuring 3cm x 25cm, raffia, scissors, sticky tape, pva glue, 20 cm length of dowel, modelling clay, paint in gold and a contrasting colour, paintbrushes, foil sweet wrappers.

1 Put the strip of card on a covered, flat surface. Cut strips of raffia. Carefully tape the strands of raffia to the card. Leave your chauri to dry.

2 Wrap the card and raffia around the dowel, and glue it in place. Keep the card 2 cm from the top, so that the dowel supports the raffia.

3 Tape the card and raffia band firmly in place to make sure that it will not come undone when you use your whisk. Leave the whisk to dry.

A KING'S HALO

The king in this procession has a halo surrounding his head. From Mughal times, rulers were thought to be blessed with the divine light of wisdom. This was represented in pictures by a halo.

ROYAL CUSHION

Raja Ram Singh of Jodhpur sits with his nobles. Only the king was allowed to sit on a cushion. The Rajputs were kings of northern India who fought against Muslim invaders in the first millennium AD. In the Mughal Empire, they were important military allies of the Muslims.

ROYAL RAMA

Rama was a Hindu king, believed to be the earthly representative of the god Vishnu. He is with his wife Sita and his brothers. He holds a bow, a symbol of courage. Attendants hold other symbols of royalty.

The fly whisk was a symbol of a Hindu king's power.

4 Make lots of small beads from modelling clay. Glue these on to the dowel in a circle, about 2.5 cm below the strip of card. Leave to dry.

5 Paint the dowel and beads with two coats of gold paint. Leave it to dry. Then paint a pattern on the strip of card and the dowel, in different colours.

6 When the paint is dry, glue bits of coloured foil paper to your chauri. The more decorations you add, the more it will look like a real chauri.

The Mughal Empire

I N 1526, A PRINCE called Babur invaded India from the north-west. He swept across the country with a powerful army and soon arrived in Delhi. The city was the heart of the Sultanate, the kingdom that Islamic invaders had founded 300 years before. Babur defeated the Sultanate and founded the Mughal Empire. It was the last important dynasty of India before the British arrived in the 1700s.

Babur's grandson, Akbar was a great Mughal leader from 1556 to 1605. Although a Muslim, he was tolerant of other religions and took Hindu princesses as his wives. Forty years later, the warlike Mughal ruler Aurangzeb returned to a stricter form of Islam and expanded the Empire. The Mughals were patrons of the arts, and built glorious palaces,

gardens and tombs. Many of India's most precious works of art date from this era. Persian was the language of their court, but they also spoke Urdu, a mixture of Persian, Arabic and Hindi.

ORDERLY COURTIERS
Mughal nobles had to take part in court rituals. They had to arrive punctually at court, and line up in rows. Dress and posture were very important. The cummerbund tied around the waist and the turban were signs of self-control. Courtiers guarded the palace strictly in turn.

THE FIRST MUGHAL EMPEROR
Babur defeats Ibrahim Lodi, the last sultan of Delhi, at the Battle of Panipat in 1526. Babur invaded India because he was unable to recapture his own homeland in Samarkand.

MAKE A LACQUERED STORAGE BOX
You will need: pencil, ruler, sheets of card, scissors, sticky tape, newspaper, wallpaper paste or flour and water, bowl, fine sandpaper, paint in white and bright colours, paintbrushes, non-toxic varnish.

1 Scale up the shape shown here to the size you want your box to be and copy the shape on to card. Cut out the shape and fix the edges with sticky tape to form a box.

2 Draw 4 card triangles with sides the same length as the top of the box. Tape the triangles together to form a pyramid and cut off the top.

3 Add newspaper strips to the paste, or flour and water, to make papier mâché. Cover the box and lid with three layers of papier mâché. Dry between layers.

A POEM IN STONE

The Mughal emperor Shah Jahan commemorated his wife Mumtaz Mahal (who died in childbirth) by building this magnificent mausoleum. It was built between 1631 and 1648, and came to be known as the Taj Mahal. It is built of white marble from Rajasthan. The Taj Mahal is one of the most magnificent buildings in the world, and is the high point of Mughal art.

JADE HOOKAH

This Mughal period *hookah* (pipe) is made from precious green jade. During Mughal times, the culture of the court reached a high point in Indian history. Many fine objects and ornaments like this were made.

RED PALACE

The Red Fort in Agra is one of the palaces built by Akbar. The Mughal emperors broke with the tradition of kings living in tents, and built sumptuous residences in their capital cities.

Lacquered boxes were popular with women of the royal court for storing jewellery.

4 When the papier mâché is dry, smooth any rough edges with sandpaper. Add squares of cardboard as feet. Paint the box and the lid white.

5 Allow the painted box and lid to dry. Draw a pattern on to the box and lid. You could copy the pattern shown here, or use your own design.

6 Paint the lid and the box, including the feet, with brightly coloured paints. Use the pattern that you have drawn as a guide. Leave to dry.

7 To finish, paint the box and lid with a coat of non-toxic varnish. Leave to dry completely, then add a final coat of varnish. Your storage box is now finished.

Lives of the Chinese Rulers

THE FIRST CHINESE RULERS lived about 4,000 years ago. This early dynasty (period of rule) was known as the Xia. We know little about the Xia rulers, because Chinese history of this time is mixed up with ancient myths and legends. Excavations have told us more about the Shang dynasty rulers about 1,000 years later. They were waited on by slaves and had fabulous treasures.

During the next period of rule, the Zhou dynasty, an idea grew up that Chinese rulers were Sons of Heaven, placed on the throne by the will of the gods. After China became a powerful, united empire in 221BC, this idea helped keep the emperors in power. Rule of the Empire was passed down from father to son. Anyone who seized the throne by force had to show that the overthrown ruler had offended the gods. Earthquakes and natural disasters were often taken as signs of the gods' displeasure.

Chinese emperors were among the world's most powerful rulers ever. Emperors of China's last dynasty, the Qing (1644–1912), lived in luxurious palaces that were cut off from the world. When they travelled through the streets, the common people had to stay indoors.

WHERE EMPERORS PRAYED
There are beautifully decorated pillars inside the Hall of Prayer for Good Harvests at Tiantan in Beijing. An emperor was a religious leader as well as a political ruler. Each New Year, the emperor arrived at the hall at the head of a great procession. The evening was spent praying to the gods for a plentiful harvest in the coming year.

TO THE HOLY MOUNTAIN
This stele (inscribed stone) is located on the summit of China's holiest mountain, Taishan, in Shandong province. To the ancient Chinese, Taishan was the home of the gods. For over 2,000 years the emperors climbed the carved steps to the temple to offer prayers.

IN THE FORBIDDEN CITY
The vast Imperial Palace in Beijing is best described as 'a city within a city'. It was built between 1407 and 1420 by hundreds of thousands of labourers under the command of Emperor Yongle. Behind its high, red walls and moats were 800 beautiful halls and temples, set among gardens, courtyards and bridges. No fewer than 24 emperors lived here in incredible luxury, set apart from their subjects. The Imperial Palace was also known as the Forbidden City. Ordinary Chinese people were not even allowed to approach its gates.

'WE POSSESS ALL THINGS'

This was the message sent from Emperor Qianlong to the British King George III in 1793. Here the emperor is being presented with a gift of fine horses from the Kyrgyz people of Central Asia. By the late 1800s, Chinese rule took in Mongolia, Tibet and Central Asia. All kinds of fabulous gifts were sent to the emperor from every corner of the Empire, as everyone wanted to win his favour.

RITUALS AND CEREMONIES

During the Qing dynasty, an emperor's duties included many long ceremonies and official receptions. Here in Beijing's Forbidden City, a long carpet leads to the ruler's throne. Officials in silk robes line the steps and terraces, holding their banners and ceremonial umbrellas high. Courtiers kneel and bow before the emperor. Behaviour at the royal court was set out in the greatest detail. Rules decreed which kind of clothes could be worn and in which colours.

CARRIED BY HAND

The first Chinese emperor, Qin Shi Huangdi, is carried to a monastery high in the mountains in the 200s BC. He rides in a litter (a type of chair) that is carried on his servants' shoulders. Emperors always travelled with a large following of guards and courtiers.

Japan's Emperors of the Sun

HANIWA FIGURE
From around AD300-550, clay *haniwa* figures were put around tombs. Statues of soldiers, servants and animals were placed in an emperor's tomb to look after him in his next life.

THE JAPANESE PEOPLE began to live in villages in about 300BC. Over the next 600 years, the richest and most powerful of these villages became the centres of small kingdoms, controlling the surrounding lands. By about AD300, a kingdom based on the Yamato Plain in south-central Japan became bigger and stronger than the rest. It was ruled by chiefs of an *uji* (clan) who claimed to be descended from the Sun goddess. The chiefs of the Sun-clan were not only army commanders. They were priests, governors, law-makers and controllers of their people's treasure and food supply as well. Over the years, their powers increased.

By around AD500, Sun-clan chiefs from Yamato ruled over most of Japan. They claimed power as emperors, and organized lesser chiefs to work for them, giving them noble titles as a reward. Each emperor chose his own successor from within the Sun-clan, and handed over the sacred symbols of imperial power – a jewel, a mirror and a sword. If a male successor to the throne was too young to rule, an empress might act for a time as regent.

Descendants of these early emperors still rule Japan today, although their role is purely ceremonial. In other periods of Japan's history, too, the emperors had very little power. Some did play an active part in politics, while others spent their time shut away from the outside world.

NARA
This shrine is in the ancient city of Nara. Originally called Heijokyo, Nara was founded by Empress Gemmei (ruled AD707–715) as a new capital for her court. The city was planned and built in Chinese style, with streets arranged in a grid pattern. The Imperial Palace was situated at the northern edge.

FANTASTIC STORIES

Prince Shotoku (AD574–622) was descended from the imperial family and from another powerful clan, the Soga. He never became emperor, but ruled as regent for 30 years on behalf of Empress Suiko. Many fantastic stories were told about him. One was that he was able to speak as soon as he was born. It was also said that he could see into the future. More accurate reports of Shotoku's achievements list his introduction of a new calendar, and his reform of government, based on Chinese ideas. He was also a supporter of the new Buddhist faith, introduced from China.

LARGEST WOODEN STRUCTURE

The Hall of the Great Buddha at Nara was founded on the orders of Emperor Shomu in AD745. The whole temple complex is said to be the largest wooden structure in the world. It houses a bronze statue of the Buddha, 16m tall and weighing 500 tonnes. It was also designed to display the emperor's wealth and power. There is a treasury close to the Hall of the Great Buddha, built in AD756. This housed the belongings of Emperor Shomu and his wife, Empress Komyo. The treasury still contains many rare and valuable items.

BURIAL MOUNDS

The Yamato emperors were buried in huge, mound-shaped tombs surrounded by lakes. The largest, built for Emperor Nintoku, is 480m long. From above, the tombs have a keyhole-shaped layout. Inside, they contain many buried treasures.

THE SUN GODDESS

The Sun goddess Amaterasu Omikami is shown emerging from the earth in this print. She was both honoured and feared by Japanese farmers. One of the emperor's tasks was to act as a link between the goddess and his people, asking for her help on their behalf. The goddess's main shrine was at Ise, in central Japan. Some of its buildings were designed to look like grain stores – a reminder of the Sun's power to cause a good or a bad harvest.

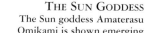

Keeping Control in Japan

DANCE
A Bugaku performer makes a slow, stately movement. Bugaku is an ancient form of dance that was popular at the emperor's court over 1,000 years ago. It is still performed today.

I N EARLY JAPAN, everyone, from the proudest chief to the poorest peasant, owed loyalty to the emperor. However, many nobles ignored the emperor's orders – especially when they were safely out of reach of his court. There were plots and secret schemes as rival nobles struggled to influence the emperor or even to seize power for themselves.

Successive emperors passed laws to try to keep their nobles and courtiers under control. The most important new laws were introduced by Prince Shotoku (AD574–622) and Prince Naka no Oe (AD626–671). Prince Naka considered his laws to be so important that he gave them the name *Taika* (Great Change). The Taika laws created a strong central government, run by a Grand Council of State, and a well-organized network of officials to oversee the 67 provinces.

POLITE BEHAVIOUR
A group of ladies watches an archery contest from behind a screen at the edge of a firing range. The behaviour of courtiers was governed by rigid etiquette. Noble ladies had to follow especially strict rules. It was bad manners for them to show their faces in public. Whenever men were present, the ladies crouched behind a low curtain or a screen, or hid their faces behind their wide sleeves or their fans. When travelling, they concealed themselves behind curtains or sliding panels fitted to their ox-carts. They also often left one sleeve dangling outside.

THE SHELL GAME

You will need: fresh clams, water bowl, paintbrush, gold paint, white paint, black paint, red paint, green paint, water pot.

1 Ask an adult to boil the clams. Allow them to cool and then remove the insides. Wash the shells and leave them to dry. When dry, paint the shells gold.

2 Carefully pull each pair of shells apart. Now paint an identical design on to each of a pair of clam shells. Start by painting a white, round face.

3 Add features to the face. In the past, popular pictures, such as scenes from the *Tale of Genji*, were painted on to the shell pairs.

NOBLES AT COURT

Two nobles are shown here riding a splendid horse. Noblemen at the imperial court spent much of their time on government business.

They also practised their riding and fighting skills, took part in court ceremonies, and read and wrote poetry.

THE FUJIWARA CLAN

Fujiwara Teika (1162–1241) was a poet and a member of the Fujiwara clan. This influential family gained power at court by arranging the marriages of their daughters to young princes and emperors. Between AD724 and 1900, 54 of the 76 emperors of Japan had mothers who were related to the Fujiwara clan.

THE IMPERIAL COURT

Life at court was both elegant and refined. The buildings were exquisite and set in beautiful gardens. Paintings based on the writings of courtiers show some of the famous places they enjoyed visiting.

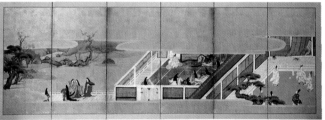

A LOOK INSIDE

This scroll-painting shows rooms inside the emperor's palace and groups of courtiers strolling in the gardens outside. Indoors, the rooms are divided up by silken blinds and the courtiers sit on mats and cushions.

4 Paint several pairs of clam shells with various designs. Make sure that each pair of shells has an identical picture. Leave the painted shells to dry.

5 Turn all your shells face down and mix them up well. Turn over one shell then challenge your opponent to pick the matching shell to yours.

6 If the two shells do not match, turn them over and try again. If they do match, your opponent takes the shells. Take it in turns to challenge each other.

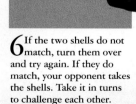

The person with the most shells wins! Noble ladies at the imperial court enjoyed playing the shell game. This is a simplified version of the game they used to play.

Japanese Military Power

I N 1159, a bloody civil war, known as the Heiji War, broke out in Japan between two powerful clans, the Taira and the Minamoto. The Taira were victorious in the Heiji War, and they controlled the government of the country for 26 years. However, the Minamoto rose again and regrouped to defeat the Taira in 1185.

Yoritomo, leader of the Minamoto clan, became the most powerful man in Japan and set up a new headquarters in the city of Kamakura. The emperor continued to act as head of the government in Kyoto, but he was effectively powerless. For almost the next 700 years, until 1868, military commanders such as Yoritomo, rather than the emperors, were the real rulers of Japan. They were known by the title *sei i tai shogun* (Great General Subduing the Barbarians).

SHOGUN FOR LIFE
Minamoto Yoritomo was the first person to take the title shogun and to hand the title on to his sons. In fact, the title did not stay in the Minamoto family for long because the family line died out in 1219. But new shogun families soon took its place.

FIRE! FIRE!
This scroll-painting illustrates the end of a siege during the Heiji War. The war was fought between two powerful clans, the Taira and the Minamoto. The rival armies set fire to buildings by shooting burning arrows and so drove the inhabitants out into the open where they could be killed.

MAKE A KITE
You will need: A1 card, ruler, pencil, dowelling sticks tapered at each end (5 x 50cm, 2 x 70cm), masking tape, scissors, glue, brush, thread, paintbrush, paints, water pot, paper (52cm x 52cm), string, bamboo stick.

1 Draw a square 50cm x 50cm on card with a line down the centre. Lay the dowelling sticks on the square. Glue the sticks to each other and then tape.

2 When the glue has dried, remove the masking tape. Take the frame off the card. Bind the corners of the frame with the strong thread.

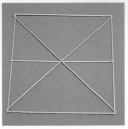

3 Now position your two longer dowelling sticks so that they cross in the middle of the square. Glue and then bind the corners with the strong thread.

DYNASTY FOUNDER

Tokugawa Ieyasu (1542-1616) was a noble from eastern Japan. He was one of three powerful warlords who brought long years of civil war to an end and unified Japan. In 1603 he won the battle of Sekigahara and became shogun. His family, the Tokugawa, ruled Japan for the next 267 years.

RESTING PLACE

This mausoleum (burial chamber) was built at Nikko in north-central Japan. It was created to house the body of the mighty shogun Tokugawa Ieyasu. Three times a year, Ieyasu's descendants travelled to Nikko to pay homage to their great ancestor.

UNDER ATTACK

Life in Nijo Castle, Kyoto, is shown in great detail on this painted screen. The castle belonged to the Tokugawa family of shoguns. Like emperors, great shoguns built themselves fine castles, which they used as centres of government or as fortresses in times of war. Nijo Castle was one of the finest buildings in Japan. It had 'nightingale' floors that creaked loudly when an intruder stepped on them, raising the alarm. The noise was made to sound like a bird call.

Kites were sometimes used for signalling during times of war. The Japanese have also enjoyed playing with kites for over 1,000 years.

4 Paint a colourful kite pattern on to the paper. It is a good idea to tape the edges of the paper down so it does not move around or curl up.

5 Draw light pencil marks 1cm in from the corners of the paper on all four sides. Carefully cut out the corners of the paper, as shown.

6 Glue the paper on to the kite frame. You will need to glue along the wooden frame and fold the paper over the edge of the frame. Leave to dry.

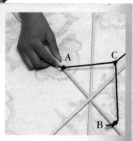

7 Tie a short length of string across the centre of the kite frame (A to B). Knot a long kite string on to it as shown (C). Wind the string on the bamboo.

Imperial Life in Japan

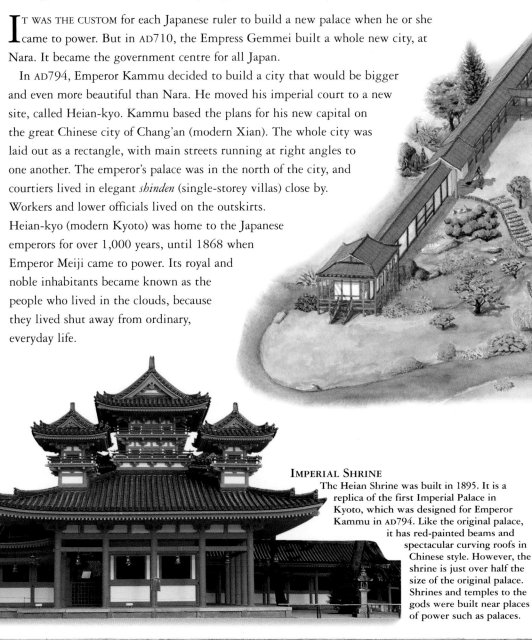

IT WAS THE CUSTOM for each Japanese ruler to build a new palace when he or she came to power. But in AD710, the Empress Gemmei built a whole new city, at Nara. It became the government centre for all Japan.

In AD794, Emperor Kammu decided to build a city that would be bigger and even more beautiful than Nara. He moved his imperial court to a new site, called Heian-kyo. Kammu based the plans for his new capital on the great Chinese city of Chang'an (modern Xian). The whole city was laid out as a rectangle, with main streets running at right angles to one another. The emperor's palace was in the north of the city, and courtiers lived in elegant *shinden* (single-storey villas) close by. Workers and lower officials lived on the outskirts. Heian-kyo (modern Kyoto) was home to the Japanese emperors for over 1,000 years, until 1868 when Emperor Meiji came to power. Its royal and noble inhabitants became known as the people who lived in the clouds, because they lived shut away from ordinary, everyday life.

IMPERIAL SHRINE
The Heian Shrine was built in 1895. It is a replica of the first Imperial Palace in Kyoto, which was designed for Emperor Kammu in AD794. Like the original palace, it has red-painted beams and spectacular curving roofs in Chinese style. However, the shrine is just over half the size of the original palace. Shrines and temples to the gods were built near places of power such as palaces.

LIFE IN A *SHINDEN*

In *Heian-kyo*, nobles and courtiers lived in splendid *shinden* (houses) like this one. Each *shinden* was designed as a number of separate buildings, linked by covered walkways. It was usually set in a landscaped garden, with artificial hills, ornamental trees, bridges, pavilions and ponds. Sometimes a stream flowed through the garden – and through parts of the house, as well. The various members of the noble family, and their servants, lived in different parts of the *shinden*.

GOLDEN PAVILION

This is a replica of the Kinkakuji (Temple of the Golden Pavilion). The original was completed in 1397 and survived until 1950. But, like many of Kyoto's old wooden buildings, it was destroyed by fire. The walls of the pavilion are covered in gold leaf. The golden glow is reflected in the calm waters of a shallow lake.

SILVER TEMPLE

The Ginkakuji (Temple of the Silver Pavilion) in Kyoto was completed in 1483. Despite its name, it was never painted silver, but left as natural wood.

THRONE ROOM

The Shishinden Enthronement Hall is within the palace compound in Kyoto. The emperor would have sat on the raised platform (left) while his courtiers bowed low before him. This palace was the main residence for all emperors from 1331 to 1868.

Organized Government in Greece

ANCIENT GREECE WAS MADE UP of about 300 separate city states. Some were no bigger than villages, while others centred around cities such as Sparta or Athens. Each city state was known as a *polis* (from which we take our word politics) and had its own laws and government. In the 4th century BC, the Greek philosopher Aristotle wrote that there were various types of government. Autocracy was power held by one person. This might be a monarch, on account of his royal birth, or a tyrant who had siezed power by force. Oligarchy was government by a few people. These might be aristocrats who assumed control by right of noble birth, or a group of rich and powerful people. Democratic government was rule by many and was only practised in Athens. It gave every male citizen the right to vote, hold public office or serve on a jury. However, women, slaves and foreigners were not counted as full citizens.

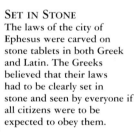

SET IN STONE
The laws of the city of Ephesus were carved on stone tablets in both Greek and Latin. The Greeks believed that their laws had to be clearly set in stone and seen by everyone if all citizens were to be expected to obey them.

BEHIND THE SCENES
Women were not allowed to take an active part in politics in ancient Greece. However, some played an important role behind the scenes. One such woman was Aspasia, a professional entertainer. She met and became mistress to Pericles, one of the most influential Athenian statesmen of the 5th century BC. Pericles confided in his mistress about affairs of state. He came to rely on her insight and wisdom in his judgement of people and situations.

VOTING TOKENS
You will need: pair of compasses, thin card, pencil, ruler, scissors, rolling pin, cutting board, self-hardening clay, modelling tool, balsa wood stick 5cm long, piece of drinking straw 5cm long, bronze-coloured paint, paintbrush, water pot.

1 Make two templates. Use a pair of compasses to draw two circles, on a piece of thin card. Make each one 4cm in diameter. Cut them out.

2 Use a rolling pin to roll out the clay to 3cm thickness. Use a modelling tool to cut around the card circles into the clay. Press down hard as you do this.

3 Make a hole in the centre of each clay circle. Use the balsa wood to make one hole (innocent token). Use the straw to make the other hole (guilty token).

PEOPLE POWER

Solon the Lawgiver was an Athenian statesman and poet who lived from 640 to 559BC. Around 594BC, he served as chief magistrate. He gave Athens new laws that enabled more people to take part in politics. His actions prevented a civil war from breaking out between the few nobles in power and the people who suffered under their rule.

VOTE HERE

This terracotta urn was used to collect voting tokens. They were used in Athens when votes needed to be taken in law courts or when the voters' intentions needed to be kept secret. Each voter put a bronze disc in the urn to register his decision. Normally, voting was done by a show of hands, which was difficult to count precisely.

FACE TO FACE

The ruins of this council chamber at Priene in present-day Turkey show how seating was arranged. The tiered, three-sided square enabled each councillor to see and hear clearly all of the speakers involved in a debate. Even in the democracies of ancient Greece, most everyday decisions were taken by committees or councils and not by the assembly of voters.

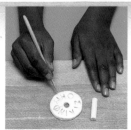

4 Write a name on the innocent token using the modelling tool. Carefully push the balsa stick through the hole. Leave it to dry.

5 Write another name on the guilty token using the modelling tool. Carefully push the drinking straw through the hole. Leave it to dry.

6 Wait until the clay tokens are dry before painting them. The original tokens were made from bronze, so use a bronze-coloured paint.

Jurors were issued with two tokens to vote with. A hollow centre meant that the juror thought the accused was guilty. A solid centre meant that the juror thought the accused was innocent.

Inequality in Greece

GREEK SOCIETY WAS DIVIDED by a strict social structure that was enforced by its governments. Most city states were ruled by a small group of people (oligarchy). Two exceptions were the powerful cities of Sparta and Athens. Sparta held on to its monarchy, while Athens introduced the first democratic government in history. In the city of Athens, all citizens could vote and hold office. However to be a citizen, it was necessary to be an adult male, born in the city itself. Even so-called democratic Athens was ruled by a minority of the people who lived there. The treatment of *metics* (foreign residents), women, slaves and children was just the same as in other city states.

Women had no legal rights and rarely took part in public life. Metics had to pay extra taxes and serve in the army, but could not own land or marry an Athenian. The Athenians felt uneasy about the large number of metics living in their city, but depended upon their skills.

Slaves made up half the population of Athens. Most of them had been born to slaves, were prisoners of war or captives of pirates. Even native Greeks could become slaves by falling into debt, but they were freed once the debt was paid off.

WARRIORS AND WEALTH
Only the wealthiest members of society could afford to arm themselves for war. Bronze weapons were expensive. In early centuries, the poor were given supporting jobs, such as slingers or carriers of supplies. However, as cities grew richer, weapons were manufactured at public expense by slaves, and most male citizens were expected to carry arms.

A WOMAN'S PLACE
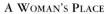
Greek women spent their lives at home. On this vase, made about 450BC, a woman ties her sandal before going out. As she has attendants, she must be wealthy. Poor women would leave the house to fetch water, work in the fields or shop in the market. Women with slaves, like this one, might leave the home to visit relatives or to pray at a shrine or temple.

LOVED ONES

A young girl and her pet dog are seen on this tombstone from the 4th century BC. The likely expense of such a detailed carving suggests that she was dearly loved. Not all children were cherished. Girl babies, and sick babies of either sex, were often left outside to die. Some were underfed and fell victim to diseases. Greek law required children to support their parents in old age. Childless couples were always keen to adopt, and sometimes rescued abandoned children.

CRAFTSMAN

This smith could be a slave working in a factory owned by a wealthy man. Most craftsmen were slaves, ex-slaves or *metics* (foreign residents). They were looked down upon by other citizens. If a master owned a talented slave, he might set the slave up to run his own business. In return, the master would receive a share of the profits. This smith might also have been a free, self-employed man, with his own workshop and a slave or two working as his assistants.

PATH TO POWER?

Being able to read and write in ancient Greece was not an automatic key to success. The Greek alphabet could be learned quite easily. Even slaves could become highly educated scribes. However, illiterate men were unlikely to hold high positions, except perhaps in Sparta, where written records were rarely kept. Although women were denied the right to a formal education, they were often able to read and write enough to keep a record of household stores.

ENSLAVED BY LANGUAGE

This Roman bottle is made in the shape of an African slave girl's head. The Greeks also owned slaves. The Greek philosopher Aristotle argued that some people were "naturally" meant to be slaves. His opinion was shared by many of his countrymen. He felt that this applied most obviously to people who did not speak Greek. Slaves were treated with varying degrees of kindness and hostility. Some were worked to death by their owners, but others had good jobs as clerks or bailiffs. A few hundred slaves were owned by the city of Athens and served as policemen, coin-inspectors and clerks of the court.

Rulers of Rome

IN ITS EARLY DAYS, the city of Rome was ruled by kings. The first king was said to be Romulus, the founder of the city in 753BC. The last king, a hated tyrant called Tarquinius the Proud, was thrown out in 509BC. The Romans then set up a republic. The Senate, an assembly of powerful and wealthy citizens, chose two consuls to lead them each year. By 493BC, the common people had their own representatives – the tribunes – to defend their rights in the Senate. In times of crisis, rulers could take on emergency powers and become dictators. The first Roman emperor, Augustus, was appointed by the Senate in 27BC. The emperors were given great powers and were even worshipped as gods. Some lived simply and ruled well, but others were violent and cruel. They were surrounded by flatterers, and yet were in constant fear of their lives.

TRIUMPHAL PROCESSION
When a Roman general won a great victory, he was honoured with a military parade called a triumph. Cheering crowds lined the streets as the grand procession passed by. If a general was successful and popular, the way to power was often open to him. Probably the most famous Roman ruler of all, Julius Caesar, came to power after a series of brilliant military conquests.

STATE SACRIFICE
Roman emperors had religious as well as political duties. As *pontifex maximus*, or high priest, an emperor would make sacrifices as offerings to the gods at important festivals.

DEADLY FRUIT

figs

Who killed Augustus, the first Roman emperor, in AD14? It was hard to say. It might have been a natural death... but then again, it might have been caused by his wife Livia. She was said to have coated the figs in his garden with a deadly poison. Roman emperors were much feared, but they were surrounded by enemies and could trust no one, least of all their own families.

GUARDING THE EMPEROR

The Praetorian Guards were the emperor's personal bodyguards. They wore special uniforms, were well paid and they were the only armed soldiers allowed in the city of Rome. They became very powerful and sometimes took power into their own hands. Guards assassinated the emperor Caligula and elected Claudius to succeed him.

In Rome, wreaths made from leaves of the laurel tree were worn by emperors, victorious soldiers and athletes. The wreath was a badge of honour. The Romans copied the idea from the ancient Greeks.

WREATH OF HONOUR

You will need: tape measure, garden wire, pliers, scissors, clear tape, green ribbon, bay or laurel leaves (real or fake).

1 Measure around your head with the tape measure. Cut some wire the same length, so the wreath will fit you. Bend the wire as shown and tape the ribbon round it.

2 Start to tape the leaves by their stems on to the wire, as shown above. Work your way around to the middle of the wire, fanning out the leaves as you go.

3 Then reverse the direction of the leaves and work your way around the rest of the wire. Fit the finished wreath to your head. Hail, Caesar!

Masters and Slaves in Rome

ROMAN SOCIETY was never very fair. In the early days of the Republic, a group of rich and powerful noble families, called the patricians, controlled the city and the Senate. A citizen who wanted his voice heard had to persuade a senator to speak on his behalf. Over the centuries the common citizens, known as plebeians, became more powerful. By 287BC, they shared equally in government. Eventually, in the days of the Empire, even people of humble birth could become emperor, provided they were wealthy or had the support of the army. Emperors always feared riots by the common people of Rome, so they tried to keep the people happy with handouts of free food and lavish entertainments. Roman women could not vote. Most had little power outside the family, but some were successful in business or influenced political events through their husbands. Slaves had very few rights, even though Roman society was dependent on their labour. Prisoners of war were sold as slaves, Many were treated cruelly and revolts were common.

A ROMAN CONSUL
This is a statue of a Roman consul, or leader of the Senate, in the days of the Republic. At first, only members of the noble and wealthy class could be senators. However, under the emperors, the power and influence of the Senate slowly grew less.

LIFE AS A SLAVE
The everyday running of the Empire depended on slavery. This mosaic shows a young slave boy carrying fruit. In about AD100, a wealthy family might have had as many as 500 slaves. Some families treated their slaves well, and slaves who gave good service might earn thei freedom. However, many more led miserable lives, toiling in the mines or labouring in the fields.

SLAVE TAG
This bronze disc was probably worn like a dog tag around the neck of a slave. The Latin words on it say: 'Hold me, in case I run away, and return me to my master Viventius on the estate of Callistus'. Slaves had few rights and could be branded on the forehead or leg as the property of their owners.

COLLECTING TAXES

This stone carving probably shows people paying their annual taxes. Officials counted the population of the Empire and registered them for paying tax. Money from taxes paid for the army and running the government. However, many of the tax collectors took bribes, and even emperors seized public money to add to their private fortunes.

ARISTOCRATS

This Italian painting of the 1700s imagines how a noble Roman lady might dress after bathing. Wealthy people had personal slaves to help them bathe, dress and look after their hair. Household slaves were sometimes almost part of the family, and their children might be brought up and educated with their owner's children.

Celtic Societies

T HE CELTS WERE NEVER a single, unified nation. Instead there were many separate tribes throughout Europe. Greek and Roman writers recorded many Celtic tribal names, for example, the Helvetii (who lived in Switzerland) and the Caledones (who lived in Scotland). Tribes sometimes made friendly alliances with one another, or with a stronger power such as Rome. This usually happened when a tribe was threatened by invaders or at war. Within each tribe, there were many clans. These were families who traced their descent from a single ancestor, and who shared ties of loyalty and a family name.

Each tribe was headed by a king (or chieftain). His task was to lead men in battle and on raids, and to maintain peace and prosperity. Kings were chosen from rich noble families. Senior noblemen were expected to support the king and to lead their own bands of warriors. Druids (Celtic priests) and bards (well-educated poets) also came from noble families. Farmers and craftworkers ranked lower, but they were highly valued for their important skills. There were also servants and slaves.

GUARDIAN GODDESS
Many Celtic tribes had their own special god or goddess, to protect them and to bring fertility to their farm animals and crops. This mother goddess was the special guardian of a Celtic tribe who lived in Austria. She is shown gently cradling twin babies, looking after them with her magical protective powers. After a battle, the Celts sacrificed a share of all they had captured to their favourite gods and goddesses.

PROUD LEADER
This stone statue of a Celtic king or chieftain from Gaul (modern France) was made around 50BC. He is dressed ready to lead his tribe into war, in a chainmail tunic and a magic torc. His torc (neck ornament) is an indication of high rank, but we have no idea who he actually was.

Religious support, knowledge, rituals

Protection and offerings

Gifts and prestige

Loyalty and help in battle

Chieftains

Protection and offerings

Religious support

Druids and bards

Farmers and craftworkers

Nobles and warriors

Religious support

Respect and offerings

Respect and manpower

Protection and access to land

THE STRUCTURE OF SOCIETY

All the different groups within Celtic society had an important part to play. They relied on one another to survive. This diagram shows what each different group gave to society, and what it received in return. Chieftains offered leadership and inspired loyalty. Nobles and warriors protected the tribe from attack. Farmers and craftworkers produced food and goods. Druids and bards provided religious support and celebrated tribal pride. The lowest social rank was held by labourers and slaves. They did jobs that were often hard and dirty.

TRIBAL COIN

Many Celtic tribes issued coins, marked with their own special design. This coin was made for the Catuvellauni tribe who lived in southern England. It shows a warrior on horseback riding into battle brandishing a carnyx (war-trumpet). It was designed to tell everyone what a brave and warlike people the Catuvellauni were.

SLAVE CHAIN

Chains like these were used to stop slaves running away. The round iron bracelets, joined by links of heavy metal, were fastened round a slave's wrists or ankles and locked shut. Slavery was never very important in Celtic society. There were many more free people than slaves. However, slaves were used for dirty, difficult, dangerous work (for example, in the salt mines at Hallstatt, Germany).

Viking Rulers and Freemen

MOST VIKINGS WERE KARLS (freemen) who owned some land and a farm, and went to sea for raids and adventures. Other karls were merchants, ship builders or craft workers. The free Vikings used *thralls* (slaves) as labourers and servants on farms and in workshops. Many Vikings were slave-traders. Prisoners who had been captured on raids all over Europe were sold as thralls. Viking society allowed thralls few rights. Their children were slaves as well.

The most powerful and wealthy Vikings were chieftains or *jarls* (earls). They controlled large areas in Norway and Sweden, and some jarls became local kings. Viking kings became more powerful as they conquered new lands and united them into kingdoms. By 900, Harald Finehair, King of Vestfold, had brought all of Norway under his control. Denmark had always been ruled by a single person, and in the reign of Harald Bluetooth, government became even more centralized. Yet the early Vikings had been quarrelsome and proud people, who bridled against any centralized control. This remained true in colonies such as Iceland. Many people, including Eirik the Red, fled to Iceland to escape the law, or because they did not want to be ruled by a distant king. Iceland remained an independent republic throughout the Viking Age. However, after 1100, it was forced to recognize a Norwegian king.

STRONG RULERS
This king is a piece in a chess set from the Isle of Lewis, Scotland. Viking kings were often violent men who were hungry for power. They led their men into battle and fought with them to the bitter end.

FIGHTING FORCE
Karls (freemen), formed the backbone of a Scandinavian invasion force when the Normans attacked England in 1066. This scene is part of the Bayeux tapestry and shows Norman karls preparing for conquest.

FARMERS
Viking karls (freemen) built farmhouses on the Shetland islands to the north of Scotland. The search for new land to farm led many karls to travel overseas. The buildings on Shetland were made of timber, stone and turf. This Viking site is known as Jarlshof today.

LOYAL TO YOUR LORD

This reconstruction of a Viking raid is taking place on the island of Lindisfarne in northern England. Viking raiders first attacked Lindisfarne in the year 793. A typical war band would have been made up of karls (freemen). In battle, they followed their jarl (earl), into the thick of the fighting without hesitation. They formed a tight guard around him when the fighting got tough. In the early Viking days, it was more important to show loyalty to one's family or lord than to a kingdom.

DEFENSIVE FORT

King Harald Bluetooth had a series of forts built to defend the Danish kingdom in the 980s. This one is at Fyrkat, in Jutland. By the end of the Viking period, it was very rare for independent Viking chieftains to lead small bands of karls on raids.

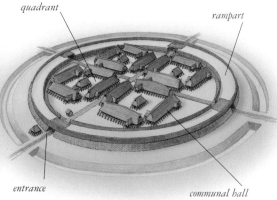

quadrant

rampart

entrance

communal hall

A RESTLESS PEOPLE

Poor farmhands prepare wool in this reconstruction showing Vikings at work. Families of all social classes left Scandinavia to settle new lands during the Viking age. They were driven by the need for land and wealth. They faced long sea voyages and years of hard work building new farms or towns.

Viking Assemblies

EACH REGION AND LAND where the Vikings settled had its own public assembly called the *Thing*, where laws and judgements were passed. The Thing met at regular intervals and was made up only of karls (freemen). Women and slaves had no right to speak there.

The Thing had great powers, and it could even decide who should be king. If someone was murdered or robbed, the victim's relatives could go to the Thing and demand justice. Everybody in the assembly considered the case. If they all agreed that a person was guilty, then judgement was passed. The person sentenced might have to pay a fine of money or other valuable goods. Sometimes the only way a dispute could be settled was by mortal combat (a fight to the death). However, mortal combat was made illegal in Iceland and Norway around AD1000. The assembly also dealt with arguments over property, marriage and divorce.

In Iceland there was no king at all in the Viking period. Instead, an *Althing* or national assembly was held each midsummer. The Althing was a cross between a court, a parliament and a festival. It was a chance for families to come in from their isolated farmhouses and meet up with each other. The assembly approved laws that had been drafted by the jarls and elected a Law Speaker.

PAY UP
The Thing could order a criminal to pay the victim, in the form of money or goods. If the criminal failed to do so, he was made an outlaw. This entitled anyone to kill him.

MEETING PLACE
The Icelandic Althing met on the Thingvellir, a rocky plain east of the city of Reykjavik. A Law Speaker read out the laws, which had been passed by a group of 39 chieftains, from the Law Rock. The Althing is the world's oldest surviving law-making assembly on record. It met from 930 until 1800 and again from 1843. Today it is Iceland's parliament.

A Difficult Decision

This carving shows an important gathering of the Althing in 1000. The assembly was split over a difficult decision – should Iceland become Christian? It was left to the Law Speaker to decide. After a lot of thought, he ruled that the country should be officially Christian, but that people who wished to worship the old gods could do so in private.

Manx Law

An earth mound marks the site of the old Viking assembly on the Isle of Man. The Vikings who settled on the island, off the west coast of Great Britain, called this assembly field the Tynwald. This is also the name of the island's parliament today. The Tynwald still has the power to make the island's laws.

Mortal Combat

A Viking duel is re-enacted today. Life was cheap in Viking times, and violent death was common. A fight to the death was an official way of settling a serious dispute, such as an accusation of murder. This system of justice was taken to England by the Normans in 1066.

Law Makers

Viking chieftains would ride to Iceland's Thingvellir (Assembly Plain) from all over the island. This 19th-century painting by W.G. Collingwood shows chieftains gathering for the Althing. This assembly was held only once a year.

Aztec and Maya Social Order

THE LAND BETWEEN North and South America, known as Mesoamerica, was never a single, united country. During the Maya (AD250-900) and later Aztec civilizations, it was divided into several, separate states. The rulers of these states often combined the roles of army commanders, law-makers and priests. Some claimed to be descended from the gods. Rulers were almost always men. Mesoamerican women – especially among the Maya – had important religious duties but rarely took part in law-making or army life. Maya rulers were called *ahaw* (lord) or *mahk'ina* (great Sun lord), and each city-state had its own royal family.

The supreme Aztec leader was called the *tlatoani* (speaker). Originally, he was elected from army commanders by the Aztec people. Later, he was chosen from the family of the previous leader. He ruled all Aztec lands, helped by a deputy called *cihuacoatl* (snake woman), nobles and army commanders. Rulers, priests and nobles made up a tiny part of society. Ordinary citizens were called *macehualtin*. Men were farmers, fishermen or craftworkers. There were thousands of slaves, who were criminals, enemy captives or poor people who had given up their freedom in return for food and shelter.

OFFICIAL HELP
This Maya clay figure shows a scribe at work. Well-trained officials, such as scribes, helped Mesoamerican rulers by keeping careful records. Scribes also painted ceremonial pottery.

HONOUR TO THE KING
Painted pottery vases like this were buried alongside powerful Maya people. They show scenes from legends and royal palace life. Here, a lord presents tribute to the king.

MAYA NOBLEWOMAN
This terracotta figure of a Maya noblewoman dates from between AD600 and 900. She is richly attired and is protecting her face with a parasol. Women did not usually hold official positions in Mesoamerican lands. Instead noblewomen influenced their husbands by offering tactful suggestions and wise advice. Whether she was rich or poor, a woman's main duty was to provide children for her husband and to support him in all aspects of his work.

THE RULING CLASS

A noble is shown getting ready for a ceremony in this Aztec picture. Aztec nobles played an important part in government. They were chosen by rulers to be judges, army commanders and officials. Nobles with government jobs paid no taxes and were given a free house to live in. Noble men and women came from ancient families who were related to the rulers. It was, however, possible for an ordinary man to achieve higher rank if he fought very bravely in battle and captured four enemy soldiers alive.

MEN AT WORK

Aztec farmers are harvesting ripe cobs of maize. This painting comes from the Florentine Codex. This 12-volume manuscript was made by a Spanish friar. Codex pictures like this tell us a lot about ordinary peoples' everyday lives. Notice how simply the farmers are dressed compared to the more powerful people on these pages.

WAR LEADER

A Maya stone carving shows ruler Shield Jaguar (below left) getting ready to lead his army in AD724. He is wearing a padded tunic and holding a knife in his right hand. His wife, Lady Xoc, is handing him his jaguar headdress. Maya rulers also took part in religious ceremonies, where they offered drops of their blood to the gods in return for their help.

Life at the Top in Mesoamerica

THE RULERS OF EACH Maya and Aztec city-state lived in splendid palaces that were a reflection of their power and wealth. The palace of the Aztec ruler Moctezuma II in Tenochtitlan was vast. It had banqueting rooms big enough to seat 3,000 guests, private apartments, a library, a schoolroom, kitchens, stores, an arsenal for weapons, separate women's quarters, spectacular gardens and a large zoo. Etiquette around the emperor was very strict. Captains of the royal bodyguard had to approach Moctezuma barefoot, with downcast eyes, making low bows and murmuring, 'Lord, my lord, my great lord.' When they left, they had to walk backwards, keeping their gaze away from his face.

Palaces were also the government headquarters where rulers greeted ambassadors from neighbouring city-states and talked with advisors.

Rulers had the power to make strict laws. Each city-state had its own law-courts, where formidable judges had the power of life and death.

ROYAL RECORD
Maya rulers set up stelae (stone pillars) in their cities. Carved pictures recorded major people and events of their reigns. This one celebrates a Maya ruler in Copan, Honduras.

THE SEAT OF POWER
This carved jade ornament shows a seated Maya king. Aztec and Maya leaders had the final say in any decision. However, they were advised by judges, officials and scribes.

MAKE A FEATHER FAN

You will need: pencil, thick card, scissors, thin red card, green paper, double-sided tape, feathers (real or paper), masking tape, paints, paintbrushes, coloured felt, pva glue and brush, sticky tape, coloured wool, bamboo cane.

1 Draw two rings about 45cm in diameter and 8cm wide on thick card. Cut them out. Make another ring the same size from thin red card, as above.

2 Cut lots of leaf shapes from green paper. Stick them around the edge of one thick card ring using double-sided tape. Add some real or paper feathers.

3 Cut two circles about 12cm in diameter from thin red card. Draw around something the right size, such as a reel of tape. These are for the centre of the fan.

LOCKED UP

A group of Aztec judges discusses how best to punish prisoners in the cage. Punishments were very severe. If ordinary citizens broke the law, they might be beaten or speared with cactus spines. For a second offence, they might be stoned to death.

THE RULE OF THE GODS

In this stone carving, a human face is being swallowed by a magic serpent. Royal and government buildings were often decorated with carvings like this. They signified the religious power of the ruler of a particular city.

FIT FOR A KING

An Aztec picture shows visitors at a ruler's palace. Spanish explorers in the 1500s reported that over 600 nobles visited the Aztec ruler's palace every day. They attended council meetings, consulted palace officials, asked favours from the ruler and made their views heard. It was the Aztec tradition that the ruler sat on a mat on the floor with his council.

Beautiful feather fans rather like this were used by Aztec nobles and rulers to keep themselves cool.

4 Paint a flower on one of the two smaller red circles and a butterfly on the other. Cut v-shapes from the felt and glue them to the large red ring.

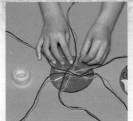

5 Using sticky tape, fix lengths of coloured wool to the back of one of the red circles, as shown. Place the red circle in the centre of the ring with leaves.

6 Tape the lengths of wool to the outer ring to look like spokes. Coat the ring with PVA glue and place the second card ring on top, putting a cane in between.

7 Use double-sided tape to stick the second red circle face up in the centre. Glue the red ring with felt v-shapes on top of the second thick card ring.

Inca Lords of the Sun

THE INCAS WERE ORIGINALLY a tribal people of the Peruvian Andes in the 1100s. As the tribes grew in size, strong leaders began to take control. Under them, the Incas began to conquer neighbouring lands in the 1300s. During the 1400s, the mighty Inca Empire had developed.

The Inca emperor was called *Sapa Inca* (Only Leader). He was regarded as a god, a descendant of the Sun. He had complete power over his subjects, and was treated with the utmost respect at all times, but was always on his guard. There were many rivals for the throne among his royal relations. Each emperor had a new palace built for himself in the royal city of Cuzco. Emperors were often veiled or screened from ordinary people.

The empress, or *Quya* (Star), was the emperor's sister or mother. She was also thought to be divine and led the worship of the Moon goddess. The next

emperor was supposed to be chosen from among her sons. An emperor had many secondary wives. Waskar was said to have fathered eighty children in just eight years.

RELIGIOUS LEADERS
Sacrifices of llamas were made to the gods each month, at special festivals and before battle. The *Sapa Inca* controlled all religious activities. In the 1400s, the emperor Wiraqocha Inka declared that worship of the god Wiraqocha, the Creator (after whom he was named), was more important than worship of Inti, the Sun god. This made some people angry.

A CHOSEN WOMAN
Figurines of young girls were originally dressed, but the specially made clothes have perished or been lost over the years. Chosen girls (*akllakuna*), were educated for four years in religion, weaving and housekeeping. Some became the emperor's secondary wives or married noblemen. Others became priestesses or *mamakuna* (virgins of the Sun).

MAKE AN EMPEROR'S FAN
You will need: pencil, card, ruler, scissors, paints in bright colours, paintbrush, water pot, masking tape, wadding, pva glue, hessian or sackcloth, needle, thread, string or twine.

1 Draw a feather shape 18cm long on to card and cut it out. The narrow part should be half of this length. Draw around the shape on card nine times.

2 Carefully paint the feathers with bright colours. Use red, orange and yellow to look like rainforest birds. Allow the paint to dry completely.

3 Cut out each feather and snip along the sides of the widest part to give a feathery effect. When the paint is dry, paint the other side as well.

COMMANDER IN CHIEF

The emperor sits on his throne. He wears a tasselled woollen headdress or *llautu*, decorated with gold and feathers, and large gold earplugs. He carries a sceptre. Around him, army chiefs await their orders. Emperors played an active part in military campaigns and relied on the army to keep them in power.

COOL SPRINGS

At Tambo Machay, to the south of Cuzco, fresh, cold water is channelled from sacred springs. Here, the great Pachakuti Inka Yupanki would bathe after a hard day's hunting.

THE LIVING DEAD

The dead body of an emperor, preserved as a mummy, is paraded through the streets. When each emperor died, his palace became his tomb. Once a year, the body was carried around Cuzco amid great celebrations. The picture is by Guamán Poma de Ayala, who was of Inca descent. In the 1600s, he made many pictures of Inca life.

Feathers from birds of the tropical forests to the east of the Andes were used to make fans for the emperor.

4 Hold the narrow ends of the feathers and spread out the tops to form a fan shape. Use masking tape to secure the ends firmly in position.

5 Cut a rectangular piece of wadding 9cm high and long enough to wrap the base of the feathers several times. Use glue on one side to keep it in place.

6 Cut a strip of hessian or sackcloth about 5cm wide. Starting at the base of the feathers, wrap the fabric around the stems. Hold it in place with a few stitches.

7 Wind string or twine firmly around the hessian to form the fan's handle. Tuck in the ends and use glue at each end to make sure they are secure.

Controlling Inca Society

FAMILY CONNECTIONS PLAYED an important part in royal power struggles and in everyday social organization in the Inca world. The nobles were grouped into family-based corporations called *panakas*. Members of each *panaka* shared rights to an area of land, its water, pasture and herds. Linked to each *panaka* was a land-holding *ayllu* (or clan) – a group of common people who were also related to each other.

The Incas managed to control an empire that contained many different peoples. Loyal Incas were sent to live in remote areas, while troublemakers from the regions were resettled nearer Cuzco, where they could be carefully watched. Conquered chiefs were called *kurakas*. They and their children were educated in Inca ways and allowed to keep some of their local powers.

The Inca system of law was quite severe. State officials and *kurakas* (conquered chiefs) acted as judges. Those who stole from the emperor's stores of grain, textiles and other goods faced a death sentence. Torture, beating, blinding and exile were all common punishments. The age of the criminal and the reason for the crime were sometimes taken into account.

A CLEVER CALCULATOR
One secret of Inca success was the *quipu*. It was used by government officials for recording all kinds of information, from the number of households in a town to the amount of goods of various kinds in a warehouse. The *quipu* was a series of strings tied to a thick cord. Each string had one or more colours and could be knotted. The colours represented anything from types of grain to groups of people. The knots represented numbers.

ONE STATE, MANY PEOPLES
The ancestors of these Bolivian women were subjects of the Incas. The Inca Empire was the largest ever known in all the Americas. It included at least a hundred different peoples. The Incas were clever governors and did not always try to force their own ideas upon other groups. Conquered peoples had to accept the Inca gods, but they were allowed to worship in their own way and keep their own customs.

A Royal Inspection

The Inca emperor Topa Inka Yupanki inspects government stores in the 1470s. In the Inca world, nearly all grain, textiles and other goods were produced for the State and stored in warehouses. Some extra produce might be bartered, or exchanged privately, but there were no big markets or shops.

Public Works

Labourers build fortifications on the borders of the Inca Empire. People paid their taxes to the Inca State in the form of labour called *mit'a*. This might be general work on the land. Men were also conscripted to work on public buildings or serve in the army. The Spanish continued to operate the *mit'a* as a form of tax long after they conquered the Inca Empire.

Ollantaytambo

This building in Ollantaytambo, in the Urubamba Valley, was once a State storehouse for the farm produce of the region. Ollantaytambo was a large town, which was probably built about 550 years ago. It protected the valley from raids by the warriors who lived in the forests to the east. Buildings dating from the Inca Empire were still being lived in by local people when the American archaeologist Dr Hiram Bingham passed through in 1911.

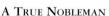

Levels of Inca Society

INCA SOCIETY was strictly graded. At the top were the *Sapa Inca* and his *Quya*. The High Priest and other important officials were normally recruited from members of the royal family.

If noblemen were loyal to the emperor, they might receive gifts of land. They might be given gold or a beautful *akllakuna* as a wife. They could expect jobs as regional governors, generals or priests. Lords and ladies wore fine clothes and were carried in splendid chairs, called litters.

Next in rank were the conquered non-Inca rulers and chiefs, the *kurakas*. They were cleverly brought into the Inca political system and given traditional honours. They served as regional judges.

Most people in the Empire were peasants. They were unable to leave their villages without official permission. They had no choice but to stay and toil on the land, sending their produce to the government stores.

CRAFT AND CLASS
A pottery figure from the Peruvian coast shows a porter carrying a water pot on his back. In the Inca Empire, craft workers such as potters and goldsmiths were employed by the State. They formed a small middle class. Unlike peasants they were never made to do *mit'a* (public service).

A TRUE NOBLEMAN
This man's headdress sets him apart as a noble or possibly a high priest. The model dates from a pre-Inca civilization 1,500-2,000 years ago. The Incas absorbed many different cultures into their own civilization.

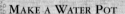

MAKE A WATER POT
You will need: self-drying clay, cutting board, rolling pin, ruler, water, water pot, acrylic paints, paintbrush.

1 Roll out a piece of clay on the board. Make a circle about 17cm in diameter and 1cm thick. This will form the base of your water pot.

2 Roll some more clay into long sausages, about as fat as your little finger. Dampen the base with water and carefully place a sausage around the edge.

3 Coil more clay sausages on top of each other to build up the pot. Make each coil slightly smaller than the one below. Water will help them stick.

A PEASANT'S LIFE

A woman harvests potatoes near Sicuani, to the south of Cuzco. Then, as now, life was hard for the peasant farmers of the Andes. Both men and women worked in the fields, and even young children and the elderly were expected to help. However, the Inca State did provide some support for the peasants, supplying free grain in times of famine.

PLUGGED IN

Earplugs like this one, made of gold, turquoise and shell, were worn as a badge of rank. Inca noblemen wore such heavy gold earplugs that the Spanish called them *orejones* (big ears). Noblewomen wore their hair long, covered with a head-cloth.

LAND AND SEASONS

One third of all land and produce belonged to the emperor, one third to the priests and one third to the peasants. It was hardly a fair division. A peasant's life, digging, planting and harvesting, was ruled by the seasons. Each new season was celebrated by religious festivals and ceremonies.

Children were expected to help their parents by fetching water from the wells and mountain springs.

4 When you reach the neck of the pot, start making the coils slightly bigger again to form a lip. Carefully smooth the coils with wet fingertips.

5 Use two more rolls of clay to make handles on opposite sides of the pot. Smooth out the joints carefully to make sure the handles stay in place.

6 Leave the clay to dry completely. Then paint the pot all over with a background colour. Choose an earthy reddish brown to look like Inca pottery.

7 Leave the reddish brown colour to dry. Use a fine paintbrush and black paint to draw Inca designs on the pot like the ones in the picture above.

Tribes in North America

Fʀᴏᴍ ᴀʀᴏᴜɴᴅ 3000ʙᴄ, many different tribal societies developed throughout North America, from the Apaches in the South to the Inuits of the far North. A single tribe might be as small as ten families or number thousands. Tribes came together in times of war, for ceremonies and for trading, or to form powerful confederacies (unions). Some Algonquin people formed the Powhatan Confederacy and controlled the coast of present-day Virginia. In the South-east, the Creek, Seminole, Cherokee, Choctaw and Chickasaw were known by Europeans as the 'Five Civilized Tribes' because their system of law courts and land rights developed from European influences.

Mᴀɢɴɪꜰɪᴄᴇɴᴛʟʏ Cᴏꜱᴛᴜᴍᴇᴅ
American Horse of the Oglala Sioux wears a double-trail war bonnet. His painted shirt shows he was a member of the Ogle Tanka'un or Shirt Wearers, who were wise and brave.

Cᴏᴍᴍɪᴛᴛᴇᴇ Mᴇᴇᴛɪɴɢ
A Sioux council gathers to hear the head chief speak. Councils were made up of several leaders or chiefs. They elected the head chief whose authority came from his knowledge of tribal lore and skill as a warrior.

Mᴀᴋᴇ ᴀ Sᴋɪɴ Rᴏʙᴇ

You will need: an old single sheet (or large piece of thin cotton fabric), scissors, tape measure or ruler, pencil, large needle, brown thread, felt in red, yellow, dark blue and light blue, pva glue, glue brush, black embroidery thread (or string), red cotton thread (or other colour).

1 Take the sheet and cut out a rectangle 140cm x 60cm. Then cut out two 40cm x 34cm rectangles for the arms. Fold the main (body) piece in half.

2 At the centre of fold, draw a neckline 22cm across and 6cm deep. Cut it out. Roll fabric over at shoulders and stitch down with an overlapping stitch.

3 Open the body fabric out flat and line up the arm pieces, with the centre on the stitched ridge. Stitch the top edge of the arm pieces on to the body.

WOMEN IN SOCIETY

The Iroquois women attended council meetings, but in most tribes women did not join councils or become warriors. Women held a respected place in society. In many tribes, such as the Algonquan, people traced their descent through their mother. When a man married, he left his home to live with his wife's family.

DISPLAYS OF WEALTH

Potlatch ceremonies could last for several days. The gathering was a big feast celebrated by tribes on the Northwest Coast. Gifts were exchanged. The status of a tribe was judged by the value of the gifts.

IN COMMAND

This chief comes from the Kainah group of Blackfoot Indians. The Kainah were also known by Europeans as the Blood Indians because of the red face paint they wore. The Blackfoot headdress had feathers that stood upright as opposed to the Sioux bonnet which sloped backwards sometimes, with trailing eagle feathers.

FEATHER PIPE OF PEACE

North American Indians had a long tradition of smoking pipes. Plants were often smoked for religious and ritual reasons. Early peace talks involved passing around a pipe for all to smoke to show they had good intentions of keeping agreements.

4 Fold the fabric in half again to see the shirt's shape. Now stitch up the undersides of the sleeves. The sides of the shirt were usually not sewn together.

5 Your shirt is ready to decorate. Cut out strips and triangles of felt and glue them on to the shirt. Make fringes by cutting into one side of a felt strip.

6 Make fake hair pieces by cutting 8cm lengths of black thread and tying them together in bunches. Wind red thread tightly around the top, as here.

7 Glue or sew the fake hair (or scalplocks) on to your shirt. You can follow the pattern we used as shown in the picture (top), or create your own.

Survival of a Tribal Tradition

MODERN CEREMONIES
This couple are joining other American Indian descendants at a powwow (tribal gathering). The meetings are popular because of a recent surge of interest in the culture of the tribes. Powwows give the people a chance to dress in traditional costume, speak their native language and learn more about their tribal history.

Some TRIBAL SOCIETIES have had to fight to hold on to their social structure and traditions. The North American Indian culture was nearly wiped out forever. From the 1600s onwards, settlers from Europe took over the land of North America and imposed their own laws. By 1900 the population of tribes north of Mexico had dropped from just below three million to 400,000.

The foreign settlers formed the United States of America at the end of the 1700s, but did not regard the native tribes as 'Americans'. Over the next 200 years, the US Government moved the native Indian peoples from their homelands to areas of land known as reserves or reservations. About 300 US federal reservations still exist today, some for a single tribe, others as home to a number of groups.

In the 1900s, Indians became more politically active. Tribes began to demand financial compensation for lost land. The Cherokees were awarded $15 million. Today, many reservations are governed by the tribes, although the US Government still controls a lot of surviving Indian land. Since 1970, tribes have been allowed to run their reservation schools and teach ancestral history.

TRIBAL PROTEST
In July 1978 these American Indians walked for five months to Washington from their reservations to protest to Congress. At protest meetings, leaders read from a list of 400 treaties – promises that the United States had made and broken. For years, many tribes tried to get back land taken from them. In 1992, Navajo and Hopi tribes were given back 1.8 million acres of their land in Northern Arizona to be divided between the tribes.

SODA BAR STOP
A Seminole family enjoy sodas in 1948 in a Miami store. Tribes gradually adapted to the American ways of life, but some kept their own customs and dress. Seminoles were forced from Florida to Oklahoma in 1878. Almost 300 refused to leave the Everglades and around 2,000 live there today.

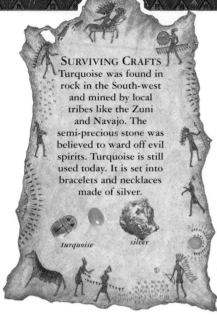

SURVIVING CRAFTS
Turquoise was found in rock in the South-west and mined by local tribes like the Zuni and Navajo. The semi-precious stone was believed to ward off evil spirits. Turquoise is still used today. It is set into bracelets and necklaces made of silver.

turquoise   *silver*

THE TOURIST TRAIL
A traditional Inuit scene of snowshoes propped outside an igloo. Most people in Alaska and Greenland live in modern, centrally heated homes. However, the ancient skills of building temporary shelters from ice bricks still survive. They are passed down to each generation and occasionally used by hunters or tourists keen to experience North American Indian customs.

CHEERLEADING CHIEF
Dressed in full ceremonial costume, this North American Indian helps conduct celebrations at a football stadium. It is a way of raising awareness of the existence of tribes. The cheerleading is not far removed from a war chief's tribal role of encouraging warriors in battle.

STITCHING THE PAST
Traditional American Indian crafts are still made today. The method of curing hides has remained the same. No chemicals are used during the tanning process and the scraping is still done by hand. However, styles of the crafts had already changed to suit the European market in the 1600s when traders brought in new materials.

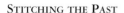

TRADITIONAL SKILLS
An Indian craftsman produces beautiful jewellery in silver and turquoise. Zuni and Navajo people were among the finest jewellery makers in this style. Other tribes, such as the Crow, are famous for their beadwork.

Travel, Conquest & Warfare

Discover how people conquered new lands and how they harnessed existing technologies for transport and weaponry

Breaking New Frontiers

EARLY HUMANS WERE ALWAYS on the move, searching for wild animals and plants for food. They had to walk everywhere. They had not learned how to tame such animals as wild oxen or asses to carry them. But then, the hunter-gatherers did not feel the need to develop new methods of transport, because they did not have much to carry around.

Gradually, some humans learned how to cultivate wild grasses into reliable crops. They built permanent shelters in the fertile river valleys and farmed there.

They wanted and needed to find out how to grow better food, and to store and transport it. Life was no longer the scrabble for survival that it had been for their earliest ancestors.

They had time to work out how to make improvements. New and better methods of transport and travel were used in peacetime and in war.

Populations increased in the fertile farmlands. People moved in search of new places to live, and with this, came the need to

Primitive humans were hunter-gatherers. They were always on the move, looking for food. They had not learned how to tame animals that could be ridden or used to pull vehicles.

The Polynesians roamed the ocean of the South Pacific seeking new islands to settle. Over 2,000 years ago they could navigate the seas successfully, and travel over vast expanses of empty ocean in sail-powered canoes.

TIMELINE 100,000–200BC

100,000 years ago. Nomadic bands of hunter-gatherers migrate north out of Africa into the Middle East in search of new hunting grounds.

50,000 years ago. The ancestors of the Aborigines become the earliest people to build boats or rafts when they sail from Asia to Australia.

Early humans used their upright stance to gather berries

10,000BC Humans discover every continent except ice-covered Antarctica.

8000BC Beginning of farming in the Middle East.

4500BC The first Mesopotamian sailing ships are built.

3800BC Metal weapons, made of bronze, come into use in the Middle East.

3500BC The first wheeled vehicles are made in Mesopotamia.

3000BC Age of the oldest surviving large ships, discovered buried in the desert in Egypt.

1500BC War chariots are used by the Assyrians and Egyptians to carry archers into battle.

bronze spearheads

100,000BC.   10,000BC   3500BC   2500B

travel. As people travelled to lands already settled by others, they had to fight to win new territory. Both travel and war led to the spread of new inventions and ideas, and the incentive to create ever better transport and weapons.

Farming communities were producing more goods than they needed for themselves. Surplus produce could be transported to other regions and traded. With

Horsedrawn chariots could travel fast over the battlefield. The Hittites, who lived in a region that is now part of modern Turkey, were among the first to use horses in warfare. They made the chariot one of the most feared weapons of war around 1600 to 1200BC.

expansion and trade, came the need for faster, safer and more reliable methods of travel. Farmers tamed animals such as the horse and ox for carrying goods and people from place to place, and then realized that the animals could also pull ploughs to till the soil.

About 6,000 years ago, the Mesopotamians harnessed the wind by hoisting sails on their boats. Sailing in the open ocean is dangerous even in today's yachts. Imagine then what it must have been like for Phoenician traders, who, from about 850BC, were sailing from the eastern Mediterranean into the Atlantic Ocean.

Expert horsemen were at an advantage over footsoldiers. Persian soldiers had horses that were strong and nimble, and the rider could wield a weapon from a height.

Sometimes, people wanted to travel and conquer just because they were greedy. A successful farmer might fancy taking over someone else's land just to increase the size of his own farm and give him more wealth and power. A neighbouring tribe or region

Assyrian war chariot

1500BC The Saami in Arctic Europe invent skis for travelling over snow.

1000BC Iron weapons and tools come into widespread use in the Middle East and Europe.

800BC The Greeks begin to fight as hoplites (armoured infantry).

387BC The Celts sack Rome.

312BC The Romans start to build a road system throughout the Empire.

221BC Qin Shi Huangdi founds the Chinese Empire.

Greek galley

1500BC   350BC   200BC

might have something another tribe wanted such as fertile soil, timber or metal. Conflict was an inevitable result. Celts and Vikings fought over cattle and land. Monarchs and emperors fought for control of whole countries.

Unfortunately it is often a war that provides the spur to technological improvements. If you want to win a race or a battle, you make sure you have the best equipment. The warlike Hittites were among the first to ride horses into battle and use iron weapons. Their country in south-eastern Europe (present day Turkey) was landlocked, and they fought for control of ports and trade in the Mediterranean Sea. The Mesopotamians upgraded the solid-wheeled cart into an effective war chariot with spoked wheels.

Early Egyptian life centred on the River Nile, so the Egyptians were experts in making river boats. Later, they wanted to trade farther afield and built seagoing boats like this one with huge sails.

Both trade and empire-building encouraged the spread and exchange of ideas and technology. European invaders introduced the horse to America in the 1500s, which completely transformed how North American Indians hunted, travelled and fought. Phoenician traders and Greek adventurers

In the Crusades, a series of conflicts between Christians and Saracen Muslims during the Middle Ages, the knights of both sides fought on horseback. The Europeans also picked up some useful ideas on castle and weapon design from their foes.

TIMELINE 200BC–AD1900

191BC–AD43 The Romans conquer the Celts in northern Europe.

AD476 Fall of the Western Roman Empire. The Eastern Empire survives until 1453.

AD793 Viking pirates begin to attack Britain and Ireland.

AD800 The Chinese build their first large ships, called junks, with many masts and proper rudders.

Viking longship

AD969 Gunpowder is used in war for the first time, in China.

AD1000 The Viking Leif Eriksson becomes the first European to reach America.

1100 Samurai warriors become important in warfare in Japan.

Chinese fireworks

200BC   AD800   AD900   AD130

took their shipbuilding expertise throughout the Mediterranean and beyond. The superb metalworking craftsmanship of the Saracen Muslims east of the Mediterranean, spread to northern Europe.

Roman galleys were used mostly for war. They had picked up the galley design from the Greeks. Oarpower allowed for manoeuvrability in close combat.

The geography of a country shapes the way in which its transport and warfare develops. The Greeks were great seafarers partly because of their endless coastline, but also because there was a limited amount of fertile land in their rugged country. The Vikings, trapped in narrow coastal strips beneath the mountains of Scandinavia, built ships that crossed the Atlantic Ocean to America. They were also fearsome warriors. The Incas in South America had a major road network and wheeled toys, but no wheeled vehicles. As in the mountains of Japan, walking over steep, narrow tracks was faster and safer than wheeled transport.

As you turn these pages, you will see how different countries and cultures travelled and conquered – and developed transport and weapons.

The Spanish went to Mesoamerica greedy for Aztec gold. The Aztecs were fierce fighters but no match for the Spanish, on horseback, with their gunpowder and steel.

1492 Columbus 'discovers' America while searching for a route to China.

1521 The Spanish under Cortes conquer the Aztecs.

1526 The Mughals begin to conquer India.

Christopher Columbus

1532 The Spanish under Francisco Pizarro conquer the Incas.

1607 The English begin to settle in Virginia in North America.

1776 The United States declares independence from Britain.

Francisco Pizarro

1868 The Tokugawa dynasty of shoguns comes to an end in Japan.

1890 The 'Battle' of Wounded Knee ends the Indian Wars in the United States. Native Indians are confined to reservations.

a Huron brave

AD1500   AD1800   AD1900

Stone Age People on the Move

THE EARLIEST MEANS of transport, apart from travelling on foot, was by boat. The first people to reach Australia, around 50,000BC, probably paddled log or bamboo rafts across the open ocean. Later Stone Age peoples made skin-covered coracles, kayaks (canoes) hollowed from tree trunks and boats made from reeds. Wooden sledges or *travois* (triangular platforms of poles lashed together) were dragged to carry goods and people overland. People pushed logs to act as rollers beneath very heavy objects such as rocks. The taming of horses, donkeys, camels and oxen revolutionized land transport. The first roads and causeways in Europe were built around the same time. By about 3500BC, the wheel had been invented in Egypt and Mesopotamia.

HORSE'S HEAD
This rock engraving of a horse's head comes from a cave in France. Some experts think that horses may have been tamed as early as 12,000BC. There are carvings that appear to show bridles around the heads of horses, although these could indicate manes.

CORACLE
A man fishes from a coracle, one of the oldest boat designs. Made of animal hide stretched over a wooden frame, the coracle may have been used since about 7600BC.

MAKE A MODEL CANOE
You will need: card, pencil, ruler, scissors, pva glue, glue brush, masking tape, self-drying clay, double-sided sticky tape, chamois leather, pair of compasses, thread, needle.

canoe top

———— 20cm ————

canoe top

———— 10cm ————

canoe base

———— 20cm ————

canoe base

———— 10cm ————

1 Cut card to the size of the templates shown on the left. Remember to cut semicircles from the long edge of both top pieces.

2 Glue the bases together and the tops together. Use masking tape to secure them as they dry. Join the top to the base in the same way.

STONE BRIDGE

Walla Brook bridge on Dartmoor is one of the oldest stone bridges in Britain. Bridges make travelling easier, safer and more direct. The first bridges were made by placing tree trunks across rivers, or by laying flat stones in shallow streams.

SAILING BOATS

Skin-covered boats called *umiak* were used by the Inuit of North America. The figure at the back is the helmsman, whose job is to steer the boat. The other figures are rowing the oars. The ancient Egyptians were among the first people to have sailing boats – for moving around on the River Nile.

KAYAK FRAME

This wooden frame for a kayak was made by an Inuit fisherman. It has been built without any nails. The joints were lashed together with strips of leather. Canoes like this have been in use for thousands of years.

Inuit kayaks give clues about how Stone Age boats may have looked. The outsides were covered with skin.

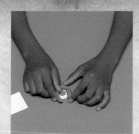

3 Draw three circles the size of the holes in the top, with smaller circles inside. Cut them out. Make clay rings the same size.

4 Cover the clay and the card rings with double-sided tape. These rings form the seats where the paddlers will sit.

5 Cover your canoe with chamois leather, leaving holes for seats. Glue it tightly in place so that all the cardboard is covered.

6 Use a needle and thread to sew up the edges of the leather on the top of the canoe. Position and fix the seats and oars.

Egyptian Sailpower

T HE ANCIENT EGYPTIANS were not great seafarers, although their ships did sail through the Mediterranean and the Red Sea, and may even have reached India. Generally, though, they mostly kept to coastal waters and became experts at river travel. The River Nile was Egypt's main road, and all kinds of boats travelled up and down. Simple boats made from papyrus reed were used for fishing and hunting. Barges transported stones to temple building sites, ferries carried people and animals across the river. There were trading vessels and royal pleasure boats. Egypt had little timber, so wooden ships had to be built from cedar imported from Lebanon in the eastern Mediterranean.

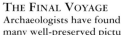

THE FINAL VOYAGE
Archaeologists have found many well-preserved pictures and models of boats in tombs. People believed that the boats carried the mummified body of a pharaoh to its final resting place on the west bank of the Nile, and carried the dead person's spirit into the Underworld.

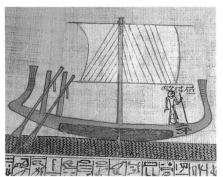

ALL ALONG THE NILE
Wooden sailing boats with graceful, triangular sails can still be seen on the River Nile today. They carry goods and people up and down the river. The design of the *felucca* has changed since the time of the ancient Egyptians. The sails on early boats were tall, upright and narrow. Later designs were broader, like the ones shown above. In Egypt, most people lived in the fertile valley of the River Nile. The river has always been the main route of communication and transport.

MAKE A BOAT

You will need: a large bundle of straw 30cm long, scissors, string, balsa wood, red and yellow card, pva glue and brush.

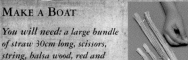

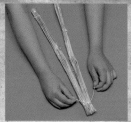

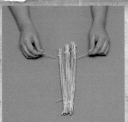

1 Divide the straw into five equal bundles and then cut three of them down to 15cm in length. Tie all five bundles securely at both ends and in the middle, as shown.

2 Take the two long bundles and tie them together at one end as shown. These bundles will form the outer frame of the boat. Put them to one side.

3 Next take the three short bundles of straw and bind them together at both ends. These will form the inner surface of the straw boat.

STEERING ROUND SAND BANKS

A wooden tomb model shows a boat from 1800BC with high, curved ends. Long steering oars kept the boat on course through the powerful currents of the flooding river. Timber was the main material for building large boats, but designs were similar to those of the simple reed vessels used for fishing.

FINAL VOYAGE

These boats are making a pilgrimage to Abydos. This was the city of Osiris, the god of death and rebirth. Mummies were taken here by boat. Ships and boats played a major part in the religious beliefs of the Egyptians. Ra the Sun god travelled on a boat across the sky to bring in each new day. In October 1991, a fleet of 12 boats dating from about 3000BC was found at Abydos near Memphis. The boats were up to 30m long and had been buried beneath the desert sands. They are the oldest surviving large ships in the world.

SIGN OF THE NORTH

The hieroglyph below means boat. It looks a bit like the papyrus reed vessels. This sign later came to mean north. Boats floated downstream with the current from south to north, and used sail power to travel the other way.

Early boats were made from papyrus reeds. These were bound with string made from reed fibres.

4 Next push the short bundles into the centre of the long pair firmly. Tie the bundles together with string at one end, as shown.

5 Bring the rear of the long pair of bundles together and tie them securely, as shown. Bind the whole boat together with string.

6 Thread a string lengthwise from one end to the other. The tension on this string should give the high curved prow and stern of your boat.

7 Finally, cut the card and glue it to the balsa sticks to make the boat's paddle and harpoon. Boats like these were used for fishing and hunting hippos.

Sailing in the Mediterranean

GALLEYS WERE SAILED and rowed in Mediterranean waters for hundreds of years, from the heyday of Phoenician traders around 1000–572BC to the merchant galleys of Venice in the 1400s. Roman galleys were very similar to the earlier Greek vessels. When the wind was favourable, a big, square sail could be set for extra speed. Continuous power, though – whatever the weather – and manoeuvrability in battle – came from one or more rows of oars. A standard Roman war galley had 270 oarsmen below deck.

Most goods, especially heavy cargoes of food or building materials, were moved around the Roman Empire by water. Barges were used on rivers.

Seafaring in the Mediterranean was dangerous, mainly because of storms and piracy. The Greeks built the first lighthouse at Alexandria around 300BC, and the Romans built many around their empire.

CONTAINERS
A large pottery jar called an amphora is being taken from one ship to another. Merchant ships were deeper, heavier and slower than galleys. They had bigger sails and longer oars. They were usually sailed, as they were too heavy to be rowed.

AT THE DOCKS
This wall painting from the port of Ostia shows a Roman merchant ship being loaded. Heavy sacks of grain are being carried on board. You can see the two large steering oars at the stern (rear) of the ship.

ROLLING ON THE RIVER
Wine and other liquids were sometimes stored in barrels. These were transported by river barges, like the one in this carving. Barrels of wine would be hauled from the vineyards of Germany or southern France to the nearest seaport.

MAKE AN AMPHORA
You will need: large sheet of thin card, ruler, two pencils, scissors, corrugated cardboard – two circles of 10cm and 20cm in diameter, two strips of 40cm x 30cm and another large piece, masking tape, pva glue, old newspaper, paintbrush, reddish-brown acrylic paint, water pot.

1 Cut two pieces of card – 5cm and 38cm in depth. Tape the short piece to the small circle. Curl the long piece to make the neck. Make two holes in the side and tape it to the large circle.

2 Roll up the strips of corrugated cardboard. Bend them, as shown, fitting one end to the hole in the neck and the other to the cardboard. Fix in place with glue and tape.

3 Cut a piece of card, 40cm square. Roll it into a cylinder shape. Cut four lines, 10cm long, at one end, so it can be tapered into a point, as shown. Bind with tape.

SAILING OFF TO BATTLE

A Roman war galley leaves harbour on its way to battle. A helmsman controlled a war galley's steering and shouted orders down to the oarsmen below deck. Slaves manned the oars, and there was a separate fighting force on board. This galley has three banks (layers) of oars and is called a trireme (meaning three oars). An underwater battering ram stuck out from the bow (front) of Greek and Roman war galleys. During battle, the mast was lowered, as the ship was easier to manoeuvre under oarpower. The galley rammed the enemy ship to disable it. Then the soldiers boarded to fight man to man.

In the ancient world, amphorae were used to transport wine and oil and fish sauce. The jars could be easily stacked in the ship's hold. Layers of brushwood provided padding.

4 To give the amphora a more solid base, roll up a cone of corrugated cardboard and stick it around the tapered end. Push a pencil into the end, as shown. Tape in position.

5 Stick the neck on to the main body. Cover the whole piece with strips of newspaper brushed on with glue. Leave to dry. Repeat until you have built up a thick layer.

6 When the paper is dry, paint the amphora. Roman amphorae were made of clay, so use a reddish-brown paint to make yours look like it is clay. Leave to dry.

Overland in China

THE ANCIENT CHINESE EMPIRE was linked by a network of roads used only by the army, officials and royal messengers. A special carriageway was reserved for the emperor. Ordinary people travelled along dusty or muddy routes and tracks.

China's mountainous landscape and large number of rivers meant that engineers became expert at bridge-building. Suspension bridges of rope and bamboo were built from about AD1 onwards. A bridge suspended from iron chains crossed the Chang Jiang (Yangzi River) as early as AD580. A stone arch bridge of AD615 still stands today at Zhouxian in Hebei province.

Most people travelled by foot, and porters carried great loads on their backs or balanced on shoulder poles. Single-wheeled barrows were useful too, 1,000 years before they were invented in the West. China's small native ponies were interbred with larger, stronger horses from central Asia sometime after 100BC. This provided fast, powerful mounts that were suitable for messengers and officials, and could also pull chariots and carriages. Mules and camels were the animals used on the trade routes of the north, while shaggy yaks carried loads in the high mountains. Carts were usually hauled by oxen.

HEADING OUT WEST
Chinese horsemen escort the camels of a caravan (trading expedition). The traders are about to set out along the Silk Road. This trading route ran all the way from Chang'an (Xian) in China to Europe and the lands of the Mediterranean.

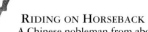

RIDING ON HORSEBACK
A Chinese nobleman from about 2,000 years ago reins in his elegant horse. Breaking in the horse would have been difficult, as the rider has no stirrups and could easily be unseated. Metal stirrups were in general use in China by AD302. They provided more stability and helped the rider control his horse.

CAMEL POWER

Bactrian (two-humped) camels were originally bred in central Asia. They could endure extremes of heat and cold for long distances without water. This toughness made them ideal for transporting goods through the mountains and deserts of the Silk Road.

CARRIED BY HAND

A lazy landowner of the Qing Dynasty travels around his estates. Wealthy people were often carried in a litter (a portable chair). An umbrella shades the landowner from the heat of the summer sun.

HAN CARRIAGE

During the Han Dynasty (202BC–AD 220), three-horse carriages were used by the imperial family only. This carving from a tomb brick probably shows a messenger carrying an important order from the emperor.

TRAVELLING IN STYLE

Han Dynasty government officials travelled in stylish horse-drawn carriages. New breeds of large strong horses became a status symbol for the rich and powerful. The animals were considered celestial (heavenly). The Han civilization developed around the Huang He (Yellow River). Han people invented the chariot by 1500BC, around 500 years later than in Mesopotamia.

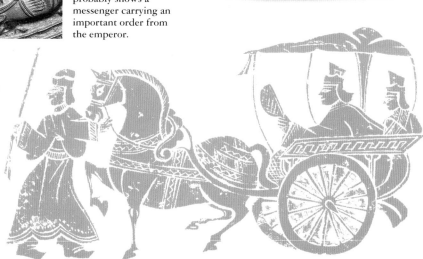

The Chinese Afloat

IN FULL SAIL
Junks were a type of sailing vessel used by merchants in the East and South China seas. They were also used by pirates. The China seas could be blue and peaceful, but they were often whipped into a fury by typhoons (tropical storms).

From early in China's history, the country's rivers, lakes and man-made canals were its main highways. Fishermen propelled small wooden boats with a single oar or pole at the stern. These small boats were often roofed with mats, like the sampans (meaning 'three planks') still seen today. Large, wooden, ocean-sailing ships called junks were either keeled or flat-bottomed, with a high stern and square bows. Matting sails were stiffened with strips of bamboo.

By the 1st century AD, the Chinese had built the first ships with rudders instead of steering oars, and soon went on to make ships with several masts. In the 1400s, admirals Zheng He and Wang Jinghong led expeditions to South-east Asia, India, Arabia and East Africa. The flagship of their 300-strong naval fleet was over five times the size of the largest European ships of the time.

RIVER TRAFFIC
All sorts of small trading boats were sailed or rowed along China's rivers in the 1850s. River travel had always been difficult and could be dangerous. The Huang He (Yellow River) often flooded and changed course. The upper parts of China's longest river, the Chang Jiang (Yangzi River), were rocky and had powerful currents.

MAKE A SAMPAN
You will need: ruler, pencil, thick and thin card, scissors, glue and brush, masking tape, 6 wooden barbecue sticks, string, thin yellow paper, paint (black, dark brown), paintbrush, water pot.

Runner A (x2) — 39cm, 1cm

Side B (x2) — 33.5cm, 15cm, 5cm

Base C (x2) — 15cm, 7cm

Base D — 18cm

Floor E — 10cm, 7cm

Floor F (x2) — 4cm, 7cm

Edge G (x2) — 6.5cm, 1cm

Cut pieces B, C, D and G from thick card. Cut pieces A, E, and F from thin card.

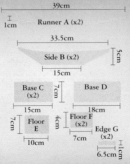

1 Glue base pieces C and D to side B, as shown. Hold the pieces with masking tape while the glue dries. When dry, remove the masking tape.

2 Glue remaining side B to the boat. Stick runner A pieces to top of the sides. Make sure the ends jut out 2.5cm at the front and back of the boat.

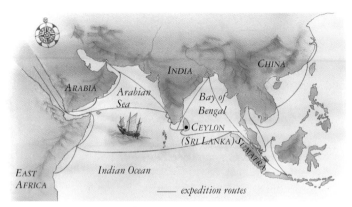

FISHERMEN'S FEASTS
Seas, lakes and rivers were an important food source in imperial China. Drying fish was often the only way to preserve it in the days before refrigeration. Dried fish made strong-tasting sauces and soups. Popular seafoods included crabs, prawns and squid.

dried fish

dried squid

THE VOYAGES OF ZHENG HE
Chinese admirals Zheng He and Wang Jinghong carried out seven fantastic voyages of exploration between 1405 and 1433. This map shows how far and wide they travelled on these expeditions. Their impressive fleets included over 60 ships crewed by about 27,000 seamen, officers and interpreters. The biggest of their vessels was 147m long and 60m wide.

THE FISHING TRIP
A fisherman poles his boat across the river in the 1500s. The bird shown in the picture is a tamed cormorant, used for catching the fish. The cormorant was normally attached to a line, with a ring around its neck to prevent it from swallowing the fish.

To add the finishing touch to your sampan, make a boatman and oar to propel the vessel through the waterways.

3 Glue floor E to centre of base. Add floor F pieces to the ends of the base, as shown. Stick edge G pieces in between the ends of the runners.

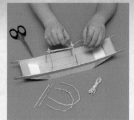

4 Bend 2 barbecue sticks into 10cm high arches. Cut 2 more sticks into five 10cm struts. Glue and tie 2 struts to sides of arches and 1 to the top.

5 Repeat step 4 to make a second roof. To make roof matting, cut thin yellow paper into 1cm x 10cm strips. Fold strips in half and stick to roofs.

6 Paint boat and roofs. Allow to dry. Glue the matting strips to the roofs, as shown. When the glue is dry, place roofs inside the boat.

Over the Mountains of Japan

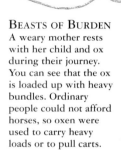

JAPAN IS A RUGGED and mountainous country. Until the 1900s, the only routes through the countryside were narrow, winding tracks. Paths and fragile wooden bridges across deep gullies and streams were often swept away by landslides or floods.

During the Heian period (from around AD794), wealthy warriors rode fine horses, while important officials, wealthy women, children and priests travelled in lightweight wood and bamboo carts. The carts were pulled by oxen and fitted with screens and curtains for privacy. If the route was impassable for ox-carts, wealthy people were carried on palanquins (lightweight portable boxes or litters). Ordinary people usually travelled on foot.

During the Tokugawa period (1600–1868) the shoguns (military rulers) encouraged new road building as a way of increasing trade and keeping control of their lands. The Eastern Sea Road ran for 480km between Kyoto and the shogun's capital, Edo, and took 20-30 days to travel on foot. Some people said it was the busiest road in the world.

BEASTS OF BURDEN
A weary mother rests with her child and ox during their journey. You can see that the ox is loaded up with heavy bundles. Ordinary people could not afford horses, so oxen were used to carry heavy loads or to pull carts.

SHOULDER HIGH
Noblewomen on palanquins (litters) are being taken by porters across a deep river. Some women have decided to disembark so that they can be carried across the river. Palanquins were used in Japan right up to the Tokugawa period (1600–1868). Daimyos (warlords) and their wives might be carried the whole journey to or from the capital city of Edo in a palanquin.

HUGGING THE COASTLINE

Ships sail into harbour at Tempozan, Osaka. The marks on the sails show the company that owned them. Cargo between the shogun's city of Edo and Osaka was mostly carried by ships that hugged the coastline.

CARRYING CARGO

Little cargo-boats, such as these at Edobashi in Edo, carried goods along rivers or around the coast. They were driven through the water by men rowing with oars or pushing against the river bed with a long pole.

STEEP MOUNTAIN PATHS

Travellers on mountain paths hoped to find shelter for the night in villages, temples or monasteries. It could take all day to walk 16km along rough mountain tracks.

IN THE HARBOUR

Sea-going sailing ships, laden with cargo, are shown here at anchor in the harbour of Osaka, an important port in south-central Japan. In front of them you can see smaller river-boats with tall sails. Some families both lived and worked on river-boats.

Viking Specialities

IT WAS OFTEN QUICKER for the Vikings to travel around the coast than over the icy mountains. However, they used horses for carrying baggage and pulling wheeled carts and wagons over their wooden causeways. Sledges hauled goods over grass as well as ice and snow. The Vikings became best known, however, for their shipbuilding skills. Longships were designed for ocean voyages and warfare. They were up to 23m long but were shallow enough to row on rivers. A single oak beam was used for the keel – the backbone of the ship. Planks were caulked (made watertight) with wool or animal hair and coated with a tar made of pine resin. Oar holes ran the length of the ship, and there was a broad steering oar at the stern (back). The large square or rectangular sail was made of heavy woollen or linen cloth.

The Vikings also made broad-beamed cargo and trading vessels and small rowing and sailing boats.

DRAGON SHIPS
The hulls were clinker-built. This means that long, wedge shaped strakes (planks) were nailed to the frame so that they overlapped.

MAKE A SLEDGE

You will need: cardboard, balsa wood, ruler, pencil, craft knife, red acrylic paint, paint brush, brown construction paper, pva glue, glue brush, paper fasteners, masking tape, red string, fur fabric.

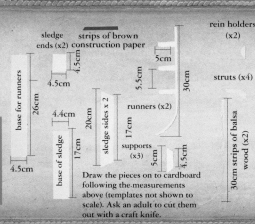

sledge ends (x2)
strips of brown construction paper
base for runners 26cm
4.5cm
4.5cm
4.4cm
base of sledge 17cm
20cm
sledge sides x 2
17cm
supports (x3) 5cm
5cm
5.5cm
30cm
4.5cm
rein holders (x2)
struts (x4)
runners (x2)
30cm strips of balsa wood (x2)
4.5cm

Draw the pieces on to cardboard following the measurements above (templates not shown to scale). Ask an adult to cut them out with a craft knife.

1 Paint one side of each of the 9 pieces that will form the top of the sledge, as shown. When they have dried, turn them over and paint the other side.

MODERN VIKINGS

In recent years modern replicas of longships have proved to be strong, fast and easy to sail. The planking bends well to the waves and the ships are light enough to be hauled overland.

PUTTING TO SEA

A longship put to sea with a crew of 30 or more fighting men. In Greek and Roman galleys, there was a separate fighting force. The Vikings, though, were both warriors and sailors. They sometimes slung their round shields along the side of the ship.

Many Viking sledges were designed to be pulled by horses and were often finely carved.

SHIPS' TIMBERS

In the Viking Age, much of northern Europe was still densely forested. In most places there was no shortage of timber for building or repairing longships. Oak was always the shipbuilders' first choice of wood, followed by pine, beech and ash.

beech

oak

2 Cut several strips of brown construction paper. Arrange them to form diamond patterns along the sides of the sledge. Trim and glue in place.

3 Ask an adult to make cuts with a craft knife. Push paper fasteners through to form patterns. Glue the top of the sledge. Hold it together with masking tape.

4 While you wait for the top to dry, glue the 8 pieces that form the base of the sledge together. Glue the 2 rein holders on the top of the base.

5 Paint the base red. When it is dry, brush plenty of glue on to it and carefully stick on the top. Leave it to dry. Attach the reins and trim with fur fabric.

Wheel-less in Mesoamerica

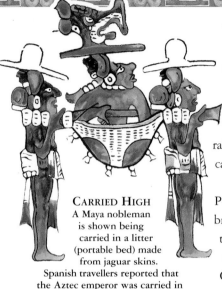

THE AZTEC AND MAYA PEOPLE of Central America knew about wheels and built an intricate system of roads – but they did not make wheeled transport of any kind. Carriages and carts would not have been able to travel through dense rainforests, along steep, narrow mountain tracks or the raised causeways that linked many cities.

Most people travelled on foot, carrying goods on their backs. Porters carried heavy loads with the help of a *tumpline*. This was a broad band of cloth that went across their foreheads and under the bundles on their backs, leaving their arms free. Rulers and nobles were carried in portable beds, called litters.

On rivers and lakes, Mesoamericans used simple dug-out boats. Maya sailors travelled in huge wooden canoes that were able to make long voyages, even in the rough, open sea.

CARRIED HIGH
A Maya nobleman is shown being carried in a litter (portable bed) made from jaguar skins.
Spanish travellers reported that the Aztec emperor was carried in the same way. When the emperor walked, blankets were spread in front of him so that his feet did not touch the ground.

MEN OR MONSTERS?
Until the Spaniards arrived with horses in 1519, there were no animals big and strong enough to ride in the Mesoamerican lands. There were horses in America in prehistoric times, but they died out around 10,000BC. When the Aztecs saw the Spanish riding, they thought the animals were monsters – half man, half beast.

MAKE A WHEELED DOG

You will need: board, self-drying clay, 4 lengths of thin dowel about 5cm long and 2 lengths about 7cm long, water bowl, thick card, scissors, pva glue, glue brush, paintbrush, paint, masking tape.

1 Roll a large piece of clay into a fat sausage to form the dog's body. Push the 5cm pieces of dowel into the body to make the legs. Leave to dry.

2 Cover the dowel legs with clay, extending the clay 2cm beyond the end of the dowel. Make a hole at the end of each leg with a piece of dowel. Leave to dry.

3 Push the dowel through the holes in the legs to join them horizontally. Make the dog's head and ears from clay. Join them to the body using water.

HARDWORKING PORTERS

This engraving from the 1900s shows Aztec slaves and commoners carrying loads for Spanish conquerors. Being a porter was very hard work. They were expected to cover up to 100km per day, carrying about 25–30kg on their backs. Like most Mesoamerican people, they travelled these long distances barefoot.

BY BOAT

The city of Tenochtitlan was built on artificial islands on a lake. Transport around the city was by flat-bottomed boat. The boats ferried people and transported fruits and vegetables to market. Dug-out canoes made from hollowed-out tree trunks were popular too.

AZTEC WATERWAYS

The Aztecs paddled their canoes and flat-bottomed boats on Lake Texcoco. Today most of this lake has dried up. The lakeside *chinampas*, where they grew food and flowers, have almost disappeared. This photograph shows modern punts sailing along one of the last remaining Aztec waterways between the few *chinampas* that survive.

Toys such as this dog are proof that the wheel was known in Mesoamerica. Wheeled vehicles were not suitable for rugged Mesoamerican land.

4 Cut four circles 3.5cm in diameter from card to make wheels. Pierce a hole in the centre of each. Make the holes big enough for the dowel to fit through.

5 Make four wheels from clay, the same size as the card wheels. Glue the clay and card wheels together. Make holes through the clay wheels and leave to dry.

6 Paint the dog's head, body, legs and wheels with Aztec patterns. When the paint is dry, give the dog a thin coat of pva glue to act as a varnish.

7 Fit the wheels on to the ends of the dowels that pass through the dog's legs. Wrap strips of masking tape around the ends to stop the wheels falling off.

Arctic Travel

DURING THE WINTER, the surface of the Arctic Ocean freezes and snow covers the land. In the past, sledges were the most common way of travelling over the ice and snow. They were made from bone or timber lashed together with strips of hide or whale sinew. They glided over the snow on runners made from walrus tusks or wood. Arctic sledges had to be light enough to be pulled by animals, yet strong enough to carry an entire family and its belongings. In North America, huskies pulled the sledges. In Siberia and Scandinavia, however, reindeer were used.

From ancient times, Arctic peoples have needed skis and snowshoes to travel over snow. Skis are thought to have been invented by the Saami people of Lapland more than 3,500 years ago. Snowshoes enabled Arctic hunters to stalk prey without sinking into deep snowdrifts.

REINDEER SLEDGES
Three reindeer stand by a family and their sledge in Siberia. In Arctic Russia and Scandinavia, reindeer were commonly used to pull sledges. Small, narrow sledges carried just one person. Larger, wider models could take much heavier loads.

HITCHING A DOG TEAM
A husky team struggles up a hill in eastern Greenland. Traditionally, the traces (reins) that connected the dogs to the sledge were made of walrus hide. Different Arctic cultures used one of two arrangements to hitch the dogs together. Some people hitched them in the shape of a fan. Others hitched the dogs in pairs in a long line.

MAKE A MODEL SLEDGE

You will need: thick card, balsa wood, ruler, pencil, scissors, pva glue, glue brush, masking tape, compass, barbecue stick, string, shammy leather, brown paint, paint brush, water pot.

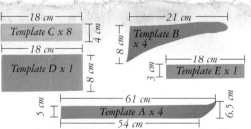

Template C x 8 — 18 cm, 4 cm
Template D x 1 — 18 cm, 8 cm
Template B x 4 — 21 cm, 8 cm
Template E x 1 — 18 cm, 3 cm
Template A x 4 — 61 cm, 54 cm, 5 cm, 6.5 cm

Using the shapes above for reference, measure out the shapes on the card (use balsa wood for template C). Cut the shapes out using your scissors. You will need to make 4 A templates, 4 B templates, 8 C templates (balsa wood), 1 D template and 1 E template. Always remember to cut away from your body when using scissors.

1 Glue 2 A templates together. Repeat this for the other 2 A templates. Repeat this with the 4 B templates. Cover all the edges with masking tape.

SNOWSHOES

Snowshoes are used to walk across deep snowdrifts without sinking into the snow. They spread the person's weight across a large area. To make the snowshoe, thin, flexible birch saplings were steamed to make them supple. The saplings were then bent into the shape of the snowshoe frame. Some shoes were rounded but others were long and narrow. The netting was woven from long strips of animal hide.

birch sapling

snowshoes

rawhide thongs

MAN'S BEST FRIEND

This picture, painted around 1890, shows an Inuit hunter harnessing one of his huskies. Huskies were vital to Inuit society. On the hunt, the dogs helped to nose out seals hiding in their dens. They hauled heavy loads of meat back to camp.

SAAMI SKIS

The Saami have used skis for thousands of years. Early skis were made of wood and the undersides were covered with strips of reindeer skin. The hairs on the skin pointed backwards, giving the skier grip when walking uphill.

LET SLEEPING DOGS LIE

A husky's thick coat keeps it warm in temperatures as low as −50°C. These hardy animals can sleep peacefully in the fiercest of blizzards. The snow builds up against their fur and insulates them.

Inuit hunters used wooden sledges pulled by huskies to hunt for food over a large area. The wood was lashed together with animal hide or sinew.

2 Using a compass, make small holes along the top edge of the glued A templates. Use the end of a barbecue stick to make the holes a little larger.

3 Glue the balsa wood slats C in position over the holes along the A templates as shown above. You will need to use all 8 balsa wood slats.

4 Carefully glue the B templates and the E and D templates to the end of the sledge, as shown above. Allow to dry, then paint the model.

5 Thread string through the holes to secure the slats on each side. Decorate the sledge with a shammy-covered card box and secure it to the sledge.

Early Conflicts in Mesopotamia

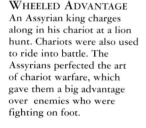

T HE CITY-STATES of Mesopotamia were frequently at war with one another. Usually, the disputes were local affairs over pieces of land or the ownership of canals. Later, powerful kings created empires and warred with foreign countries. King Sargon of Agade, for example, subdued all the cities of Sumer and then conquered great cities in northern Syria. Assyria and Babylonia were often at war in the first millennium BC. The walls of Assyrian palaces were decorated with reliefs (painted carvings) that celebrate battle scenes.

The Mesopotamians were among the first people to invent the wheel. They put this to good use in chariot warfare and wheeled siege machines.

WHEELED ADVANTAGE
An Assyrian king charges along in his chariot at a lion hunt. Chariots were also used to ride into battle. The Assyrians perfected the art of chariot warfare, which gave them a big advantage over enemies who were fighting on foot.

IN THE BEGINNING
A model of a very early chariot, about 4,000 years old, shows the first wheel designs of solid wood. By the time of the Assyrian Empire, about 900-600 BC, war chariots had spoked wooden wheels with metal rims.

THE KING'S GUARDS
A panel from the palace of the Persian kings at Susa shows a long procession of king's guards. The guards are armed with spears, and carry quivers full of arrows. King Cyrus of Persia conquered Babylon in 539BC.

MAKE A CHARIOT
You will need: pen, cardboard, scissors, paints and paintbrushes, flour, water and newspaper to make papier mâché, glue, masking tape, 2 x dowel 16cm long, card tubes, needle, 4 cocktail sticks.

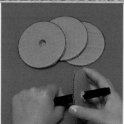

1 Cut four circles about 7cm in width out of the card. Use the scissors to make a hole in the centre of each circle. Enlarge the holes with a pen.

2 Cut out two sides for the chariot 12cm long x 8cm high as shown, one back 9 x 8cm, one front 9 x 15cm, one top 9 x 7cm and one base 12 x 9cm.

3 Trim the top of the front to two curves as shown. Stick the side pieces to the front and back using masking tape. Stick on the base and top.

SLINGS AND ARROWS

Assyrian foot-soldiers used rope slings and stone balls the size of modern tennis balls. Others fired arrows while sheltering behind tall wicker shields. They wore helmets of bronze or iron and were protected by metal scale armour and leather boots.

GOING INTO BATTLE

Sumerian chariot drivers charge into battle. A soldier armed with spears stands on the footplate of each chariot ready to jump off and fight. They are all protected by thick leather cloaks and helmets. The chariots were drawn by onegars (wild asses).

Your chariot copies a clay model made in northern Mesopotamia over 4,000 years ago.

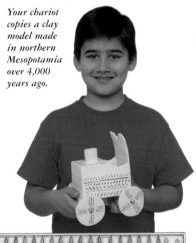

STORMING A CITY

Many Assyrian fighting methods can be seen in the palace reliefs at the city of Nimrud. In this scene, the Assyrians storm an enemy city which stands on a hill. A siege engine with spears projecting from the front breaks down the walls. Attacking soldiers climbed the walls with the help of siege ladders, and they were protected by archers.

4 Roll up a piece of newspaper to make a cylinder shape 3cm long, and attach it to the chariot. Attach the cardboard tubes to the bottom of the chariot.

5 Mix a paste of flour and water. Dip newspaper strips into the paste to make papier mâché. Cover the chariot with layers of papier mâché. Leave to dry.

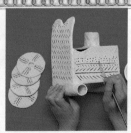

6 Paint the whole chariot cream. Add detail using brown paint. Paint the wheels, too. Make a hole with the needle in each end of the dowels.

7 Insert a cocktail stick in the dowel, add a wheel and insert into the tube. Fix another wheel and stick to the other end. Repeat with the other wheels.

Indian Armies

Conflict was a fact of life in India from the time when people invaded from central Asia around 1750BC. At first, tribes fought and stole each others' cattle. Gradually, empires grew and warfare became more elaborate. By the time of the emperor Ashoka in 250BC, armies were divided into four parts – infantry (footsoldiers), cavalry (horses), chariots and elephants. The infantry was the core of all Indian armies, but was often made up of poorly trained peasants. Elephants were symbols of royalty, majesty and prestige.

In the first millennium AD, when the Turks invaded, chariots became less important. This was because the Turks had excellent horses and could use bows on horseback. Soon, all Indian armies copied them and developed a top-grade cavalry. The first recorded use of gunpowder in Indian warfare was in the 1400s. Later, the Mughals combined field artillery (guns) with cavalry and elephants.

UNEQUAL CONTEST
A mounted warrior and a footsoldier attack each other. From the 1200s, nobles preferred to fight on horseback. Footsoldiers faced a height disadvantage when fighting mounted soldiers. The horsemen could also use swords as well as bows.

SUPERIOR WARRIOR
A Mongol warrior draws his bow and aims behind him as he rides. The Mongols were great fighters, especially on horseback. In 1398, they devastated Delhi and took many of its citizens as slaves.

MUGHAL HELMET
You will need: strips of newspaper, flour and water or wallpaper paste, bowl, inflated balloon, scissors, fine sandpaper, thin card, sticky tape or pva glue, gold and black paint, paintbrushes, 20 x 10 cm piece of black card, ruler.

1 Soak the newspaper in the paste or flour and water. Cover half the balloon with three layers of newspaper. Leave to dry between layers.

2 When dry, burst the balloon and remove it. Smooth edges of helmet with sandpaper. Wrap a strip of card around the base. Fix with tape or glue.

3 Place a longer piece of card inside the helmet. It should be long enough to cover your ears and neck. Glue or tape it into position and trim to fit.

LIGHT PROTECTION

A Hindu warrior on horseback prepares to hurl his spear. Warriors had little armour besides shields. They often wore ornaments and lucky charms.

BEST WEAPON

The Hindu footsoldier's favoured weapons were the bow and arrow, and the sword. However, they also fought with maces, lances, spears and daggers.

FORTIFIED CHAIR

A king at war travels in a fortified howdah (chair) on an elephant's back. The combination of howdah and elephant was like the armoured tank of modern warfare. The best elephants for army use came mainly from eastern and southern India, and Sri Lanka.

FINE WEAPONRY

This Mughal dagger handle is inlaid with gold and jewels. Weapons were often crafted from the finest materials.

A Mughal warrior wore a plumed helmet to protect his head in battle.

4 Paint the entire helmet with two coats of gold paint, using a medium-sized paintbrush. Allow the paint to dry completely between coats.

5 Add detail with black paint and a fine paintbrush. You could use a Mughal pattern like the one shown here, or design your own.

6 Cut narrow slits 5 mm apart in the black card. Leave 5 cm uncut at the bottom of the card. Cover this patch with glue and roll the card up tightly.

7 When the glue is dry, fix the plume to the top of your helmet with glue, or you can cut a small hole in the helmet and push the plume through.

Shoguns and Samurai

BETWEEN 1185 AND 1600 there were a great many wars throughout Japan. Rival warlords fought to become shogun – the title held by the military ruler. Some former emperors also tried, unsuccessfully, to restore imperial rule. During this troubled time in Japanese history, emperors, shoguns and daimyo all relied on armies of well-trained samurai to fight their battles. The samurai were highly trained warriors from noble families. Members of each samurai army were bound by a solemn oath, sworn to their lord. They stayed loyal from a sense of honour – and because their lord gave them rich rewards. The civil wars ended around 1600, when the Tokugawa dynasty of shoguns came to power. From this time onwards, samurai spent less time fighting, and served instead as officials and business managers.

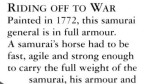

RIDING OFF TO WAR
Painted in 1772, this samurai general is in full armour. A samurai's horse had to be fast, agile and strong enough to carry the full weight of the samurai, his armour and his weapons.

TACHI
Swords were a favourite weapon of the samurai. This long sword is called a *tachi*. It was made in the 1500s for ceremonial use by a samurai.

METAL HELMET
Samurai helmets like this were made from curved metal panels, carefully fitted together, and decorated with elaborate patterns. The jutting peak protected the wearer's face and the nape-guard covered the back of the neck. This helmet dates from around 1380.

SAMURAI HELMET

You will need: thick card, pin, string, felt-tip pen, ruler, scissors, tape measure, newspaper, bowl, water, pva glue, balloon, petroleum jelly, pencil, modelling clay, bradawl, paper, gold card, paints, brush, water pot, glue brush, masking tape, paper fasteners, 2 x 20cm lengths of cord.

1 Draw a circle 18cm in diameter on card using the pin, string and felt-tip pen. Using the same method, draw two larger circles 20cm and 50cm.

2 Draw a line across the centre of the three circles using the ruler and felt-tip pen. Draw tabs in the middle semi-circle. Add two flaps as shown.

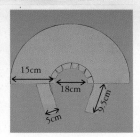

3 Now cut out the neck protector piece completely, as shown above. Make sure that you cut around the tabs and flaps exactly.

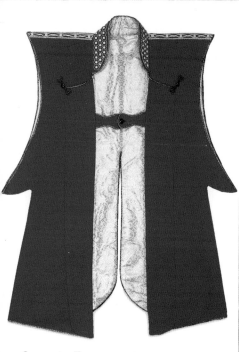

Surcoat Finery

For festivals, ceremonies and parades samurai wore surcoats (long, loose tunics) over their armour. Surcoats were made from fine, glossy silks, dyed in rich colours. This example was made during the Tokugawa period (1600–1868). Surcoats were often decorated with family crests. These were originally used to identify soldiers in battle, but later became badges of high rank.

Protective Clothing

This fine suit of samurai armour dates from the Tokugawa period (1600–1868). Armour gave the samurai life-saving protection in battle. High-ranking warriors wore suits of plate armour, made of iron panels, laced or riveted together and combined with panels of chain mail or rawhide. Lower-ranking soldiers called *ashigaru* wore thinner, lightweight armour, made of small metal plates. A full suit of samurai armour could weigh anything up to 18kg.

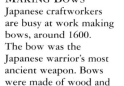

Making Bows

Japanese craftworkers are busy at work making bows, around 1600. The bow was the Japanese warrior's most ancient weapon. Bows were made of wood and bamboo and fired many different kinds of arrow.

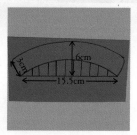

4 Draw the peak template piece on another piece of card. Follow the measurements shown in the picture. Cut out the peak template.

5 To make papier-mâché, tear the newspaper into small strips. Fill the bowl with 1 part pva glue to 3 parts water. Add the newspaper strips.

6 Blow up the balloon to the size of your head. Cover with petroleum jelly. Build up three papier-mâché layers on the top and sides. Leave to dry between layers.

7 When dry, pop the balloon and trim. Ask a friend to make a mark on either side of your head.

Instructions for the helmet continue on the next page...

Honour Among Samurai

THE TAKEDA FAMILY
The famous daimyo (warlord) Takeda Shingen (1521–1573), fires an arrow using his powerful bow. The influential Takeda family owned estates in Kai province near the city of Edo and kept a large private army of samurai warriors. Takeda Shingen fought a series of wars with his near neighbour, Uesugi Kenshin. However, in 1581, the Takeda were defeated by the army of General Nobunaga.

SAMURAI WERE HIGHLY TRAINED WARRIORS who dedicated their lives to fighting for their lords. However, being a samurai involved more than just fighting. The ideal samurai was supposed to follow a strict code of behaviour, governing all aspects of his life. This code was called *bushido* (the way of the warrior). *Bushido* called for skill, self-discipline, bravery, loyalty, honour, honesty, obedience and, at times, self-sacrifice. It taught that it was nobler to die fighting than to run away and survive.

Many samurai warriors followed the religious teachings of Zen, a branch of the Buddhist faith. Zen was introduced into Japan by two monks, Eisai and Dogen, who went to China to study in the 1100s and 1200s and brought Zen practices back with them. Teachers of Zen encouraged their followers to meditate (to free the mind of all thoughts) in order to achieve enlightenment.

SWORDSMEN
It took young samurai many years to master the skill of swordsmanship. They were trained by master swordsmen. The best swords, made of strong, springy steel, were even given their own names.

8 Place clay under the pencil marks. Make two holes – one above and one below each pencil mark – with a bradawl. Repeat on the other side.

9 Fold a piece of A4 paper and draw a horn shape on to it following the design shown above. Cut out this shape so that you have an identical pair of horns.

10 Take a piece of A4 size gold card. Place your paper horns on to the gold card and draw around them. Carefully cut the horns out of the card.

11 Paint the papier-mâché helmet brown. Paint a weave design on the neck protector and a cream block on each flap. Leave to dry.

OFF TO WAR

A samurai warrior (on horseback) and foot-soldiers set off for war. Samurai had to command and inspire confidence in others, so it was especially important for them to behave in a brave and honourable way.

MARTIAL ARTS

Several sports that people enjoy playing today have developed from samurai fighting skills. In aikido, players try to throw their opponent off-balance and topple them to the ground. In kendo, players fight one another with long swords made of split bamboo. They score points by managing to touch their opponent's body, not by cutting or stabbing them!

kendo *aikido*

SURVIVAL SKILLS

Samurai had to know how to survive in wild countryside. Each man carried emergency rations of dried rice. He also used his fighting skills to hunt wild animals for food.

ZEN

The Buddhist monk Rinzai is shown in this Japanese brush and ink scroll-painting. Rinzai was a famous teacher of Zen ideas. Many pupils, including samurai, travelled to his remote monastery in the mountains to study with him.

Samurai helmets were often decorated with crests made of lacquered wood or metal. These were mounted on the top of the helmet.

12 Bend back the tabs on the peak piece. Position it at the front of the helmet. Stick the tabs to the inside with glue. Hold in place with tape.

13 Now take the neck protector. Bend back the front flaps and the tabs. Glue the tabs to the helmet, as shown. Leave the helmet to dry.

14 Stick the horns to the front of the helmet. Use paper fasteners to secure, as shown. Decorate the ear flaps with paper fasteners.

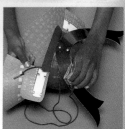

15 Thread cord through one of the holes made in step 8. Tie a knot in the end. Thread the other end of the cord through the second hole. Repeat on the other side.

Greek Fighting Forces

ALL GREEK MEN were expected to fight in their city's army. In Sparta the army was on duty all year round. In other parts of Greece men gave up fighting in autumn so that they could bring in the harvest and make the wine. The only full-time soldiers were the personal bodyguards of a ruler and mercenaries who fought for anyone who paid them. Armies consisted mainly of hoplites (armoured infantry), cavalry (soldiers on horseback) and a group of foot soldiers armed with stones and bows and arrows. The hoplites engaged in hand-to-hand combt and were the most important fighting force. The cavalry was less effective because riders had no stirrups. This made charging with a lance impossible, as the rider would fall off on contact. Instead horsemen were used for scouting, harassing a beaten enemy and carrying messages.

HARD HELMET
This bronze helmet from the city of Corinth was fashioned to protect the face. It has guards for the cheeks and the bridge of the nose. Iron later replaced bronze as the main metal for weapons.

BOWMEN
The Greek army usually employed Scythian archers from north of the Black Sea to fight for them. Archers were useful for fighting in mountainous countryside if they were positioned above the enemy. Some Greek soldiers did fight with bows and arrows. They fought in small units known as *psiloi*. But most of the soldiers in these units could only afford simple missile weapons, such as a javelin or slings from which they shot stones.

WARRIOR GREAVES
You will need: clear film, bowl of water, plaster bandages, sheet of paper, kitchen paper, scissors, cord, gold paint, paintbrush.

1 Ask a friend to help you with steps 1 to 3. Loosely cover both of your lower legs (from your ankle to the top of your knee) in clear film.

2 Soak each plaster bandage in water. Working from one side of your leg to the other, smooth the bandage over the front of each leg.

3 Carefully remove each greave. Set them on some paper. Dampen some kitchen paper and use it to smooth the greaves down. Leave them to dry.

A RARE SIGHT IN BATTLE

Chariots were not often used in Greek warfare. They could only be used on plains. There were usually two people in the chariot, one to drive it and the other to fight from the back.

FIGHTING FORCES

Tin and copper were used to make bronze, the main material for weapons and armour. Bronze is harder than pure copper and, unlike iron, does not rust. As there was no tin in Greece, it was imported from faraway lands.

copper   *tin*

MIDDLE CLASS FOOT SOLDIERS

The hoplite fighting force was made up of middle-class men who could afford to arm themselves. A hoplite's armoury consisted of a shield, helmet, spear, sword and greaves. Helmets were made of bronze and were usually crested with horsehair. The body was protected by a bronze cuirass – a one-piece breast- and back-plate. Underneath this, there was a leather cuirass. Shields were usually round and decorated with a symbol.

4 Trim the edges of the greaves, to make them look neat. Measure four lengths of cord to fit around your leg, below the knee and above the ankle.

5 Turn the greaves on to their front. Lay the cord in place at the point where you want to tie them to your leg. Fix them into place using wet bandages.

6 Leave the plaster bandages to dry, with the cord in place. Now paint each greave with gold paint. Once they are dry, tie them on.

Greaves were attached to the lower leg to protect it in battle. They were worn by hoplites.

Legions of Romans

THE ARMY OF THE EARLY ROMAN EMPIRE was divided into 28 groups called legions. Each of these numbered about 5,500 soldiers. The legion included mounted troops and foot-soldiers. They were organized into cohorts of about 500 men, and centuries, of about 80 men – even though centuries means 'hundreds'. Each legion was led into battle by soldiers carrying standards. These were decorated poles that represented the honour and bravery of the legion.

The first Roman soldiers were called up from the wealthier families in times of war. These conscripts had to supply their own weapons. In later years, the Roman army became paid professionals, with legionaries recruited from all citizens. During the period of the Empire, many foreign troops also fought for Rome as auxiliary soldiers.

Army life was tough and discipline was severe. After a long march carrying heavy kits, tents, tools and weapons, the weary soldiers would have to dig camp defences. A sentry who deserted his post would be beaten to death.

AT WAR
Trajan's Column in Rome is decorated with scenes from the Dacian wars. These were fought in the region of present-day Romania. Scenes like these can tell us much about Roman soldiers, the weapons they used, their enemies and their allies.

A LEGIONARY
This bronze statue of a legionary is about 1,800 years old. He is wearing a crested parade helmet and the overlapping bronze armour of the period. Legionaries underwent strict training and were brutally disciplined. They were tough soldiers and quite a force to be reckoned with.

ON HORSEBACK
Roman foot-soldiers were backed up by mounted troops, or cavalry. They were divided into groups, of 500 to 1,000, called *alae*. The cavalry were amongst the highest paid of Roman soldiers.

RAISING THE STANDARD

The Emperor Constantine addresses his troops, probably congratulating them on a victory. They are carrying standards, emblems of each legion. Standards were decorated with gold eagles, hands, wreaths and banners called *vexilla*. They were symbols of the honour and bravery of the legion and had to be protected at all costs.

A ROMAN FORT

The Roman army built forts of wood or stone all over the Empire. This fort is in southern Britain. It was built to defend the coast against attacks by Saxon raiders from northern Europe. Today, its surrounding area is called Porchester. The name comes from a combination of the word port and *caster*, the Latin word for fort.

HADRIAN'S WALL

This is part of Hadrian's Wall, which marks the most northerly border of the Roman Empire. It stretches for 120km across northern England, almost from coast to coast. It was built as a defensive barrier between AD122 and 128, at the command of the Emperor Hadrian.

Equipped to Kill

ROMAN SOLDIERS were renowned for their effective weapons. A legionary carried a dagger called a *pugio*, a short iron sword called a *gladius*, which was used for stabbing and slashing, and a javelin, or *pilum*. In the early days of the Empire, a foot-soldier's armour was a mail shirt, worn over a short, thick tunic. Officers wore a cuirass, a bronze casing that protected the chest and back, and crests on their helmets to show their rank. By about AD35, the mail shirt was being replaced by plate armour, in which iron sections were joined by hooks or leather straps. Early shields were oval, and later ones were oblong with curved edges. They were made of layers of wood glued together, covered in leather and linen. A metal boss, or cover, over the central handle could be used to hit an enemy who got too close.

ROMAN SOLDIERS
Artists over the ages have been inspired by the battles of the Roman legions. They imagined how fully armed Roman soldiers might have looked. This picture shows a young officer giving orders.

HEAD GEAR
Roman helmets were designed to protect the sides of the head and the neck. This cavalry helmet is made of bronze and iron. It would have been worn by an auxiliary, a foreign soldier fighting for Rome, sometime after AD43. Officers wore crests on their helmets, so that their men could see them during battle.

ROMAN ARMOUR

You will need: tape measure, A1-size sheets of silver card (one or two, depending on how big you are), scissors, pencil, pva glue, paintbrush, 2m length of cord, compass.

1 Measure yourself around your chest. Cut out three strips of card, 5cm wide and long enough to go round you. Cut out some thinner strips to stick these three together.

2 Lay the wide strips flat and glue them together with the thin strips, as shown above. The Romans would have used leather straps to hold the wide metal pieces together.

3 When the glue is dry, bend the ends together, silver side out. Make a hole in the end of each strip and thread the cord through, as shown above.

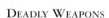

DEADLY WEAPONS

These iron spearheads were found on the site of an old Roman fort near Bath, in Britain. The wooden shafts they were on rotted long ago. Roman soldiers carried both light and heavy spears. The lighter ones were used for throwing, and the heavier ones were for thrusting at close range.

TORTOISE TACTICS

Siege tactics were one of the Roman army's great strengths. When approaching an enemy fortress, a group of soldiers could lock their shields together over their heads and crouch under them. Protected by their shields, they could safely advance toward the enemy. This was known as the *testudo* (tortoise), formation. During a siege, iron bolts and large stones were hurled over fortress walls by giant catapults.

SWORDS

Both short and long swords were kept in scabbards. This spectacular scabbard was owned by an officer who served the Emperor Tiberius. It may have been given to him by the emperor himself. It is elaborately decorated in gold and silver.

Put the shoulder piece over your head and tie the chest section round yourself. Now you are a legionary ready to do battle with the enemies of Rome. Metal strip armour was invented during the reign of the Emperor Tiberius, AD14-37. Originally, the various parts were hinged and were joined together either by hooks or by buckles and straps.

4 Cut a square of card as wide as your shoulders. Use the compass to draw a 12cm diameter circle in the centre. Cut the square in half and cut away the half circles.

5 Use smaller strips of card to glue the shoulder halves together, leaving a neck hole. Cut out four more strips, two a little shorter than the others. Attach them in the same way.

Celts versus Romans

THE ROMANS HAD TO DO some hard fighting to win over new lands for their empire. The Celts were among their fiercest foes. There were Celtic tribes scattered throughout central and northern Europe. They shared similar languages and customs – and resistance against Roman rule! The first major conflicts began soon after 400BC, when migrating bands of Celts from France arrived in northern Italy. Then, in 387BC, Celtic warriors attacked the city of Rome itself. To the Romans, the Celts were savage, barbarian and brutal, compared with their own people. However, Roman soldiers were impressed by the courage and ferocity of Celtic warriors, and the fast, two-horse chariots that the chiefs rode into battle. The Romans soon discovered that most of the Celtic troops were no match for their well-organized, disciplined way of fighting, or for their short, stabbing swords. Once ordinary Celtic warriors saw their hero chiefs dead on the battlefield, they panicked. They either hurled themselves recklessly towards the Romans, and were easily killed, or else retreated in confusion and despair.

It took many years for the Romans to conquer all the Celtic tribes, but in the end, they succeeded.

ROMANS RIDING HIGH
This tombstone was carved as a memorial to a Roman soldier named Flavinus. He served as a standard-bearer in a cavalry regiment that was sent to enforce the Roman conquest of Britain in about AD50. The carving shows his horse trampling a Celtic warrior under its hoofs. The warrior has hair stiffened with lime to make him look more fierce. Despite their courage, Celtic foot soldiers had little chance of surviving a Roman cavalry charge.

CAPTIVE CELTS
Once captured by the Romans, Celtic men, women and children were either killed or sold as slaves. This painting dates from the 1800s and shows captive Celts in Rome. The artist has invented some details of the Celts' clothes and hairstyles. After success in war, the Romans paraded captured prisoners through the city.

TRIUMPH AND DEFEAT

Two Celts, captured and in chains, are depicted on a Roman triumphal arch. The arch was built around AD25 in southern France. It commemorates a Roman victory against the rebellious Gauls. The sculptor has shown the Gauls as the Romans imagined them, looking wild and ragged, and dressed in shaggy fur.

ENEMIES ON COINS

The Romans chose to show a Celtic warrior in his battle chariot on this Roman coin. They admired certain aspects of the Celtic civilization and were proud to have conquered such a people.

JULIUS CAESAR

Roman army commander Julius Caesar was very ambitious. He used his success against the Celts in France to help advance his political career in Rome. In 44BC, he declared himself "Dictator (sole ruler) for Life". He wrote a book describing his campaigns against the Celts. Although it paints a hostile picture of the Celtic people, Caesar's book has become one of the most important pieces of evidence about Celtic life. This silver coin shows Julius Caesar, represented as an elephant, crushing Gaul (France).

WALLED FRONTIER

In AD122, the Roman emperor, Hadrian, gave orders for a massive wall to be built across northern England. Its purpose was to mark the border between lands ruled by Rome and lands further north in Scotland, where Celtic chiefs still had power. Roman soldiers were stationed at forts built at intervals along the wall. They kept a look out for Celtic attackers, but also met, traded with, and sometimes married, members of the local Celtic population who lived and worked close to the wall.

Celts Fight Back

THE CELTS RELIED ON THEIR STRENGTH – and their weapons – to survive in battle. Their heavy iron swords were used for cutting and slashing. They were carried in decorated scabbards made of bronze, wood or leather. Spears and javelins were lighter. They were used for stabbing at close quarters or for throwing at an enemy many metres away. Round pebbles, hurled by cloth or leather slings, could also be deadly weapons. Archaeologists have found huge stockpiles of pebbles at Celtic hill forts. Wooden clubs were used by warriors to bludgeon their enemies in battle, but were also used for hunting birds.

For protection, Celtic warriors carried a long shield, usually made of wood and leather. Normally, Celtic men wore a thigh-length tunic over baggy trousers but, in battle, they often went naked except for a torc (twisted metal ring) around the neck and a metal helmet. This nakedness was a proud display of physical strength – even the Celts' enemies admired their tall, muscular physique. The Celts believed that torcs gave magical protection. Their helmets, topped with magic crests, gave them extra height and made them look frightening.

CHAIN MAIL
The Celts sometimes used flexible chest coverings of chain mail in battle. Several burial sites have yielded actual chain mail such as that shown above, found in St Alban's, England. However, most of the time, the Celts went into battle naked.

UNDRESSED TO KILL
This gold pin is decorated with the figure of a naked Celtic warrior, armed with sword, shield and helmet. One ancient writer described a Celtic warrior's weapons: "A long sword worn on the right side, and a long shield, tall spears and a kind of javelin. Some also use bows and slings. They have a wooden war club, which is thrown by hand with a range far greater than an arrow …"

MAKE A SHIELD
You will need: felt-tip pen, card 77cm x 38cm, scissors, ruler, pair of compasses, bottle top, bradawl, leather thongs, paper fasteners, sticky tape, drink carton lid, plasticine, pva glue, paint, paintbrushes, dowling rod 75cm long.

1 Draw a shield shape on to card. The shield should have rounded corners and curve in slightly on each of the long sides, as shown. Cut out.

77cm
38cm

2 Draw a vertical and a horizontal line through the centre of the shield. Add a large circle in the centre and two smaller circles either side, as shown.

29cm
17cm

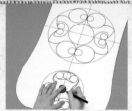

3 With a felt-tip pen draw a typical Celtic design inside the circles, as shown. Use the bottle top and compasses to help you create your design.

SPANISH SHIELDS

The design of weapons and armour varied in different Celtic lands. These Celts are carrying small, round shields that originated in Spain. Shields were made from wood and leather. All Spanish warriors usually fought with a short, single-edged sword, called a *falcata*.

HANDY WEAPON

Daggers were used for fighting at close range. By the end of the Celtic era, when this dagger was made, their strong, sharp blades were usually forged from iron. They often had finely decorated hilts (handles), with scabbards (sheaths) fashioned from softer bronze. This dagger was found in the River Thames, London.

BRAIN GUARD

Helmets were usually made of iron, padded inside with cloth and covered on the outside by a layer of bronze. The high, domed shape protected the wearer's skull. The peaked front kept slashing sword blows away from the eyes.

SHARP AND DEADLY

Celtic weapons were fitted with sharp metal blades, designed to cause terrible injuries. This bronze spear-point was made in Britain in about 1400BC, using techniques that were still employed by the Celts a thousand years later. Celtic metalworkers used moulds to make tools and weapons. Molten bronze was poured into the mould. Once the bronze object was cold and hard, rough edges were polished away, using coarse sand.

Shields were a speciality of craft workshops in southern England. A shield was one of a Celtic warrior's most prized possessions.

4 Use the bradawl to make two holes between the large and smaller circles, as shown. Thread the leather thongs through the holes.

5 With the bradawl, make small holes for the decorative paper fasteners. Push the paper fasteners through the holes and tape the ends on the back.

6 Stick the drink carton lid into the centre of the large circle. Roll long, thin plasticine snakes. Glue them along the lines of your decorative pattern.

7 Paint the front of the shield bronze. When dry, turn over and stick the dowling rod down the back. Use tape to secure. Tie the leather thongs.

The Fall of the Celts

CELTIC POWER in Europe lasted for around 800 years. It started to decline because other peoples grew strong enough to make their own claims for power and land. The first and most formidable of these were the well-trained, well-equipped soldiers of the Roman Empire. They had driven Celtic settlers from northern Italy in 191BC and from Spain in 133BC. After long campaigns led by their brilliant general, Julius Caesar, the Romans finally conquered France in 51BC. They invaded southern Britain in AD43, and at first met with resistance, such as the revolt led by the Celtic queen, Boudicca. Nevertheless, by AD61, the Romans controlled southern Britain, and they ruled there until AD410. However, they never managed to conquer the whole of the British Isles. Parts of Scotland and Ireland continued under Celtic rule until about AD1100. As Roman power weakened, new groups of migrants arrived, mostly from the north, to settle in the former Celtic lands. These invaders included many peoples with strong armies and vibrant cultures of their own, such as the Visigoths, the Angles and Saxons, the Franks and the Vikings.

GREAT CONQUEROR
Julius Caesar (*c.*100–44BC) led the Roman armies that conquered the Celts in France. He fought and won a series of battles, known as the Gallic Wars, between 58BC and 51BC. He also hoped to conquer Britain and Germany, but a political crisis in Italy forced him to return to Rome.

ROMAN STYLE
After the Romans conquered Britain in AD43, a new, mixed civilization grew up which combined both Roman and Celtic traditions. Although some Celtic chieftains rebelled against Roman rule, others decided to co-operate with the Romans, and served as local governors. They built splendid country houses, known as villas, which were decorated in the Roman style with beautiful mosaic floors such as this one.

THE VISIGOTHS

This jewelled, golden crown was made for the Visigothic kings of Spain to give as a religious offering. The Visigoths were a people from northern Europe. Celtic lands in Spain were conquered by the Romans in 133BC, and then by the Visigoths in about AD400. Even so, many Celtic skills, such as the art of fine metalworking, survived and were passed down by successive generations of settlers.

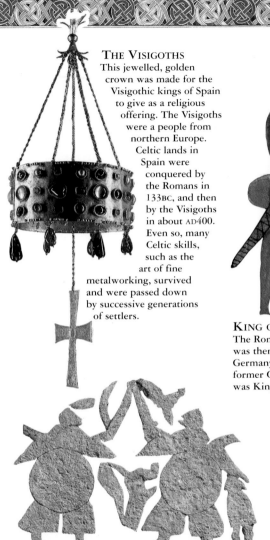
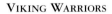

KING OF THE FRANKS

The Romans ruled France until about AD400. Northern France was then taken over by the Franks, a people from southern Germany. The Frankish kings built up a powerful empire in former Celtic France. Their most successful and powerful ruler was King Charlemagne (left), who reigned from AD771 to 814.

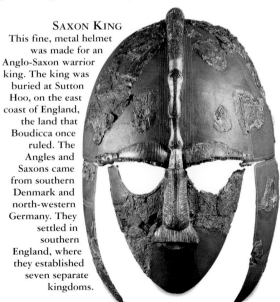

SAXON KING

This fine, metal helmet was made for an Anglo-Saxon warrior king. The king was buried at Sutton Hoo, on the east coast of England, the land that Boudicca once ruled. The Angles and Saxons came from southern Denmark and north-western Germany. They settled in southern England, where they established seven separate kingdoms.

VIKING WARRIORS

The Vikings were sailors, raiders and traders who came from Scandinavia. They first attacked Britain around AD790. Soon afterwards, Viking settlers came to live in many parts of the British Isles and northern France. This tombstone shows two Viking warriors with round shields.

Viking Raids and Piracy

IN AD793, A BAND of heavily armed Vikings ran
their longships ashore on Lindisfarne (an island
off the north-east coast of England). It was the site of
a Christian monastery. The monks tried in vain to
hide their precious crosses, silver chalices and bibles,
but the Vikings axed them down. They set fire to the
buildings and sailed away with their loot.

BLOOD AND FIRE
This gravestone is from
Lindisfarne. It shows fierce Viking warriors
armed with swords and battle axes.

This was the start of the period in which the Vikings
spread terror around western Europe. They began by
attacking easy targets, such as villages, monasteries or other ships. They took away cattle, grain,
chests of money and church bells that could be melted down. They also took women, and prisoners as
slaves. Booty was shared among members of the crew. Soon the Vikings were attacking the largest
and richest cities in Europe. In AD846, they sacked (raided), the cities of Hamburg and Paris. King
Charles the Bald of France had to pay the Viking leader Ragnar Hairy-Breeks over three tonnes of
silver to leave. From AD865 onwards, the English kings were also forced to pay over huge sums of
money, called Danegeld.
Like gangsters, the Vikings
returned time after time,
demanding more money –
as well as land on which
they could settle.

INVADING VIKINGS
This painting shows Danish
Vikings invading Northumbria.
The raiders soon realized how
easy it was to attack neighbouring
lands. They began to set up year-
round war camps on the coasts.
Soon they were occupying large
areas of territory and building
their own towns.

SAFE AND SOUND

Viking gold, silver and jewellery were locked in beautiful caskets and chests. This copy of a Viking chest is made of walrus ivory and gilded bronze.

ST CUTHBERT

This picture from the Middle Ages shows St Cuthbert praying in the sea. Cuthbert was one of Lindisfarne's most famous monks. He was made a saint on his death in AD687. In AD875, when the Danish Vikings attacked the island, the monks fled inland to safety, carrying St Cuthbert's remains.

BUILT FROM THE RUINS

In AD793 the Vikings sacked the monastery on Lindisfarne, an island off the coast of northeast England. Afterwards, the religious buildings lay in ruins. The new priory pictured here was built between 1100 and 1200. The stones used to build it were taken from the ruins left by the Vikings. Today, only bare stones remain to remind visitors of the original monastery and its terrible fate.

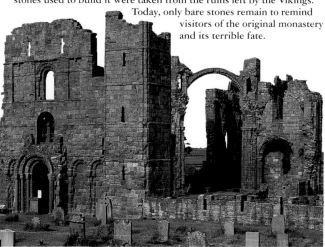

TREASURE HOARD

Part of a Viking treasure hoard was found in a chest in Cuerdale, England. It included about 40kg of chopped-up silver, fine brooches and coins from many places that the Vikings had raided. They had sailed west to North America, south to Spain, and via European rivers to Constantinople (modern Istanbul).

The Taking of America

THE VIKINGS WERE THE first Europeans to travel to North America. Later explorers, who arrived around 500 years later, made a bigger impact. They claimed the land for their own countries and set up colonies of settlers. Commissioned by Queen Isabella of Spain, the Italian explorer Christopher Columbus landed in the Bahamas in 1492, and declared the land as Spanish territory. Spaniard Ponce de León landed in Florida in 1512, and Hernando Cortés had conquered the Aztec peoples of Central America by 1521. Tales of mountains of gold in the Southwest lured a Spanish expedition headed by Vasquez de Coronado. He encountered many native American Indian tribes, but never found gold.

The native peoples were forced from their homelands, taken captive or killed in their thousands. European explorers and colonists never regarded them as equals. They tried to force tribes to change their lifestyles and beliefs and made them adapt their traditional crafts to suit European buyers.

EARLY VISITORS
Erik the Red, the Viking king, sailed to Greenland around AD982. He was probably in search of new trading partners. His son Leif later sailed to Newfoundland and established a settlement at a place now called L'Anse aux Meadows. A trade in furs and ivory was set up with northern Europe.

SETTING SAIL
Columbus and his crew prepare to set sail from Spain in 1492 in search of a trade route to India. He never reached Asia, but landed on San Salvador in the Bahamas. The Arawaks there thought that Columbus and his men came from the sky and greeted them with praise. Columbus set about claiming the islands for the Spanish Empire. He made many of the natives slaves.

A DISTANT LAND

This map from around 1550 shows a crude European impression of North America. Henry II of France ordered Descallier, a royal cartographer, to make a map of what middle and North America looked like. The French were keen to gain land there. Jacques Cartier, a French navigator, spent eight years exploring the St Lawrence River area. He made contact with the native American Huron communities. He wrote to the king that he hoped the Indians would be "easy to tame".

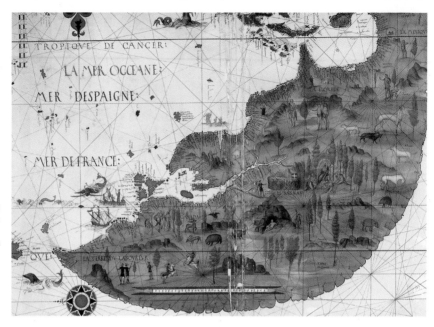

MAN WITH A MISSION

A Plains Indian views a missionary with suspicion. Eastern tribes were the first to meet French missionaries whom they called "Black Robes". In California, Indians were forced to live and work in Spanish mission villages.

SAY A LITTLE PRAYER

Young Indian girls dressed in European clothes have been separated from their families and tribal customs. Europeans could not understand the North American Indians' society and religious beliefs. They wanted to convert them to Christianity, by force if necessary. In many areas, children were taken away from their people and sent to white boarding schools, given European names and taught European religion, language and history.

Aztec Power Struggles

W AR WAS ESSENTIAL to the survival of the Aztecs in Central America. They had invaded from the north from around AD1200, winning new territory by fighting the people who already lived there. From then on, the Aztecs relied on war to keep control and to win more land and cities to keep them rich. They forced the people they conquered to pay tributes of crops, treasures and other goods in return for being left in peace. The big Aztec cities such as Tenochtitlan needed steady supplies of tribute to feed their citizens. Without such riches won from war, the whole empire would have collapsed. War was also a useful source of captives, who could be sacrificed to the gods. The Aztecs sacrificed thousands of people each year, believing that this would win the gods' help.

Each new Aztec ruler traditionally began his reign with a battle. The Empire grew rapidly during the 1400s until it included most of Mexico. Conquered cities were often controlled by garrisons of Aztec soldiers and linked to the government in Tenochtitlan by large numbers of officials, such as tax collectors and scribes.

TOTONAC TRIBUTE
Ambassadors from lands conquered by the Aztecs came to Tenochtitlan to deliver the tribute demanded from their rulers. This painting shows splendidly dressed representatives of the Totonac people meeting Aztec tax collectors. The Totonacs lived on the Gulf coast of Mexico, in Veracruz. Here they are shown offering tobacco, fruit and vanilla grown on their lands. They hated and feared the Aztecs.

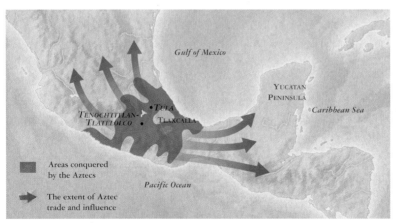

AZTEC LANDS
This map shows the area ruled by the Aztecs in 1519. Conquered cities were allowed to continue with their traditional way of life, but had to pay tribute to Aztec officials. The Aztecs also put pressure on two weaker city states, Texcoco and Tlacopan, to join with them in a Triple Alliance. One nearby city-state, Tlaxcalla, refused to make an alliance with the Aztecs and stayed fiercely independent.

Gulf of Mexico

YUCATAN PENINSULA

Caribbean Sea

TENOCHTITLAN-TLATELOLCO • *TULA* • *TLAXCALLA*

Areas conquered by the Aztecs

The extent of Aztec trade and influence

Pacific Ocean

CANNIBALS

One of the Aztecs' most important reasons for fighting was to capture prisoners for sacrifice. In this codex picture, we can see sacrificed bodies neatly chopped up. In some religious ceremonies, the Aztecs ate the arms and legs of sacrificed prisoners.

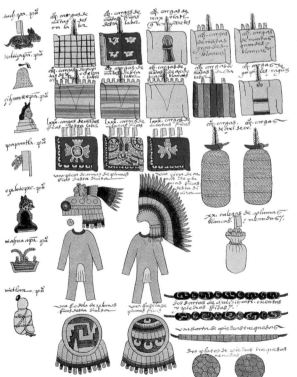

FROM HUMBLE BEGINNINGS

Aztec settlers are shown on their difficult trek through northern Mexico. The Aztecs built up their empire from humble beginnings in a short time. They first arrived in Mexico some time after AD1200. By around 1400, they had become the strongest nation in central Mesoamerica. To maintain their position, they had to be constantly ready for war. The Aztecs invented many legends to justify their success. They claimed to be descended from earlier peoples living in Mexico, and to be specially guided by the gods.

TRIBUTE LIST

The Aztecs received vast quantities of valuable goods as tribute each year. Most of the tribute was sent to their capital city of Tenochtitlan. Aztec scribes there drew up very detailed lists of tribute received, like the one on the left. Among the goods shown are shields decorated with feathers, blankets, turquoise plates, bracelets and dried chilli peppers.

End of the Aztec and Maya

IN 1493, explorer Christopher Columbus returned to Spain from his pioneering voyage to the Bahamas off the coast of Mesoamerica. He told tales of a 'new world' full of gold. Excited by Columbus' stories, a group of Spanish soldiers sailed to Mexico in 1519, hoping to make their fortunes. They were led by a nobleman called Hernando Cortés. Together with the Aztecs' enemies, he led a march on the Aztec city of Tenochtitlan. For the next two years, the Aztecs fought to keep their land. They drove the Spaniards out of Tenochtitlan in May 1520, but in 1521, Cortés attacked the city again, set fire to its buildings and killed around three-quarters of the population. In 1535, Mexico became a colony, ruled by officials sent from Spain.

Similar events happened in lands controlled by the Maya people in the south of Mesoamerica, but more slowly. The Spanish landed there in 1523, but did not conquer the last independent city-state, Tayasal, until 1697.

AGAINST THE AZTECS
This picture comes from *The History of the Indies*. It was written by Diego Duran, a Spanish friar who felt sympathy for the Aztecs. Spanish soldiers and their allies from Tlaxcalla are seen fighting against the Aztecs. Although the Aztecs fought bravely, they had no chance of defeating Spanish soldiers mounted on horseback and armed with guns.

A SAD NIGHT
On 6 May 1520, Spanish soldiers massacred Aztecs gathered for a religious festival in Tenochtitlan. The citizens were outraged and attacked the Spaniards, many of whom died. During this night, the emperor Moctezuma II was stoned to death, probably by Aztecs who believed he had betrayed them. Cortés called this the *Noche Triste* (sad night).

THE END OF AZTEC POWER
This Aztec picture shows the surrender of Cuauhtemoc, the last Aztec king, to Cortés. After Moctezuma II died in 1520, the Aztecs were led by two of Moctezuma's descendants – Cuitlahuac, who ruled for only one year, and Cuauhtemoc. He was the last king and reigned until 1524.

RUNNING FOR THEIR LIVES

This illustration from a Spanish manuscript shows Aztec people fleeing from Spanish conquerors. You can see heavily laden porters carrying stocks of food and household goods across a river to safety. On the far bank, mothers and children, with a pet bird and dog, hide behind giant cactus plants.

WORKING LIKE SLAVES

Spanish settlers in Mexico took over all the Aztec and Maya fields and forced the people to work as farm labourers. They treated them cruelly, almost like slaves. This modern picture shows a Spanish overseer giving orders.

AFTER THE CONQUEST

Mexican artist Diego Rivera shows Mesoamerica after the Spanish conquest. Throughout the 1500s and 1600s, settlers from Spain arrived there. They drove out the local nobles and forced ordinary people to work for them. Spanish missionaries tried to replace local beliefs with European customs and Christianity. In Tenochtitlan, the Spaniards pulled down splendid Aztec palaces and temples to build churches and fine homes for themselves. You can see gangs of Aztec men working as labourers in the background of this picture.

Holding on to an Empire

THE INCA PEOPLE were one of many small tribes living in the Andes Mountains of Peru. In the 1200s, though, they began to take over other tribes and lands. By the 1400s, the Inca Empire covered 3,600km of the Andes and the coast. The Incas numbered only about 40,000, but they controlled a population of 12 million. They hung on to their power by military force. Borders were defended by a string of forts, and cities became walled refuges when the surrounding countryside was under attack. The permanent army of some 10,000 elite troops, could be increased substantially by those serving their *mit'a*, a system of enforced labour.

TAKE THAT!
This star may have looked pretty, but it was deadly when whirled from the leather strap. It was made of obsidian, a glassy black volcanic rock. Inca warriors also fought with spikes set in wooden clubs. Some troops favoured the *bolas*, corded weights that were also used in hunting. Slings were used for scaring birds. However, in the hands of an experienced soldier, they could bring down a hail of stones on enemies and crack their heads open.

WAITING FOR THE CHARGE
A Moche warrior goes down on one knee and brings up his shield in defence. He is bracing himself for an enemy charge. All South American armies fought on foot. The horse was not seen in Peru until the Spanish introduced it.

IN THE BARRACKS
Many towns of the Inca Empire were garrisoned by troops. These restored barrack blocks at Machu Picchu may once have housed soldiers serving out their *mit'a* (enforced labour for the State). They would have been inspected by a high-ranking general from Cuzco. During the Spanish invasion, Machu Picchu may have been a base for desperate resistance fighters.

MAKE AN INCA HELMET
You will need: scissors, cream calico fabric, ruler, balloon, pva glue, paintbrush, paints, water pot, yellow and black felt, black wool.

1 Cut the fabric into strips about 8cm x 2cm as shown in the picture. You will need enough to cover the top half of a blown-up balloon three times.

2 Blow up the balloon to the same size as your head. Glue the strips of fabric over the top half. Leave each layer to dry before adding the next.

3 When the last layer is dry, pop the balloon and carefully pull it away. Use scissors to trim round the edge of the helmet. Paint it a reddish orange.

KINGS OF THE CASTLE

The massive fortress of Sacsahuaman at Cuzco was built on a hill. One edge was formed by a cliff and the other defended by massive terraces and zigzag walls. When the Spanish invaded in the 1500s, they were awestruck by Sacsahuaman's size and defences. The Incas regarded warfare as an extension of religious ritual. Sacsahuaman was certainly used for religious ceremonies. Some historians claim that the Inca capital was laid out in the shape of a giant puma, with Sacsahuaman as its head.

SIEGE WARFARE

An Inca army takes on the enemy at Pukara, near Lake Titicaca. Most South American cities were walled and well defended. Siege warfare was common. The attackers blocked the defenders' ways of escape from the town. After the Spanish Conquest in 1536, Inca rebels under Manko Inka trapped Spanish troops in Cuzco and besieged them for over a year.

Inca helmets were round in shape and made of wood or cane. They were decorated with braids and crests.

4 Take the felt. Measure and cut a 3cm yellow square, a yellow circle with a diameter of 3cm, a 9cm yellow square and a 5.5cm black square.

5 Glue the felt shapes on to the helmet as shown above. Glue a 2cm-wide strip of yellow felt along the edge of the helmet to neaten the edge.

6 Take 12 strands of black wool, each 30cm long. Divide them into 3 hanks of 4 strands. Knot the ends together, then plait to the end.

7 Knot the end of the finished braid. Make two more. Glue them inside the back of the helmet. Wait until it is dry before trying it on.

Spaniards Eclipse the Inca Sun

IN 1532, SPANISH SOLDIERS UNDER their commander Francisco Pizarro, landed in Peru, greedy for gold. In November, they met the Inca emperor, Ataw Wallpa, in the great square of Cajamarca. The *Sapa Inca* (Only Leader) was riding in a litter that was covered in feathers. Surrounding him, his troops glinted with gold. The sound of conch trumpets and flutes echoed around the buildings. The Spanish were amazed by the sight; the Incas looked uneasily at the strangers with their strange, fidgeting horses.

Within an hour, thousands of Incas were killed, and their emperor was in the hands of the Spanish. Ataw Wallpa offered to raise a ransom for his release, and he filled a whole room with silver and gold. Even so, in the summer of 1533, the Spanish accused Ataw Wallpa of treason, and he was garrotted (executed by strangulation). Inca resistance to the Spanish continued for another 39 years, but South American civilization had changed for ever that day.

THE WORD OF GOD?
When emperor Ataw Wallpa met the Spanish invaders in Cajamarca, he was approached by a Christian priest called Vincente de Valverde. The priest raised a Bible and said that it contained the words of God. Ataw Wallpa grabbed the book and listened to it. No words came out, so he hurled it to the ground. The Spanish were enraged, and the invasion began.

CONQUEST AND SLAVERY
The Incas were fierce fighters, but they stood no chance against the guns and steel of the Spanish. Their defeat was a disaster for all the native peoples of the Americas. Many were murdered, enslaved or worked to death in the mines. The Spanish became wealthy at the expense of the native peoples.

"SANTIAGO!"
Before the 1532 meeting with Ataw Wallpa in the great square of Cajamarca, the Spanish invader Francisco Pizarro had hidden troops behind buildings. When he shouted the pre-arranged signal of *"Santiago!"* (St James), they began to shoot into the crowd. Chaos broke out as the emperor was seized and taken prisoner.

TEARS OF THE MOON
In 1545, the Spanish discovered silver at Potosí in the Bolivian Andes and began to dig mines. The wealth was incredible, but the working conditions were terrible. Local people were forced to work as slaves. Mule trains carried the silver northwards to Colombian ports, making Spain the richest country in the world.

DESCENDANTS OF THE EMPIRE
Christians of native Andean and mixed descent take part in a procession through the city of Cuzco. In the Andes, over the past few hundred years, many Inca traditions, festivals and pilgrimages have become mixed up with Christian ones. Indigenous peoples today make up 45 per cent of the total population in Peru, 55 per cent in Bolivia and 25 per cent in Ecuador.

THE TREASURE FLEETS
The Spanish plundered the treasure of the Incas and the minerals of the Andes. Big sailing ships called galleons carried the gold and silver back to Europe from ports in Central and South America. The region was known as the Spanish Main. Rival European ships, many of them pirates from England, France and the Netherlands, began to prey on the Spanish fleets. This led to long years of piracy on the seas. Between 1820 and 1824, Spain's South American colonies finally broke away from European rule to become independent countries, but most of the region's native peoples remained poor and powerless.

Invasion of North America

LEADING THE WAY
Sacawagea, a Shoshoni girl, guides US captains Meriwether Lewis and William Clark from Mississippi to the Pacific coast, in 1804. The journey took nearly a year. President Thomas Jefferson asked them to map out the land from the Mississippi River to the Rockies. This helped to pave the way for settlers to move to the far West.

F ROM 1500, NORTH AMERICA was visited by the English, French and Spanish in increasing numbers. Each country laid claim to land and established colonies of settlers. It was mainly the British and the French who stayed. The first settlements were on the east coast, but gradually spread farther inland, encountering more and more tribes of native American Indians. The Europeans introduced diseases previously unknown to the Indians. A smallpox epidemic of 1837 almost wiped out the Mandan people. Fewer than 200 people survived from a tribe that had once numbered over 2,500.

From the 1760s to 1780s, colonists fought for independence from their parent countries, and in 1783, the United States became an independent country. It doubled in size in 1803, when Louisiana Territory was bought from France for $15 million. This marked the end of French rule, and native tribes from the East could be moved west of the Mississippi River. As frontiers edged farther and farther west, more native tribes were pushed out of their homelands.

ROLLING ACROSS THE PLAINS
From around 1850, wagon trains were signs that times were changing for the Plains tribes. Although settlers had been living in North America for around 300 years, they had mostly remained on the east coast. The US government encouraged white families to move inland.

SOD HOUSE
This is a fine example of a soddy, a house literally made from sod, or turf, cut out of the ground. Settlers had to build homes from whatever material was to hand. Life was hard for the children, they had to do chores, such as feeding chickens. If they were lucky, they went to school.

NEW TOWN
Plains Indians watch a train steaming into a new town. Land was sacred to the tribes who called it their Earth Mother. The settlers thought that the tribes wasted their land and wanted to build towns and railways on it. At first the federal government just took land for settlers. Later, they bought millions of acres of Indian land in various treaties (agreements), using force if the Indians did not agree.

PANNING FOR GOLD
A man is sifting through sand in search of gold. When gold was discovered in late 1848 in California, it started the Gold Rush. Thousands of immigrants came to the west coast from all over the world. The sheer numbers forced the tribes off their land.

TRAIN ATTACK
Plains warriors attack a train crossing their hunting grounds. The Plains tribes had always been fiercely defensive of their territory. Now they turned on the new invaders. More and more settlers were encouraged to move on to the Plains. In the 1860s, railways were constructed across Indian lands. They were built over sacred sites and destroyed buffalo hunting grounds which were essential to the tribes' livelihood. Attacks on settlers, trains and white trading posts became more frequent.

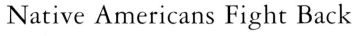

Native Americans Fight Back

WHEN THE EUROPEAN SETTLERS in North America began to fight for independence from their home countries from 1775 to 1783, some native tribes remained neutral, others took sides. Tribes who had banded together in the Iroquois League of Nations did not want to be involved in a white man's quarrel at first. They had, however, allied with the British against the French in other European wars. The League was split and eventually most of the tribes supported the British. In 1777, they ended up fighting some of their own people, the Oneidas.

Once independence had been won, the United States Government could make its own laws. In 1830, it introduced the Indian Removal Act and relocated tribes from their homelands to areas set aside for Indians called reservations. The Choctaws were relocated in 1830 to Oklahoma. They were followed by the Chickasaws, Creeks and Seminoles. Bitter battles were fought as the Indians struggled to keep their homelands. Reservation land was often less fertile and productive than the old tribal land, and some tribes faced starvation.

WILD WEST
There were many conflicts between US soldiers and different tribes, such as this attack in the 1800s. Some attempts at peaceful talks were made. However, military records show that between 1863 and 1891, there were 1,065 fights.

TRAIL OF TEARS
The heartbroken Cherokee nation is being forced to leave its homelands in 1838-39. During the trek west, rain and snow fell and soldiers made the Indians move on too quickly. It is estimated that almost 4,000 Cherokees died from exhaustion and exposure.

MAKE ANKLE BELLS

You will need: white felt, ruler, pencil or felt tip pen, scissors, strong thread, needle, 10 to 16 small bells – between five and eight for each anklet.

1 Cut out two strips of white felt 75cm x 5cm. Measure and mark a line across the felt strips, 24cm in from one end. Do the same at the other end.

2 Now make a series of marks in the middle section of the strips. Start 3cm away from one line, then mark every 3cm. This is where the bells will go.

3 Create the fringing at each end of the anklet. Do this by cutting into both ends of the band up to the pencilled lines. Do the same for the other anklet.

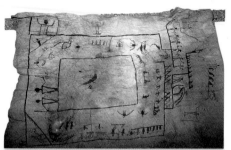

WAR BUNDLE

This buckskin was used to wrap a personal war bundle. It has been painted with the Thunderbird and other supernatural beings for spiritual protection. A bundle might carry a warrior's medicine herbs or warpaint.

THE SHIELD SURVIVED

This warrior's shield belonged to a Dakota (Sioux) warrior in the late 1800s. It may have been used in the Battle of Little Bighorn. The Sioux tribes fought in many battles with the US around that time. In 1851 their lands were defined by a treaty. Then, when gold was found in Montana, gold hunters broke the treaties by travelling through Sioux land, and war raged again.

THE END OF GENERAL CUSTER

The Battle of Little Bighorn, in 1876, is counted as the last major victory of the North American Indian. Custer and his entire 7th Cavalry were defeated by Sioux sub-tribes, after they attacked an Indian village. Sadly, this made US soldiers even more brutal in their dealings with tribes.

WAR DANCE

Sioux warriors are performing a war dance. During the dance a medicine man would chant and ask for spiritual guidance and protection for warriors going into battle. Other dances were performed after a battle.

4 Thread a large needle with strong, doubled and knotted thread. Insert the needle into the fabric and pull through until the knot hits the fabric.

5 Thread the needle through the bell and slip the bell up to the felt. Then insert the needle back into the felt very near to the place it came out.

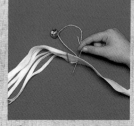

6 Push the needle through and pull tight. Knot the end (opposite side to the bell) to secure and cut away the excess thread. Repeat with the other bells.

The bells of the North American Indians were sewn on to strips of animal skins. They were tied around the ankles or just under the knees, for ceremonial dances.

Science, Crafts & Technology

Explore the inventions, engineering
skills and metalwork techniques of
the ancient world

Making Life Easier

MANY OF THE ANIMALS of prehistoric times were faster, bigger, or stronger than the early humans who hunted them. The humans had one great advantage: they had bigger brains. The humans fought – and survived – by using their brains. They looked at the world they lived in and worked out how to make use of it. Their questioning, learning and understanding is what we call science. Their ability to shape and alter natural materials and turn them into tools, weapons and clothes was the beginning of technology.

The early species of human called *Homo habilis* (meaning handy man) was a pioneer of technology. *Homo habilis* had big enough brains to work things out, and hands that could grip objects firmly. They were the first humans to make simple stone tools.

Early humans had to take meat they had hunted to the safety of a cave before other, fiercer animals came along. Smaller pieces were easier to carry. Speed was vital. The humans found hard pebbles that they could split to reveal sharp edges to cut with. Technological breakthroughs such as this were gradually perfected and crafted into an ever-wider and more complex range of tools, all of which made human life safer and easier.

Because humans learned to make use of whatever local materials were available, they adapted to new environments instead of being confined to particular habitats like most animals. They moved all over the

The wheelbarrow was invented in China more than 1,000 years earlier than in the West. This was partly because there was a huge population of rice farmers who needed to find ways of making their back-breaking work easier.

TIMELINE 2,400,000BC–500BC

2,400,000 years ago. The early human *Homo habilis* (handy man) makes the first simple tools by splitting pebbles to create sharp edges.

stone spearheads

1,500,000 years ago. *Homo erectus* (upright man) makes hand axes, using flint, wood and bone. These are made over the next million years.

400,000 years ago. Date of the oldest surviving wooden tool a spear from Germany.

100,000 years ago. Following the evolution of *Homo sapiens* – fully modern humans – a greater variety of more sophisticated tools are made.

round-based pot from ancient Japan

8000-3000BC Farming becomes widespread in Asia, Europe and Africa. New tools are invented such as axes to clear forests, sickles for harvesting corn and grindstones for making flour. Pottery is used for cooking pots and storage containers.

6500BC The earliest known cloth is woven in Turkey.

6000BC The first metal tools and ornaments are made from copper in Turkey.

2,400,000BC   400,000BC   8000BC   6000B

world. The settlements and civilizations that grew up were often separated by oceans, mountains and deserts, but they often went through similar stages of discovery and invention quite independently of each other. The ancient Egyptians were sailing boats at around the same time as the Mesopotamians, for example. The Chinese, far in the East, invented a decimal system of mathematics from 300BC, although they had no known communication with the ancient Egyptians who had

The Chinese emperor Shenb Nong described 365 medicinal plants. The study of subjects such as medicine and astronomy was often left to the upper classes. Practical inventions were made by those who worked on the land or with their hands.

New technology often depended on the natural resources available. The earliest metalworkers were people who had noticed metal ore in the local rocks, and eventually learned how to extract it.

done the same thing about 350 years earlier.

The speed with which science, craft and technology developed depended on what local materials were available, and how great the need for improvement was. Some Stone Age peoples became expert potters because they lived on clay deposits. At first, however, they only made little clay figures. It was many thousands of years before someone realized that clay could be made into ideal containers for food and liquid. The Chinese development of fine, waterproof pottery called porcelain, 1,000 years before the West, was helped by rich supplies of a very fine clay called kaolin. Inca tribes became brilliant at working with gold and silver because of the rich resources of these precious metals in the South American mountains. Most new technology was invented by people who worked with their hands. Ancient China was one of the most inventive civilizations ever because it

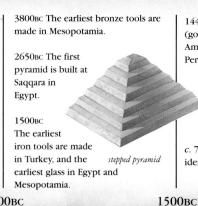

3800BC The earliest bronze tools are made in Mesopotamia.

2650BC The first pyramid is built at Saqqara in Egypt.

1500BC The earliest iron tools are made in Turkey, and the earliest glass in Egypt and Mesopotamia.

stepped pyramid

1440BC Metalworking (gold) begins in the Americas, in the Peruvian Andes.

750-54BC Celtic craftsmanship in gold and bronze flourishes in Europe.

Anglo-Saxon brooch

c. 700BC Babylonian astronomers identify the signs of the zodiac.

600BC The Chinese learn how to make cast iron.

c. 550BC Beginning of Greek science, mathematics and philosophy.

500BC Origins of the 260-day Mesoamerican calendar in Mexico.

Aztec pictures showing names for days

1000BC   1500BC   600BC   500BC

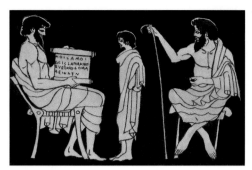

The ancient Greeks made learning a lot easier by inventing a simple alphabet. More people could read and write, so new ideas and technology spread. Ancient Greece had more scientists than any other early civilization.

was a huge country with great numbers of peasant farmers. The small, but very rich upper level of society demanded a luxurious life-style. This led to the development of fine craft skills, silk, and papermaking and printing for books.

In many civilizations, wealthy and powerful people were more interested in studying the stars and planets. Religion, astronomy and science were all closely connected in the early civilizations. The first astronomers in Babylon and Egypt believed that the movement of the stars and planets would help them discover what the gods were planning. Greek mathematicians such as Pythagoras believed that they could understand more about the gods through numbers.

The Romans were great engineers and built long, straight roads that were unsurpassed for centuries. A good road system was one way of keeping in control of their empire.

Greed and competition acted as spurs to science, craft and technology too. The person with the most efficient plough could till more land and harvest more crops than his neighbour. The country with the most deadly and effective weapons could build empires. Knowledge, science and craft skills developed very fast in empires that could call upon the resources of all the lands under their control. The rulers also had to stay in control, which was an incentive to keep one step ahead in road and transport systems, and efficient ways of trading, language, writing, and coinage. And many kings

TIMELINE 500BC–AD1800

c. 400BC The Greek Hippocrates founds one of the earliest medical schools.

384-322BC Life of the Greek philosopher Aristotle. He is widely regarded as the founder of Western science.

Hippocrates, the Greek doctor

c. 310-230BC The Greek astronomer Aristarchus claims that the Earth goes around the Sun.

c. 200BC The Romans begin the large-scale use of concrete in building.

AD1-100 The magnetic compass is invented in China.

c. AD100 Paper is invented in China.

Chinese printed paper money

c. AD350 Maya astronomy develops in Mesoamerica.

AD605-9 The Grand Canal in China is completed.

AD800-1000 Viking craftsmanship in wood and precious metals flourishes in northern Europe.

carved prow of a Viking ship

500BC   200BC   AD300   AD80

and emperors, such as the Egyptian pharaohs, masterminded amazing engineering works so that they would be remembered for eternity.

Some cultures developed slowly because they did not have the way of life or the need to invent. Native peoples in North America did not invent sophisticated methods of transport because they did not have much to carry. They did develop fine craft skills, though, making use of animal hide and bones, and dyes from plants.

As you read through these pages, you will be able to trace the special skills of different cultures, and discover what their particular contributions were to human knowledge. You will be able to see varying paces of technological development around the world and understand how different cultures had different priorities. Some cultures enjoyed remarkably intensive periods of technological advancement that provided the foundations of much of the science, craft and technology that make modern life easier.

Although the Vikings were not great inventors, their dependence on the sea for travel and invasion meant that they developed very advanced boat-building skills.

New ideas and technology were spread by war. During the Crusade wars of the 11th and 12th centuries, peoples from northern Europe picked up tips on castle building and forging steel from the Muslim Saracen armies of the East.

AD810 The Persian mathematician al-Khwarizmi invents algebra.

AD850 Gunpowder is invented in China.

AD876 Indian mathematicians invent the symbol for zero.

c. AD900-modern times. Pueblo Indian cultures in the southwest of North America make fine painted pottery.

Inca gold llama

c. 1000 The Chinese invent movable type printing.

c. 1150 The first mechanical clocks are made in Europe.

c. 1200-1533 The Incas of the Andes make fine objects in gold, silver, textiles and pottery.

the astronomer Copernicus

1500-1800 The Scientific Revolution in Europe. Great advances in astronomy, physics, chemistry and biology are made.

chronometer

1700-1800 The Industrial Revolution begins the widespread use of steam power and machines.

1720 John Harrison develops the chronometer, an accurate timepiece.

1000

1500

1800

The Beginning of Technology

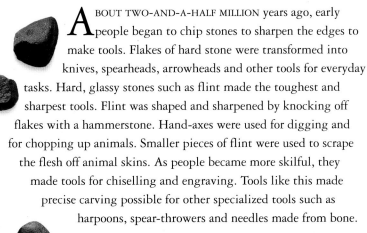

HANDY MAN

Chipped pebbles from Tanzania in Africa are some of the oldest tools ever found. They were made by *Homo habilis,* who lived almost two million years ago. *Homo habilis* (handy man) was the first human to make stone tools.

Ａbout TWO-AND-A-HALF MILLION years ago, early people began to chip stones to sharpen the edges to make tools. Flakes of hard stone were transformed into knives, spearheads, arrowheads and other tools for everyday tasks. Hard, glassy stones such as flint made the toughest and sharpest tools. Flint was shaped and sharpened by knocking off flakes with a hammerstone. Hand-axes were used for digging and for chopping up animals. Smaller pieces of flint were used to scrape the flesh off animal skins. As people became more skilful, they made tools for chiselling and engraving. Tools like this made precise carving possible for other specialized tools such as harpoons, spear-throwers and needles made from bone.

FLAKING

Some 1½ million years after *Homo habilis,* a new species of human evolved with bigger brains. Neanderthals and *Homo sapiens* were far better toolmakers. They produced pointed or oval-shaped hand-axes (*left and middle*) and chopping tools (*right*).

VALUABLE STONE

Flint was dug in this mine in England from about 2800BC. Flint was vital for survival. People would trek long distances for the stone if there were none in their area.

MAKE A MODEL AXE

You will need: self-drying clay, board, modelling tool, sandpaper, grey acrylic paint, wood stain, water pot, paintbrush, thick dowelling, craft knife, ruler, chamois leather, scissors.

1 Pull out the clay into a thick block. With a modelling tool, shape the block into an axe head with a point at one end.

2 When the clay is completely dry, lightly rub down the axe head with sandpaper to remove any rough surfaces.

3 Paint the axe head a stone colour, such as grey. You could use more than one shade if you like. Leave it to dry.

SPEAR POINT
Cro-Magnon people were top hunters, using leaf-shaped spear points to kill reindeer, wild horses, deer and woolly mammoths. They lived in Europe and Russia from around 38,000 years ago, and also learned to start fire by striking iron against flint.

STONES FOR TOOLS
The best rocks for tools were usually those that had been changed by heat. Obsidian, a glassy volcanic rock was widely used in the Near East and Mexico. It fractured easily, leaving sharp edges. In parts of Africa, quartz was made into beautiful, hardwearing hand-axes and choppers. Flint is another type of quartz. It is found in nodules in limestone rock, especially chalk. A hard igneous rock called diorite was used for making polished axe heads in Neolithic times.

quartz   *chert (a type of flint)*

AXES
Polished stone battle axes became the most important weapon in Scandinavia by the late Neolithic (New Stone Age) period. They date from about 1800BC.

TOOLMAKING LESSON
Stone Age people came to depend more and more on the quality of their tools. In this reconstruction, a father is passing on his skill in toolmaking to his son.

Prehistoric people used axes for chopping wood and cutting meat. They shaped a stone blade, then fitted it on to a

4 Ask an adult to trim one end of a piece of thick dowelling using a craft knife. Paint the piece with wood stain and leave to dry.

5 To bind the axe head to the wooden shaft, first carefully cut a long strip of leather about 2.5cm wide from a chamois cloth.

6 Place the axe head on the trimmed end of the shaft. Wrap the strip of leather around the head and shaft in a criss-cross pattern.

7 Pull the leather strip tight and wrap the ends twice round the shaft below the head. Tie the ends together and trim them.

Tools for the Job

D URING THE STONE AGE, wood, bone, antler and ivory were as important as stone for making tools and other implements. These softer materials were easily carved and shaped by stone tools. They could also be used to make more specialized stone tools. Bone and antler hammers and punches, for example, could achieve sharper cutting edges and more delicate flakes of stone. Flint blades were fitted into handles and mounts of wood. Antlers were converted into picks to dig up roots and lever lumps of rock from the ground. The broad shoulder-blade bones of cattle were turned into shovels, while smaller bones served as awls to punch small holes. Antlers and bones were also carved into spear-throwers. Ivory, from the tusks of the woolly mammoth, and bone could be crafted into fine-pointed needles, fish hooks, harpoon heads and knives. Adzes were tools for shaping wood and for making bows and arrows. Sometimes, things were made just for fun. Whistles and little paint holders were carved from small bones. Some pieces of stone, wood and bone were beautifully carved with pictures of the animals that were hunted and fine decorative patterns.

SPEAR-THROWER
This carving of a reindeer's head is probably part of a spear-thrower. The hunter slotted his spear into a hook at one end of the thrower and took aim. As he threw, the spear detached from the thrower and travelled farther and faster than if the hunter had thrown it just by hand. Hunting became safer and more accurate. Prehistoric carvers often incorporated the natural form of wood or bone into a design to suggest an animal's outlines.

SHAPING
An adze was a bit like an axe, except that its blade was at right angles to the handle. The flint blade on this adze dates from about 4000BC to 2000BC. Its wooden handle and binding are modern replacements for the originals, which have rotted away. Adzes were swung in an up-and-down movement and were used for jobs such as hollowing out tree trunks and shaping them to make dugout canoes.

AXE
Early farmers needed axes to clear land for their crops. An experiment in Denmark using a 5,000-year-old axe showed that a man could clear one hectare of woodland in about five weeks. This axe head, dating from between 4000BC and 2000BC, has been given a modern wooden handle.

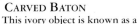

ANTLER PICK

Antlers were as useful to prehistoric humans as to the reindeer they came from! This tool comes from a Neolithic site near Avebury in England. Antler picks were used for digging and quarrying. Antler was a very hard material, but it could be carved into sharp spear points and barbed harpoons.

CRAFTSPEOPLE

A picture by an artist from the 1800s shows an imagined view of Stone Age. It shows tools being used and great care being taken over the work. Even everyday items were often finely carved and decorated by the craftspeople who made them.

CARVED BATON

This ivory object is known as a *bâton de commandement*. Several of these batons have been found, especially in France. But no one is sure what they were used for. Some experts think they were status symbols, showing the importance of the person carrying them. Others think that the holes were used to straighten arrows. Whatever their use, the batons are often decorated with fine animal carvings and geometric designs.

ANTLERS AT WORK

Two stags (male deer) fight. Male deer have large antlers, which they use to battle with each other to win territory and females. The stags shed and grow a new set of antlers each year, so prehistoric hunters and artists had a ready supply of material.

Useful Crafts

BASKET-MAKING WAS PROBABLY the very first handicraft. River reeds or twigs – whatever was found locally – were woven into shapes for carrying goods. Baskets were quick to make and easy to carry, but wore out easily and could not carry liquids. The discovery that clay turned into a hard, solid material when it was baked may have happened by accident, perhaps when a clay-lined basket was left in a bread oven. Although baked clay figures were made from about 24,000BC, it was thousands of years before pottery was used for cooking and storing food and drink. The first pots, shaped from coils or lumps of clay, were made in Japan around 10,500BC.

People learned how to spin thread from flax plants and animal hair. The loom, for weaving the thread into linen and wool cloth, was invented around 6000BC.

BAKED CLAY FIGURINE
This is one of the oldest fired-clay objects in the world. It is one of many similar figurines made around 24,000BC at Dolni Vestonice in the Czech Republic. Here, people hunted mammoths, woolly rhinoceroses and horses. They built homes with small, oval-shaped ovens, in which they fired their figurines.

CHINESE JAR
It is amazing to think that this elegant pot was for everyday use in 4500BC. It was made in Banpo, near Shanghai. The people of Banpo were some of China's earliest farmers. They grew millet and kept pigs and dogs for meat. The potters made a high quality black pottery for important occasions and this cheaper, grey pottery for everyday use.

MAKE A CLAY POT
You will need: terracotta modelling clay, wooden board, modelling tool, plastic flower pot, decorating tool, varnish, brush, sandpaper.

1 Roll out a long, thick sausage of clay on a wooden board. It should be at least 1cm in diameter.

2 Form the roll of clay into a coil to make the base of your pot. A fairly small base can be made into a pot, a larger one into a bowl.

3 Now make a fatter roll of clay . Carefully coil this around the base to make the sides of your pot.

HOUSEHOLD POTS

Many early pots were decorated with basket-like patterns. This one has a simple geometric design and was made in Thailand in about 3500BC. Clay pots like this were used for storing food, carrying water or cooking.

EASY TO CARVE

Steatite, or soapstone, has been used to make this carving from the Cycladic Islands of Greece. Soapstone is very soft and easy to carve. Figurines like this one were often used in funeral ceremonies. They could also be used either as the object of worship itself or as a ritual offering to a god. This figure has a cross around its neck. Although the symbol certainly has no Christian significance, no one really knows what it means.

WOVEN THREADS

The earliest woven objects may have looked like this rope and cane mat from Nazca in Peru. It was made around AD1000. Prehistoric people used plant-fibre rope to weave baskets and bags. The oldest known fabric dates from about 6500BC and was found at Çatal Hüyük in Turkey. Few woven objects have survived, as they rot quickly.

Fired-clay pots could only be made where there were natural deposits of clay. These areas seem to have specialized in baked-clay pottery and sculpture. The patterns used to decorate the pots vary from area to area.

4 With a modelling tool, smooth down the edges of the coil to make it flat and smooth. Make sure there are no air spaces.

5 Place your pot over a flower pot to support it. Keep adding more rolls of clay to build up the sides of your pot.

6 Smooth down the sides as you add more rolls. Then use a decorating tool with a serrated end to make different patterns.

7 Leave your pot to dry out. When the clay is dry, varnish the outside. Use sandpaper to smooth the inside of your pot.

Ceramic Skills in India

CLAY AND TERRACOTTA OBJECTS (known as ceramics) play an important part in the study of history. Because they were fired (baked), traces of carbon (burnt particles) are left on them. This enables archaeologists to date the objects quite accurately using a process called carbon-dating.

Making ceramics was one of the earliest crafts to be practised in India, for example. Many artefacts have been found at archaeological sites, dating as far back as 5000BC when a civilization began to develop in the Indus Valley. People made clay storage jars, terracotta seals and terracotta figurines of domestic animals. The animal figures may have been children's toys. Craftworkers also made terracotta figurines of gods and goddesses, though they gradually began to make stone and metal images as well. Clay containers continued to be used throughout India's history. They kept food and liquids cool in in the country's hot climate.

RECORD IN CLAY
This terracotta cart found at the ancient city of Mohenjo-Daro is about 4,000 years old. Figurines like this have been found throughout the Indus Valley. They may have been toys, but they give clues to how people lived. For example, we can see that wheeled carts drawn by animals were in use.

IDEA EXCHANGE
Painted dishes like this one found on the plains of the River Ganges, date from between 1000 and 500BC. Similar pottery has been found across the region. This shows that people travelled and shared the same technology.

SIMILAR STYLES
Black and red painted pottery has been found at sites dating from the Indus Valley civilization, and at later sites dating from around 500BC. It is found all over the Indian subcontinent.

MAKE A WATER POT
You will need: inflated balloon, large bowl, strips of newspaper, flour and water or wallpaper paste, scissors, fine sandpaper, strip of corrugated cardboard, sticky tape, terracotta and black paint, paintbrushes, pencil, pva glue.

1 Cover the balloon with 4 layers of newspaper soaked in paste. When dry, cut a slit in the papier mâché. Remove the balloon. Add more layers to give the pot a tapered top.

2 Roll the corrugated cardboard into a circle shape to fit on to the narrow end of the pot to form a base. Fix the base in place with sticky tape.

3 Cover the corrugated cardboard base with four layers of soaked newspaper. Leave to dry beween each layer. Smooth the edges with sandpaper.

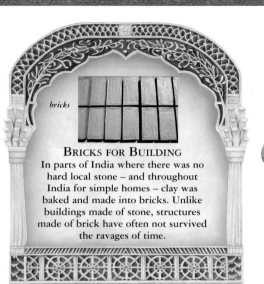

BRICKS FOR BUILDING

bricks

In parts of India where there was no hard local stone – and throughout India for simple homes – clay was baked and made into bricks. Unlike buildings made of stone, structures made of brick have often not survived the ravages of time.

TERRACOTTA GODDESS

A female terracotta figure found in Mathura, Uttar Pradesh may be an image of a mother goddess. Many terracotta images were made during the Mauryan period (400–200BC) and immediately afterwards. They were cheaper versions of the stone sculptures that were built at the imperial court.

THROWING A POT

A village potter shapes a clay vessel as it spins on his potter's wheel. Pottery was an important part of the ancient urban and village economies and is still practised in India today. Clay used for making pottery is available in most parts of the land.

Clay water pots that are 4,000 years old have been found in the Indus Valley. People carried the pots on their heads.

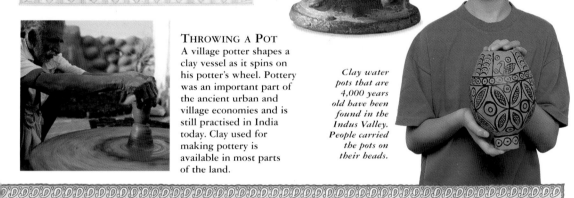

4 When it is dry, paint the water pot with two coats of terracotta paint, to make it look as though it is made of terracotta. Leave to dry between coats.

5 Draw some patterns on the water pot with a pencil. Copy the ancient Indian pattern shown here, or create your own individual design.

6 Carefully paint your designs using black paint and a fine paintbrush. Keep the edges of your lines neat and clean. Leave to dry.

7 Add final details, again using a fine paintbrush. When the paint is dry, seal the surface of the water pot with a coat of watered down pva glue.

Scientific Minds in Mesopotamia

THE SUMERIAN PEOPLE in Mesopotamia developed the world's first system of arithmetic around 2500BC. It was useful for making records of goods bought and sold. One number system used 10 as a base and the other, 60. They also calculated time in hour-long units of 60 minutes. Sumerian astronomers worked out a calendar based on 12- and 28-day cycles and 7-day weeks from studying the moon and the seasons. Later, the Babylonians made a detailed study of the heavens, and could predict events such as eclipses.

Mesopotamian doctors did not fully understand how the body worked, but they did make lists of symptoms. Their observations passed on to the Greeks centuries later and so became one of the foundations of modern medicine.

HEAVY COUGH CURE
Inscriptions on a clay tablet suggest mixing balsam (a herb) with strong beer, honey and oil to cure a cough. The mixture was taken hot, without food. Then the patient's throat was tickled with a feather to make him sick. Other prescriptions used mice, dogs' tails and urine.

BAD OMEN
Mesopotamians thought that eclipses were a bad sign – unless they were obscured by cloud. If an eclipse was covered by cloud in a particular city, the local king was told that it had nothing to do with him or his country.

MEDICINAL BREW
Servants are distilling essence of cedar, a vital ingredient for a Mesopotamian headache cure. Cedar twigs were heated to give off a vapour. This condensed against the cooler lid and trickled into the rim of the pot from where it was collected. The essence was mixed with honey, resin from pine, myrrh and spruce trees, and fat from a sheep's kidney.

MAKE A SET OF LION WEIGHTS

You will need: pebbles of various sizes, kitchen scales, modelling clay, cutting board, cocktail stick, paints and paintbrushes.

1 Weigh a pebble and add modelling clay to make it up to a weight of 225g. Once the clay has dried out, the final weight will be only about 200g.

2 Take a portion of the weighed modelling clay and shape it into a rectangle roughly 12cm by 7cm. This will be the base for your weight.

3 Wrap another piece of the weighed modelling clay around the weighed pebble to make the lion's body. Shape the body into a pear shape.

Sky Map

The sky in this Mesopotamian astronomical map is divided into eight parts and the stars in each section are indicated. The heavens were seen as a source of information about the future, so the kings often consulted astronomers. One astronomer wrote to the king in the 600s BC: "I am always looking at the sky but nothing unusual has appeared above the horizon".

Medicine Men

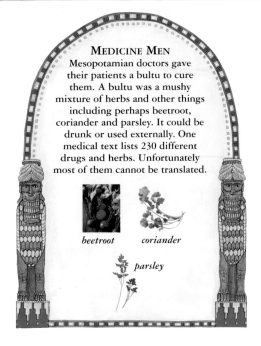

Mesopotamian doctors gave their patients a bultu to cure them. A bultu was a mushy mixture of herbs and other things including perhaps beetroot, coriander and parsley. It could be drunk or used externally. One medical text lists 230 different drugs and herbs. Unfortunately most of them cannot be translated.

beetroot   coriander

parsley

Weights and Measures

Officials weigh metal objects that have been taken as booty after a victory. The duck-shaped object is a weight. The kings were responsible for seeing that weights and measures were exact and that nobody cheated customers. Prices were fixed by law and calculated in shekels (1 shekel was about 8g of silver).

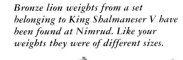

Bronze lion weights from a set belonging to King Shalmaneser V have been found at Nimrud. Like your weights they were of different sizes.

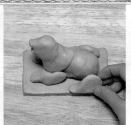

4 Position the pebble and clay on to its base. Add another piece of weighed clay to form the head and mane. Shape the face and jaw with your fingers.

5 Model four pieces of weighed clay to make the lion's four legs and stick them on to the body. Flatten the clay slightly at each end for the paws.

6 Make a tail and ears using up the remaining weighed clay. Using the cocktail stick, add extra detail to the face, mane, paws and tail. Leave to dry.

7 Paint the lion and the base cream. Flick with brown paint for a mottled appearance. Add details to the face, mane and paws. Make more lions for a set.

Mesopotamian Technology

A WHOLE CULTURE OF SPECIALIST craftworkers grew up in Mesopotamia and quickened the pace of improvement and invention. The Sumerians learned to make pottery by shaping the wet clay on a potter's wheel by about 3500BC, and became experts at making cloth, leatherwork and making fine jewellery. They were among the first people in the world to use metal. A copper sculpture of a lion-headed eagle found near the ancient city of Ur, dates from around 2600BC. Mesopotamian armies used weapons and armour of bronze, an alloy of copper and tin, which is stronger than plain copper. The Mesopotamians were also experts at irrigation and flood control, building elaborate canals, water storage and drainage systems.

SUPPLYING THE CITY
Water wheels and aqueducts like these are still used in the Middle East today. The Assyrians built aqueducts to take water to the cities to meet the needs of their growing populations. The Assyrian king Sennacherib had 10km of canals cut. They led from the mountains to the city of Nineveh. He built dams and weirs to control the flow of water, and created an artificial marsh, where he bred wild animals and birds.

A WEIGHTY CHALLENGE
Workers in a quarry near the Assyrian city of Nineveh prepare to move an enormous block of stone roughly hewn in the shape of a lamassu (human-headed winged bull). The stone is on a sledge carried on wooden rollers. At the back of the sledge, some men have thrown ropes over a giant lever and pull hard. This raises the end of the sledge and other workers push a wedge underneath. More workers stand ready to haul on ropes at the front of the sledge. At a signal everyone pulls or pushes and the sledge moves forward.

MAKE A PAINTED PLATE
You will need: a plate, flour, water and newspaper to make papier mâché, scissors, pencil, fine sandpaper, ruler, paints and paintbrushes.

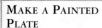

1 Tear strips of newspaper and dip them in the water. Cover the whole surface of the plate with the wet newspaper strips.

2 Mix up a paste of flour and water. Cover the newspaper strips with the paste. Allow to dry, then add two more layers, leaving it to dry each time.

3 When the papier mâché is dry, trim around the plate to make a neat edge. Remove the plate. Add more papier mâché to strengthen the plate.

MAKING CLOTH

Spinning and weaving were usually done by women in the home or in state or temple factories. Large herds of sheep and goats were kept to produce wool, to make clothing. Flax was grown for its fibres, which were used to make linen as early as 3000BC. Cotton was not introduced until the reign of the Assyrian king, Sennacherib, in the 700s BC.

wool

sheep's wool

sheep's fleece

METALWORKERS

Ceremonial daggers demonstrate the Sumerians' skill at working with gold as far back as 2600BC. Real weapons had bronze blades. The Sumerians made a wax model of the object required. They covered this with clay to make a mould. They heated the mould to harden the clay. The melted wax was poured out through a small hole, and molten metal poured in to replace it. When cool, the clay mould was broken, to reveal the metal object inside.

You have copied a plate from Tell Halaf, a small town where some of the finest pots in the ancient world were made. They were decorated with orange and brown paints made from oxides found in clay.

HAND-MADE VASES

Vases found in Samarra in the north of Mesopotamia were produced about 6,000 years ago. They were shaped by hand and fired in a kiln, then painted with geometric designs. Later, a wheel like a turntable was used to shape the clay, which speeded up the process.

4 When the papier mâché is completely dry, smooth it down with fine sandpaper. Then paint the plate on both sides with a white base coat.

5 When the paint is dry, use a pencil and ruler to mark a dot in the centre of the plate. Draw four large petals around this point and add details as shown above.

6 When you are happy with your design, paint in the patterns using three colours for the basic pattern. Allow each colour to dry before adding the next.

7 Add more detail to your plate, using more colours, including wavy lines around the edge. When you have finished painting, leave it to dry.

Egyptian Calculations

THE ANCIENT EGYPTIANS had advanced systems of numbering and measuring. They put this knowledge to good use in building, engineering and surveying the land. However, their knowledge of science was often mixed up with superstitions and belief in magic. For example, doctors understood a lot about broken bones and surgery, but at the same time they used all kinds of spells, amulets (charms) and magic potions to ward off disease. Much of their knowledge about the human body came from their experience of preparing the dead for burial.

The priests studied the stars carefully. They thought that the planets must be gods. The Egyptians also worked out a calendar, which was very important for working out when the Nile floods were due and when to plant crops.

MATHEMATICAL PAPYRUS
This papyrus shows methods for working out the areas of squares, circles and triangles. It dates from around 850BC. These methods would have been used in calculations for land areas and pyramid heights on Egyptian building projects. Other surviving writings show mathematical calculations for working out how much grain might fit into a store. The Egyptians used a decimal system of numbering with separate symbols for one, ten, 100 and 1,000. Eight was shown by eight one symbols – 11111111.

CUBIT MEASURE
Units of measurement included the royal cubit of about 52cm and the short cubit of 45cm. A cubit was the length of a man's forearm and was subdivided into palms and fingers.

MAKE A WATER CLOCK

You will need: self-drying clay, plastic flowerpot, modelling tool, skewer, pencil, ruler, masking tape, scissors, yellow acrylic paint , varnish, water pot and brush. Optional: rolling pin and board.

1 Begin by rolling out the clay. Take the plastic flowerpot and press its base firmly into the clay. This will be the bottom of your water clock.

2 Cut out an oblong of clay large enough to mould around the flowerpot. Add the base and use your modelling tool to make the joints smooth.

3 Make a small hole near the bottom of the pot with a skewer, as shown. Leave it in a warm place to dry. When the clay has dried, remove the flowerpot.

HOW DEEP IS THE RIVER?

A series of steps called a nilometer was used to measure the depth of water in the River Nile. The annual floods were desperately important for the farmers living alongside the Nile. A good flood measured about 7m. More than this and farm buildings and channels might be destroyed. Less, and the fields might go dry.

STAR OF THE NILE

This astronomical painting is from the ceiling of the tomb of Seti I. The study of the stars, as in most of the ancient civilizations, was part religion, part science. The brightest star in the sky was Sirius, which we call the dog star. The Egyptians called it Sopdet, after a goddess. This star rose into view at the time when the Nile floods were due and was greeted with a special festival.

MEDICINE

Most Egyptian medicines were based on plants. One cure for headaches included juniper berries, coriander, wormwood and honey. The mixture was rubbed into the scalp. Other remedies included natron (a kind of salt), myrrh and even crocodile droppings. Some Egyptian medicines probably did heal the patients, but others did more harm than good.

coriander

garlic

Time was calculated on water clocks by calculating how long it took for water to drop from level to level. The water level lowered as it dripped through the hole in the bottom of the pot.

4 Mark out lines at 3mm intervals inside the pot. Mask the ends with tape and paint the lines yellow. When dry, remove the tape. Ask an adult to varnish the pot inside.

5 Find or make another two pots and position them as shown. Ask a partner to put their finger over the hole in the clock while you pour water into it.

6 Now ask your partner to take their finger away. The length of time it takes for the level of the water to drop from mark to mark is the measure of time.

Pyramid Construction

QUARRYING
The core of the pyramid was of rough stone, from local quarries. Better quality stone was shipped from Aswan, 966km away. Workers used wooden mallets to drive wedges and chisels into the stone to split it.

F OR MANY YEARS the Great Pyramid at Giza was the largest building in the world. Its base is about 230m square, and its original point was 147m high. It is made up of about 2,300,000 massive blocks of stone, each one weighing about 2.5 tonnes. The blocks were secured by rope on wooden rollers. Labourers hauled them up ramps of solid earth that were built up the side of the pyramid as it grew higher and higher. The ramps were destroyed when the pyramid was completed.

The Great Pyramid was amazingly accurate and symmetrical in shape. The land had to be absolutely flat for this to be possible. The Egyptians cut channels across the building site and filled them with water. They used the water line as a marker for making the site level. The four corners of the pyramid are aligned exactly to face north, south, east and west. This was worked out by astronomers, by observing the stars.

INSIDE WORK
Inside the pyramid were narrow passages, and tomb chambers. They were lined with good quality granite. Flickering light came from pottery lamps that consisted of a wick of twine or grass soaked in animal or fish oil. Bundles of papyrus (reeds) were dipped in resin or pitch and lit to use as torches.

MAKE A PYRAMID

You will need: card, pencil, ruler, scissors, pva glue and brush, masking tape, acrylic paint (yellow, white, gold), plaster paste, sandpaper, water pot and brush.

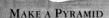

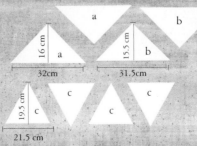

a

b

16 cm

a

15.5 cm

b

32cm

31.5cm

19.5 cm

c

c

c

c

21.5 cm

Make the pyramid in two halves. Cut out one triangle (a) for the base, one triangle (b) for the inside and two of triangle (c) for the sides of each half section.

1 Glue the half section of the pyramid together, binding the joints with pieces of masking tape, as shown. Now make the second half section in the same way.

INSIDE A PYRAMID

This cross-section shows the inside of the Great Pyramid. The design of the interior changed several times during its construction. An underground chamber may originally have been intended as the pharaoh Khufu's burial place. This was never finished. The Queen's Chamber was also found empty. The pharaoh was actually buried in the King's Chamber. Once the funeral was over, the tomb was sealed from the inside to prevent people breaking in. Blocks of stone were slid down the Grand Gallery. The workmen left through a shaft and along a corridor before the stones thudded into place.

THE KING'S CHAMBER

The burial chamber in the Great Pyramid is known as the King's Chamber. It was the final resting place of the sarcophagus containing King Khufu's body. The chamber is made of granite. Each of the nine slabs which make up its roof weighs 50 tonnes. Strangely, the only place in the pyramid where Khufu's name can be seen is above the roof. Here graffiti was left by the workmen who built the pyramid.

ventilation shafts

King's Chamber

Grand Gallery

Queen's Chamber

escape shaft for workers

corridor

unfinished chamber

2 Mix up yellow and white paint with a little plaster paste to achieve a sandy texture. Then add a little glue so that it sticks to the card. Paint the pyramid sections.

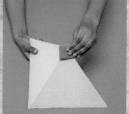

3 Leave the painted pyramid sections to dry in a warm place. When they are completely dry, sand down the tips until they are smooth and mask them off with tape.

4 Now paint the tips of each half of the pyramid gold and leave to dry. Finally, glue the two halves together and place your pyramid on a bed of sand to display.

The building of the Great Pyramid probably took about 23 years. Originally the pyramids were cased in pale limestone, so they would have looked a brilliant white. The capstone at the very top of the pyramid was probably covered in gold.

The Thinking Greeks

THE ANCIENT GREEKS COULD AFFORD time for studying and thinking because their civilization was both wealthy and secure. They learned astrology from the Babylonians and mathematics from the Egyptians. They used their scientific knowledge to develop many practical inventions, including water clocks, cogwheels, gearing systems, slot machines and steam engines. However, these devices were not widely used as there were many slave workers to do the jobs.

The word 'philosophy' comes from the Greek word *philosophos*, meaning love of knowledge. The Greeks developed many different branches of philosophy. Three of these were politics (how best to govern), ethics (how to behave well) and cosmology (how the universe worked). Greek philosophers recognized the value of experimenting. But they could not always see their limitations. Aristotle discovered that distillation turned salt water into fresh water, and wrongly assumed wine would turn into water by the same process.

GREAT THINKER
The philosopher Aristotle (384–322BC) is often recognized as the founder of Western science. He pioneered a rational approach to the world, that was based on observing and recording evidence. For three years, he was the tutor of Alexander the Great.

CLOCK TOWER
The Tower of the Winds in Athens contains a water clock. The original Egyptian invention was a bucket of water with a tiny hole in the bottom. As the water dripped out of it, the water level fell past scored marks on the inside of the bucket, measuring time. The Greeks improved on this design, using the flow of water to work a dial with a moving pointer.

ARCHIMEDES SCREW
You will need: clean, empty plastic bottle, scissors, modelling clay, strong tape, length of clear plastic tube, bowl of water, blue food colouring, empty bowl.

1 Cut off the bottle top. Place the modelling clay into the middle of the bottle, about 5cm from the end. Punch a hole here with the scissors.

2 Cut a strip of tape the same length as the bottle. Tape it to the middle of the bottle. This will give the tube extra grip later on.

3 Twist the length of tube around the bottle. Go from one end of the bottle to the other. Tape the tube into place over the first piece of tape.

WATER LIFTER

When an Archimedes screw is turned, it lifts water from one level to another. It is named after its inventor, the scientist Archimedes, who lived about 287–211BC, in Syracuse, Sicily. The device is still used today.

FATHER OF GEOMETRY

Euclid (about 330–260BC) was a mathematician. He lived in the Greek-Egyptian city of Alexandria. He is known as the father of geometry, which comes from the Greek word for 'measuring land'. Geometry is the study of points, lines, curves, surfaces and their measurements. His geometry textbook was called *Elements*. It was still widely used in the early part of the 1900s, over 2,000 years after Euclid's death. This picture shows the front page of an edition of the book that was printed in London in 1732.

4 Place a few drops of the blue food colouring into the bowl of water. Stir it in so that the colour mixes evenly throughout the water.

5 Place one end of the bottle into the bowl of blue water. Make sure that the tube at the opposite end is pointing towards the empty bowl.

6 Twist the bottle around in the blue water. As you do so, you will see the water start travelling up the tube and gradually filling the other bowl.

The invention of the Archimedes screw made it possible for farmers to water their fields with irrigation channels. It saved them from walking back and forth to the river with buckets.

Greek Medical Foundations

THE ANCIENT GREEKS LAID the foundations of modern medicine. Although they believed that only the gods had the power to heal wounds and cure sickness, they also developed a scientific approach to medicine. Greek doctors treated injuries and battle wounds by bandaging and bone-setting. They prescribed rest, diet and herbal drugs to cure diseases, although they were powerless against epidemics, such as plague. Doctors believed that good health was dependent on the balance between four main body fluids – blood, phlegm and yellow and black bile. If this balance was disturbed, they attempted to restore it by applying heated metal cups to the body to draw off harmful fluids. This mistaken practice continued in Europe until the 1600s.

FATHER OF MEDICINE
Hippocrates founded a medical school around 400BC. He taught that observation of symptoms was more important than theory. His students took an oath to use their skills to heal and never to harm. Doctors still take the Hippocratic oath today.

BODY BALANCE
Bleeding was a common procedure, intended to restore the body's internal balance. This carving shows surgical instruments and cups used for catching blood. Sometimes bleeding may have helped to drain off poisons, but more often it can only have weakened the patient.

HEALING GOD
The Greeks worshipped Asclepius, as the god of healing. He is shown here with a serpent, representing wisdom. Invalids seeking a cure made a visit to his shrine.

LEG OFFERING
You will need: self-drying modelling clay, rolling pin, board, ruler, modelling tool, paintbrush, cream acrylic paint.

1 Divide the clay into two pieces. With the rolling pin, roll out one piece to 15cm length, 10cm width and 2cm depth. This is the base for the leg.

2 Roll out the second piece of clay. With the modelling tool, carve out a leg and foot shape. It should be big enough to fit on one side of the base.

3 Gently place the leg on the right-hand side of the base. With the tool, draw a shallow outline around the leg into the base. Remove the leg.

NATURAL HEALING

The Greeks used a large variety of natural treatments to cure illnesses. Herbal remedies were particularly popular. Lentils, mustard and honey may have been combined in a poultice and applied to a wound.

lentils

honey

mustard

THEORY AND PRACTICE

Patients would explain their dreams to doctors, who then prescribed treatment. In this relief, a healing spirit in the shape of a serpent visits a sleeping patient. In the foreground, the physician bandages the wounded arm.

TOOL KIT

The Greeks used bronze surgical instruments, including forceps and probes. Surgery was usually a last resort. Even when it was successful, patients often died from the shock and pain, or from infection afterwards. Operations on limbs were more successful than those on body cavities such as the chest or stomach.

4 With the tool, score the outline with lines. Carve the ancient Greek message seen in the picture above next to the leg.

5 Mould the leg onto the scored area of the base. Use your fingers to press the sides of the leg in place. Carve toes and toenails into the foot.

6 Paint over the entire leg offering with a cream colour, to give it an aged look. Leave to dry overnight. Your leg offering is done.

This model is based on a real one that was left as a thanks offering to the god Asclepius by someone whose leg was affected by illness. This was a common practice in ancient Greece.

Roman Empire Builders

THE ROMANS ADOPTED many of the ideas of the Greeks, such as the principles of architecture, and developed them further. They built magnificent domes, arched bridges and grand public buildings throughout the Empire, spreading their ideas and their expert skills.

They built long, straight roads to carry supplies, and messengers to the farthest corners of the Empire. The roads had a slight hump in the middle so that rainwater drained to the sides. Some were paved with stone and others were covered with gravel or stone chippings. Engineers designed aqueducts to carry water supplies to their cities. If possible, local stone and timber were used for building works. The Romans were the first to develop concrete, which was cheaper and stronger than stone. The rule of the Romans came to an end in western Europe over 1,500 years ago. Yet many of their techniques and principles of building are still in use today.

ROMAN ROADS
A typical Roman road stretches into the distance. It runs through the town of Ostia, in Italy. Roman road-building techniques remained unmatched in Europe until the 1800s.

MUSCLE POWER
Romans used big wooden cranes to lift heavy building materials. The crane is powered by a huge treadwheel. Slaves walk round and round in the wheel, making it turn. The turning wheel pulls on the rope, that is tied round the heavy block of stone, raising it off the ground.

MAKE A GROMA

You will need: large, strong piece of cardboard, scissors, ruler, pencil, square of card, pva glue, masking tape, balsa wood pole, Plasticine, silver foil, string, large sewing needle, acrylic paints, paintbrush, water pot, broom handle.

1 Cut out three pieces of cardboard – two 20cm x 6cm, one 40cm x 6cm. Cut another piece, 15cm x 12cm, for the handle. Then cut them into shape, as shown above.

2 Measure to the centre of the long piece. Use a pencil to make a slot here, between the layers of cardboard. The slot is for the balsa wood pole.

3 Slide the balsa wood pole into the slot and tape the cardboard pieces in a cross. Use the card square to make sure the four arms of the groma are at right angles. Glue in place.

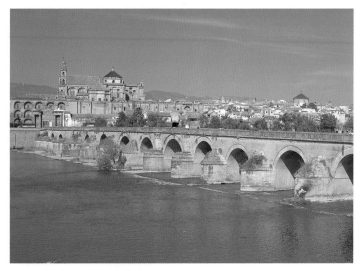

BUILDING MATERIALS

The Romans used a variety of stones for building, usually from local quarries. Limestone and a volcanic rock called tufa were used in the city of Pompeii. Slate was used for roofing in parts of Britain. Fine marble, used for temples and other public buildings, was available in the Carrara region of Italy, as it still is today. Marble was also imported from overseas.

marble

slate

ARCHING STRENGTH

The Roman bridge over the River Guadalquivir at Cordoba in Spain still stands today. The arch was a key element in many Roman buildings, including domed roofs. It gave stronger support than a simple beam.

WALLS OF ROME

The city of Rome's defences were built at many stages in its history. These sturdy walls were raised during the reign of the Emperor Marcus Aurelius, AD121–180. The Aurelian Walls were so well built that they are still in good condition.

Slot the arms on to the balsa wood pole. Use the plumb lines as a guide to make sure the pole is vertical. The arms can then be used to line up objects in the distance. Romans used a groma to measure right angles and to make sure roads were straight.

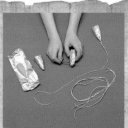

4 Roll the Plasticine into four small cones and cover them with foil. Thread string through the tops, as shown. These are the groma's plumb lines, or vertical guides.

5 Tie the plumb lines to each arm, as shown. They must all hang at the same length – 20cm will do. If the Plasticine is too heavy, use wet newspaper rolled up in the foil.

6 Split the top of the handle piece, and wrap it round the balsa wood pole. Glue it in place, as shown. Do the same on the other end with the broom handle. Paint the groma.

Roman Healing Powers

SOME ROMANS lived to old age, but most died before they reached the age of 50. Archaeologists have found out a lot about health and disease in Roman times by examining skeletons that have survived. They can tell, for example, how old a person was when he or she died and their general state of health during life. Ancient writings also provide information about Roman medical knowledge.

Roman doctors knew very little science. They healed the sick through a mixture of common sense, trust in the gods and magic. Most cures and treatments had come to Rome from the doctors of ancient Greece. The Greeks and Romans also shared the same god of healing, Aesculapius (the Greek Asclepius). There were doctors in most parts of the Empire, as well as midwives, dentists and eye specialists. Surgeons operated on wounds received in battle, on broken bones and even skulls. The only pain killers were made from poppy juice.

GODDESS OF HEALTH
Greeks and Romans honoured the daughter of the god Aesculapius as a goddess of health. She was called Hygieia. The word hygienic, which comes from her name, is still used today to mean free of germs.

A CHEMIST'S SHOP
This pharmacy, or chemist's shop, is run by a woman. This was quite unusual for Roman times, as women were rarely given positions of responsibility. Roman pharmacists collected herbs and often mixed them for doctors.

MEDICINE BOX
Boxes like this one would have been used by Roman doctors to store various drugs. Many of the treatments used by doctors were herbal, and not always pleasant to take!

MEDICAL INSTRUMENTS
The Romans used a variety of surgical and other instruments. These are made in bronze and include a scalpel, forceps and a spatula for mixing and applying various ointments.

TAKING THE CURE

These are the ruins of a medical clinic in Asia Minor (present-day Turkey). It was built around AD150, in honour of Aesculapius, the god of healing. Clinics like this one were known as therapy buildings. People would come to them seeking cures for all kinds of ailments.

BATHING THE BABY

This stone carving from Rome shows a newborn baby being bathed. The Romans were well aware of the importance of regular bathing in clean water. However, childbirth itself was dangerous for both mother and baby. Despite the dangers, the Romans liked to have large families, and many women died giving birth.

HERBAL MEDICINE

Doctors and travelling healers sold all kinds of potions and ointments. Many were made from herbs such as rosemary, sage and fennel. Other natural remedies included garlic, mustard and cabbage. Many of the remedies would have done little good, but some of them did have the power to heal.

garlic

sage

rosemary

Chinese Metalworkers

THE CHINESE MASTERED THE secrets of making alloys (mixtures of two or more metals) during the Shang dynasty (c.1600BC–1122BC). They made bronze by melting copper and tin to separate each metal from its ore, a process called smelting. Nine parts of copper were then mixed with one part of tin and heated in a charcoal furnace. When the metals melted, they were piped into clay moulds. Bronze was used to make objects such as ceremonial pots, statues, bells, mirrors, tools and weapons.

By about 600BC, the Chinese were smelting iron ore. They then became the first people to make cast iron – around 1500 years before the process was discovered in the West – by adding carbon to the molten metal. Cast iron is tougher than bronze and was soon being used to make weapons, tools and plough blades. By AD1000, the Chinese were mining and working a vast amount of iron. Coke (a type of coal) had replaced the charcoal used in furnaces, which were fired up by water-driven bellows.

SILVER SCISSORS
This pair of scissors is made of silver. They are proof of the foreign influences that entered China in the AD700s, during the boom years of the Tang dynasty. The metal is beaten, rather than cast in the Chinese way. It is decorated in the Persian style of the Silk Road, with engraving and punching.

BEWARE OF THE LION
This gilded lion is on guard at Beijing's imperial palace, the Forbidden City, built in the 1400s. The Chinese were expert at elaborately decorated metalwork, sometimes inlaying it with gold, silver and precious stones.

MAKE A NECKLACE

You will need: tape measure, thick wire, thin wire, masking tape, scissors, tin foil, measuring spoon, glue and brush, fuse wire.

1 Measure around your neck using a tape measure. Ask an adult to cut a piece of thick wire to 1½ times this length. Shape it into a rough circle.

2 Cut two 4cm pieces of thin wire. Coil loosely around sides of thick wire. Tape ends to thick wire. Slide thick wire through coils to adjust fit.

3 Cut out an oval-shaped piece of tin foil. Shape it into a pendant half, using a measuring spoon or teaspoon. Make 9 more halves.

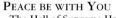

PEACE BE WITH YOU

The Hall of Supreme Harmony in Beijing's Forbidden City is guarded by this bronze statue of a turtle. Despite its rather fearsome appearance, the turtle was actually a symbol of peace.

MINERAL WEALTH

The Chinese probably learned to smelt ore in furnaces from their experience with high-temperature pottery kilns. The land was rich in copper, tin and iron, and the Chinese were very skilled miners. Large amounts of precious metals, such as gold and silver, had to be imported.

gold nugget *silver ore*

GOLDEN FIREBIRDS

Chinese craftsmen fashioned these beautiful phoenix birds from thin sheets of delicate gold. The mythical Arabian phoenix was said to set fire to its nest and die, only to rise again from the ashes. During the Tang dynasty, the phoenix became a symbol of the Chinese empress Wu Zetian, who came to power in AD660. It later came to be a more general symbol for all empresses.

DECORATIVE PROTECTION

A network of gold threads makes up these fingernail protectors of the 1800s. The blue decoration is enamel (glass) that was put into parts of the pattern in paste form, and then fired to melt and harden it.

4 Glue the 2 pendant halves together, leaving one end open. Drop some rolled-up balls of foil into the opening. Seal the opening with glue.

5 Make 4 more pendants in the same way. Thread each pendant on to the neckband with pieces of thin fuse wire. Leave a gap between each one.

People of all classes wore decorative jewellery in imperial China. The design of this necklace is based on the metal bell bracelets worn by Chinese children.

Chinese Firsts

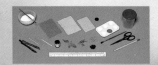

WHEN YOU WALK DOWN a shopping street in any modern city, it is very difficult to avoid seeing some object that was invented in China long ago. Printed words on paper, silk scarves, umbrellas or locks and keys are all Chinese innovations. Over the centuries, Chinese ingenuity and technical skill have changed the world in which we live.

A seismoscope is a very useful instrument in an earthquake-prone country such as China. It was invented in AD132 by a Chinese scientist called Zhang Heng. It could record the direction of even a distant earth tremor. Another key invention was the magnetic compass. Around AD1–100, the Chinese discovered that lodestone (a type of iron ore) could be made to point north. They realized that they could magnetize needles to do the same. By about AD1000, they worked out the difference between true north and magnetic north and began using compasses to keep ships on course.

Gunpowder is another Chinese invention, from about AD850. At first it was used to blast rocks apart and to make fireworks. Later, it was used in warfare.

SHADE AND SHELTER
A Qing dynasty woman uses an umbrella as a sunshade to protect her skin. The Chinese invented umbrellas about 1,600 years ago and they soon spread throughout the rest of Asia. Umbrellas became fashionable with both women and men and were regarded as a symbol of high rank.

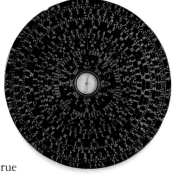

THE SAILOR'S FRIEND
The magnetic compass was invented in China around AD1–100. At first it was used as a planning aid to ensure new houses faced in a direction that was in harmony with nature. Later it was used to plot courses on long sea voyages.

MAKE A WHEELBARROW
You will need: thick card, ruler, pencil, scissors, compasses, 0.5cm diameter balsa strips, glue and brush, paintbrush, paint (black and brown), water pot, 3.5cm x 0.5cm dowel, 2cm diameter rubber washers (x4).

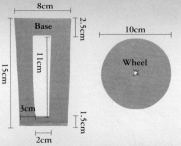

Using the measurements above, draw the pieces on to thick card. Draw the wheel with the compasses. Cut out pieces with scissors.

1 Cut 7cm, 8cm and 26cm (x2) balsa strips. Glue 7cm strip to short edge of base and 8cm strip to top edge. Glue 26cm strips to side of base.

Su Song's Masterpiece

This fantastic machine is a clock tower that can tell the time, chime the hours and follow the movement of the planets around the Sun. It was designed by an official called Su Song, in the city of Kaifeng in AD1092. The machine uses a mechanism called an escapement, which controls and regulates the timing of the clock. The escapement mechanism was invented in the AD700s by a Chinese inventor called Yi Xing.

Earthquake Warning

The decorative object shown above is the scientist Zhang Heng's seismoscope. When there was an earthquake, a ball was released from one of the dragons and fell into a frog's mouth. This showed the direction of the vibrations. According to records, in AD138 the instrument detected a earth tremor some 500km away.

One-Wheeled Transport

In about AD100, the Chinese invented the wheelbarrow. They then designed a model with a large central wheel that could bear great weights. This became a form of transport, pushed along by muscle power.

The single wheelbarrow was used by farmers and gardeners. Traders wheeled their goods to market, then used the barrow as a stall. They sold a variety of goods, such as seeds, grain, plants and dried herbs.

2 Turn the base over. Cut two 2cm x 1cm pieces of thick card. Make a small hole in the middle of each, for the wheel axle. Glue pieces to base.

3 Use compasses and a pencil to draw 1 circle around centre of wheel and 1 close to the rim. Mark on spokes. Paint spaces between spokes black.

4 Paint the barrow, leave to dry. Cut two 7cm balsa strips with tapered ends to make legs, and paint them brown. When dry, glue to bottom of barrow.

5 Feed dowel axle between axle supports, via 2 washers, wheel, and 2 more washers. Dab glue on ends of axle to keep the wheel in place.

Extraordinary Chinese Engineering

THE ENGINEERING WONDER of ancient China was the Great
Wall. It was known as *Wan Li Chang Cheng*, or the Wall of
Ten Thousand *Li* (a unit of length). The Great Wall's main
length was an incredible 6,400km. Work began on the wall in
the 400s BC and lasted until the AD1500s. Its purpose was to
protect China's borders from the fierce tribes who lived to the
north. Despite this intention, Mongol invaders managed to
breach its defences time after time. However, the Great Wall did
serve as a useful communications route. It also extended the
Chinese Empire's control over a very long distance.

The Grand Canal is another engineering project that amazes
us today. It was started in the 400s BC, but was mostly built
during the Sui Dynasty (AD581–618). Its aim was to link the
north of China with the rice-growing regions in the south via
the Chang Jiang (Yangzi River). It is still in use and runs
northwards from Hangzhou to Beijing, a distance of 1,794 km.
Other great engineering feats were made by Chinese mining
engineers, who were already digging deep mine shafts with
drainage and ventilation systems in about 160BC.

LIFE IN THE SALT MINES
Workers busily excavate and purify
salt from an underground mine.
Inside a tower *(shown bottom left)*
you can see workers using a pulley
to raise baskets of mined salt. The
picture comes from a relief (raised
carving) found inside a Han dynasty
tomb in the province of Sichuan.

MINING ENGINEERING
A Qing Dynasty official tours an
open-cast coalmine in the 1800s.
China has rich natural resources
and may have been the first
country in the world to mine coal
to burn as a fuel. Coal was
probably discovered in about
200BC in what is now Jiangxi
province. Other mines extracted
metals and valuable minerals
needed for the great empire. In
the Han dynasty, engineers
invented methods of drilling
boreholes to extract brine (salty
water) from the ground. They
also used derricks (rigid frame-
works) to support iron drills –
over 1,800 years before engineers
in other parts of the world.

HARD LABOUR
Chinese peasants use their spades to dig roads instead of fields. Imperial China produced its great building and engineering works without the machines we rely on today. For big projects, workforces could number hundreds of thousands. Dangerous working conditions and a harsh climate killed many labourers.

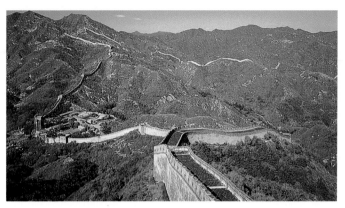

BUILDING THE WALL
The Great Wall snakes over mountain ridges at Badaling, to the northwest of Beijing. The Great Wall and Grand Canal were built by millions of workers. All men aged between 23 and 56 were called up to work on them for one month each year. Only noblemen and civil servants were exempt.

A GRAND OPENING
This painting from the 1700s imagines the Sui emperor Yangdi opening the first stage of the Grand Canal. Most of the work on this massive engineering project was carried out from AD605–609. A road was also built along the route. The transport network built up during the Sui dynasty (AD561–618) enabled food and other supplies to be moved easily from one part of the empire to another.

THE CITY OF SIX THOUSAND BRIDGES
The reports about China supposedly made by Marco Polo in the 1200s described 6,000 bridges in the city of Suzhou. The Baodai Bridge *(shown above)* is one of them. It has 53 arches and was built between AD618 and AD906 to run across the Grand Canal.

Chinese Science

From the Chinese Empire's earliest days, scholars published studies on medicine, astronomy and mathematics. The Chinese system of medicine had a similar aim to that of Daoist teachings, in that it attempted to make the body work harmoniously. The effects of all kinds of herbs, plants and animal parts were studied and then used to produce medicines. Acupuncture, which involves piercing the body with fine needles, was practised from about 2700BC. It is believed to release blocked channels of energy and so relieve pain.

The Chinese were also excellent mathematicians, and from 300BC they used a decimal system of counting based on tens. They may

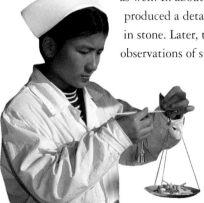

have invented the abacus, an early form of calculator, as well. In about 3000BC, Chinese astronomers produced a detailed chart of the heavens carved in stone. Later, they were the first to record observations of sunspots and exploding stars.

NEW ILLS, OLD REMEDIES
A pharmacist weighs out a traditional medicine. Hundreds of medicines used in China today go back to ancient times. Many are herbal remedies later proved to work by scientists. Doctors are still researching their uses. Other traditional medicines are of less certain value, but are still popular purchases at street stalls.

PRICKING POINTS
Acupuncturists used charts to show exactly where to position their needles. The vital *qi* (energy) is thought to flow through the body along 12 lines called meridians. The health of the patient is judged by taking their pulse. Chinese acupuncture is practised all over the world today.

MAKE AN ABACUS
You will need: thick and thin card, ruler, pencil, scissors, wood glue and brush, masking tape, self-drying clay, cutting board, modelling tool, 30cm x 0.5cm dowel (x11), paintbrush, water pot, brown paint.

Side A (x2) — 32cm, 3cm
Edge A (x2) — 32cm / 30cm, 0.5cm
Side B (x2) — 16cm, 3cm
Edge B (x2) — 16cm / 15cm, 0.5cm
Base — 32cm, 10cm
Divider — 30cm, 3cm 0.5cm
Divider edge

Using the above measurements, cut out pieces from thick brown card and thin grey card. (pieces not shown to scale).

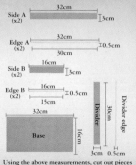

1 Glue sides A and B to the base. Hold the edges with masking tape until dry. Then glue edges A and B to the tops of the sides, as shown.

2 Roll the clay into a 2cm diameter sausage. Cut it into 77 small, flat beads. Make a hole through the centre of each bead with a dowel.

NATURAL HEALTH

Roots, seeds, leaves and flowers have been used in Chinese medicine for over 2,000 years. Today, nine out of ten Chinese medicines are herbal remedies. The Chinese yam is used to treat exhaustion. Ginseng root is used to help treat dizzy spells, while mulberry wood is said to lower blood pressure.

Chinese yam

ginseng root

A STREET DOCTOR PEDDLES HIS WARES

This European view of Chinese medicine dates from 1843. It shows snakes and all sorts of unusual potions being sold on the streets. The doctor is telling the crowd of miraculous cures.

BURNING CURES

A country doctor treats a patient with traditional techniques during the Song dynasty. Chinese doctors relieved pain by heating parts of the body with the burning leaves of a plant called moxa (mugwort). The process is called moxibustion.

The abacus is an ancient counting frame that acts as a simple but very effective calculator. Using an abacus, Chinese mathematicians and merchants could carry out very difficult calculations quickly and easily.

3 Make 11 evenly spaced holes in the divider. Edge one side with thin card. Thread a dowel through each hole. Paint all of the abacus parts. Leave to dry.

4 Thread 7 beads on to each dowel rod – 2 on the upper side of the divider, 5 on the lower. Carefully fit the beads and rods into the main frame.

5 Each upper bead on the abacus equals 5 lower beads in the same column. Each lower bead is worth 10 of the lower beads in the column to its right.

6 Here is a simple sum. To calculate 5+3, first move down one upper bead (worth 5). Then move 3 lower beads in the same column up (each worth 1).

Specialist Crafts in Japan

FROM ANCIENT TIMES, the finest quality craftsmanship was important in Japan. Although paper was invented in China, in 105AD, when the Japanese started papermaking 500 years later, they raised it to a craft of the highest level. Different papers were made into both luxury and everyday objects – from wall-screens and lanterns to clothes, windows and partitions in houses.

Working with wood was another Japanese speciality. Doorways, pillars and roofs on most large Japanese buildings, such as temples and palaces, were elaborately carved or painted, or even gilded. Inside, beams and pillars were made from strong tree trunks, floors were laid with polished wooden strips, and sliding screens had fine wooden frames. A display of woodworking skill in a building demonstrated the owner's wealth and power. However, some smaller wooden buildings were left deliberately plain, allowing the quality of the materials and craftsmanship, and the elegance of the design, to speak for themselves.

WOODEN STATUES
This statue of a Buddhist god was carved between AD800 and 900. Many powerful sculptures were inspired by religion at this time.

SCREENS WITH SCENES
Screens were movable works of art as well as providing privacy and protection from draughts. This screen of the 1700s shows Portuguese merchants and missionaries listening to Japanese musicians.

ORIGAMI BOX
You will need: a square of origami paper (15cm x 15cm), clean and even folding surface.

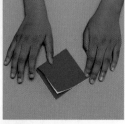

1 Place your paper on a flat surface. Fold it horizontally across the centre. Next fold it vertically across the centre and unfold.

2 Carefully fold each corner to the centre point as shown. Unfold each corner crease before starting to make the next one.

3 Using the creases, fold all the corners back into the centre. Now fold each side 2cm from the edge to make a crease and then unfold.

GRAND PILLARS

This row of red wooden pillars supports a heavy, ornate roof. It is part of the Meiji Shrine in Tokyo. Red (or cinnabar) was the traditional Japanese colour for shrines and royal palaces.

HOLY LIGHTS

Lamps of pleated paper were often hung outside Shinto shrines. They were painted with the names of people who had donated money to the shrines.

PAPER ART

Paper-making and calligraphy (beautiful writing) were two very important craft forms in Japan. These people have everything they need to decorate scrolls. Fine paper showed off a letter-writer's elegance and good taste.

PAPER RANGE

For artists such as the painter of this picture, Ando Hiroshige (1797-1858), the choice of paper was as important as the painting itself. The Japanese developed a great range of specialist papers.

Making boxes is a specialist craft in Japan. Boxes were used for storing all sorts of possessions.

4 Carefully unfold two opposite side panels. Your origami box should now look like the structure shown in the picture above.

5 Following the crease marks you have already made, turn in the side panels to make walls, as shown in the picture. Turn the origami round 90°.

6 Use your fingers to push the corners of the third side in, as shown. Use the existing crease lines as a guide. Raise the box slightly and fold the wall over.

7 Next, carefully repeat step 6 to construct the final wall. You could try making another origami box to perfect your technique.

Fine Celtic Crafts

THE CELTS WERE A PROUD people to whom appearance was important. Beautiful objects carried important messages about their owner's wealth and power. From written descriptions of their clothes, we know that the Celts were skilled weavers and dyers. While the Roman invaders of their lands wore togas and tunics, the Celtic men were wearing trousers. Celtic craftworkers made finely worked jewellery, applying their expert glassmaking, enamelling and metalworking skills. They were also excellent potters. Some decorations have magic or religious meanings to protect people from harm or to inspire warriors setting off to war.

We do not know much about the craftworkers themselves. They may have been free and independent or the skilled slaves of wealthy families. However, towards the end of the Celtic period, around 60BC, many craftworkers worked in *oppida* (fortified towns) instead of in country villages.

SMOOTH AND SHAPELY
Tall, graceful vases with smoothly curving sides were a speciality of Celtic potters working in France. They date mostly from the La Tène era (450–50BC). Pots like these were produced on a potter's wheel. They were prestige goods, produced for wealthy or noble families.

ANGULAR ART
During the Hallstatt era (750–450BC), Celtic potters decorated their wares with spiky, angular designs like the patterns on this pottery dish. After about 500BC, when compasses were introduced into Celtic lands from countries near the Mediterranean Sea, designs based on curves and circles began to replace patterns made up of angles and straight lines.

MAKE A TORC
You will need: board, modelling clay, ruler, string, scissors, pva glue and brush, gold or bronze paint, paintbrush.

1 On the board, roll out two lengths of modelling clay, as shown. Each length should be approximately 60cm long and about 1cm thick.

2 Keeping the two lengths of clay on the board, plait them together. Leave about 5cm of the clay unplaited at either end, as shown.

3 Make loops out of the free ends by joining them together. Dampen the ends with a little water to help join the clay if necessary.

GLASS JEWELS

Glass was made from salt, crushed limestone and sand, and coloured by adding powdered minerals. Craftworkers melted and twisted different coloured strands together to make jewel-like beads. Glass paste was applied to metalwork and fired to bond it to the metal in a process called enamelling.

manganese *glass* *cobalt* *lead*

PRECIOUS BOX

This gold and silver box was made in Scotland and was designed to hold Christian holy relics. It was associated with the Irish monk and Christian missionary St Columba. After the saint's death, it was kept as a lucky talisman (charm), and carried into battle by Scottish armies.

MAKING WAVES

The sides of this pot are decorated with a moulded pattern of overlapping waves. The pot has survived unbroken from the La Tène era over 2,000 years ago. It was found in France and it is made from fired clay. Celtic potters built elaborate kilns to fire (bake) their pots at high temperatures.

ELEGANT ENAMEL

This bronze plaque is decorated with red and yellow enamel. It was made in southern Britain around 50BC and was designed to be worn on a horse's harness.

Torcs were status symbols for the Celtic people. They were made from precious metals such as iron, bronze and gold.

4 With the ruler, measure an opening between the two looped ends. The ends should be about 9cm apart so that the torc fits easily around your neck.

5 When the torc is semi-dry, cut two pieces of string about 8cm long. Use the string to decorate the torc's looped ends. Glue the string in place.

6 Allow the clay to dry completely. When it is hard, cover all the clay and string with gold or bronze paint. Leave to dry.

Celtic Metalworkers

CELTIC METALWORKERS EXCELLED in several different techniques. They were among the most important people in Celtic society because they made many of the items that Celtic people valued most, from bronze and iron swords to beautiful gold jewellery. Patterns and techniques invented in one part of the Celtic world were copied and quickly spread to other parts. Designs were sketched on to the back of the metal, then gently hammered from beneath to create raised patterns. The technique was called repoussé (pushed out).

It took several years to learn all the necessary skills, and metalworkers probably began their training very young. They extracted iron from raw nuggets or lumps of ore in a very hot fire, and then forged the red-hot metal into shape. The Celts were the first to shoe horses, and invented seamless iron rims for chariot wheels to strengthen them.

PUSHED OUT DESIGN
This bronze shieldboss was made between about 200BC and 10BC. A boss is the metal plate that was fixed to the centre of a shield to protect the hand of the person holding it. The raised pattern was created by pressing out the design in the thin covering sheet of metal from behind. The technique is called repoussé (pushed out).

TOOLS OF THE TRADE
Many bronze items, such as this horse's bit (below) and harness-ring (far left), were made by pouring molten metal into clay moulds, then leaving it to cool and become solid. You can also see fragments of the clay moulds, and the little crucible used for melting the bronze (top left).

MAKE A MIRROR
You will need: pair of compasses, pencil, ruler, stiff gold mirror card, scissors, tracing paper, pen, modelling clay, board, gold paint, paintbrush, pva glue.

1 With the compasses, draw a circle 22 cm wide on to gold card. Cut out. Use this circle as a template to draw a second circle on to gold card.

2 Cut out the second gold circle. Draw another circle on tracing paper. Fold the piece of tracing paper in two and draw a Celtic pattern in pencil.

3 Lay the tracing paper on to one of the circles. Trace the pattern on to half of the gold circle, then turn the paper over and repeat. Go over the pattern with a pen.

FROM EARTH AND SEA

The most valuable materials for metalworking were difficult and sometimes dangerous to find. Silver ore was dug from mines underground, or from veins in rocks on the surface. Miners searched for nuggets of gold in gravel at the bottom of fast-flowing streams. Swimmers and divers hunted for coral that grew on little reefs in the Mediterranean Sea.

bronze ore

coral

gold nuggets

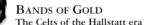

BANDS OF GOLD

The Celts of the Hallstatt era (750–450BC) liked to wear bold, dramatic jewellery, such as the armband and ankle rings shown here. They were found in a tomb in central France. Both the armband and the ankle rings were made of sheets of pure gold and twisted gold wire which were carefully hammered and soldered together.

DELICATE DESIGN

This clothing toggle was created using the lost wax method of casting. The shape of the piece was modelled in beeswax, then the fine details were added. The wax model was covered with a thick layer of clay. Then the clay-covered model was heated, and the wax ran out. Finally, molten gold was poured into the space where the wax had been.

TOOLS OF THE TRADE

These little bone spatulas (knives for scooping and spreading) were used by metalworkers to add fine details to the surface of wax models when casting bronze objects using the lost wax process.

The bronze on a Celtic mirror would have polished up so that the owner could see his or her reflection in it.

4 Roll out several snakes of modelling clay and sculpt them into a handle, as shown here. The handle should be about 15 cm long and 9 cm wide.

5 Leave the modelling clay to dry. Then paint one side of the handle with gold paint. Leave to dry, then turn over and paint the other side.

6 Stick the two pieces of mirror card together, white side to white side. Glue the handle on to one side of the mirror.

Viking Crafts

SNARL OF THE DRAGON
This masterpiece of wood carving and metalwork is a dragon-head post. It is from the Oseberg ship burial in Norway and dates from about 850. Its patterns include monsters known as 'gripping beasts'.

I N EVERY VIKING HOME, people turned their hand to craft work. The men made and repaired tools and weapons. They carved walrus ivory and wood during long winter evenings. The women made woollen cloth. They washed and combed the wool and then placed it on a long stick called a distaff. The wool was pulled out and spun into yarn on a whirling stick called a spindle. The yarn was woven on a loom, a large upright frame. Blacksmiths' furnaces roared and hammers clanged against anvils as the metal was shaped and re-shaped. Professional craftworkers worked gold, silver, bronze and pewter – a mixture of tin and lead. They made fine jewellery from amber and from a glassy black stone called jet. Beautiful objects were carved from antlers and ivory from the tusks of walruses. Homes, and later churches, had beautiful wood carvings. Patterns included swirling loops and knots, and birds and animals interlaced with writhing snakes and strange monsters.

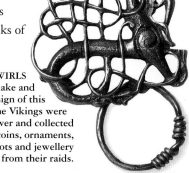

SILVER SWIRLS
Can you see a snake and a beast in the design of this silver brooch? The Vikings were very fond of silver and collected hoardes of coins, ornaments, silver ingots and jewellery from their raids.

MAKE A SILVER BRACELET

You will need: tape measure, self-drying clay, board, scissors, white cord or string, modelling tool, silver acrylic paint, paintbrush, water pot.

1 Measure your wrist with the tape measure to see how big your bracelet should be. Allow room for it to pass over your hand, but not fall off.

2 Roll the clay between the palms of your hand. Make three snakes that are just longer than your wrist measurement. Try to make them of equal thickness.

3 Lay out the three snakes on the board in a fan shape. Cut two lengths of white cord, a bit longer than the snakes, and place them in between.

COLOURS FOR CLOTH

Woollen cloth was dyed in bold colours from leaves, roots, bark and flowers. A wildflower called weld, or dyer's rocket, was used for its yellow dye. The root of the madder gave a red dye. Bright blue came from the leaves of woad plants.

woad   *madder*

THE SMITH AT WORK

This fine wood carving comes from a church in Urnes, Norway. It shows Regin the blacksmith forging a sword on an anvil, for the legendary hero Sigurd. The smith is using bellows to heat up the furnace. The skills of metal working were so important in ancient times that smiths were often seen as magical figures or gods.

TOOLS FROM THE FORGE

Viking blacksmiths used hammers for beating and shaping metal. Tongs were used for handling red-hot iron. Shears were for cutting metal sheets. The blacksmith made everything from nails and knives to farm tools.

Vikings liked to show off their wealth and rank by wearing expensive gold and silver jewellery.

4 While the clay is still soft, plait the snakes of clay and the two cords together. Ask an adult to help if you are not sure how to make a plait.

5 Trim each end of the plait with a modelling tool. At each end, press the strands firmly together and secure with a small clay snake, as shown above.

6 Carefully curl the bracelet round so that it will fit neatly over your wrist, without joining the ends. Leave it in a safe place to harden and dry.

7 When the bracelet is completely dry, paint it silver. Cover the work surface if necessary. Leave the bracelet to dry again – then try it on!

Mesoamerican Time

DIFFERENT CULTURES and civilizations devised different ways of splitting the year into seasons. The Egyptian calendar, based on a 365-day year, was linked to the annual flooding of the River Nile. The Maya and Aztec peoples in Mesoamerica had three different calendars. One, based on a 260-day year, was probably based on the time a baby spends in the womb. It was divided into 13 cycles of 20 days each. The calendar followed by Mesoamerican farmers was based on the movements of the Sun, because the seasons made their crops grow. Its 360-day year was divided into 18 months of 20 days, with five extra days that were considered unlucky. Every 52 years, measured in modern time, the two calendars ended on the same day. For five days before the end of the 52 years, people feared the world might end. There was a third calendar, of 584 days, used for calculating festival days.

SUN STONE
This massive carving was made to display the Aztec view of creation. The Aztecs believed that the world had already been created and destroyed four times and that their Fifth World was also doomed.

STUDYING THE STARS
The Caracol was constructed as an observatory to study the sky. From there, Maya astronomers could observe the planet Venus, which was important in the Mesoamericans' measurement of time.

MAKE A SUN STONE

You will need: pencil, scissors, thick card, self-drying clay, modelling tool, board, rolling pin, masking tape, pva glue, glue brush, water bowl, pencil, thin card, water-based paints, paintbrush, water pot.

1 Cut a circle about 25cm in diameter from thick card. Roll out the clay and cut out a circle, using the card as a guide. Place the clay circle on the card one.

2 With a modelling tool, mark a small circle in the centre of the clay circle. Use a roll of masking tape as a guide. Do not cut through the clay.

3 Carve the Sun-god's eyes, mouth, teeth and earrings. You can use the real Aztec Sun stone, shown at the top left of this page, as a guide.

alligator

wind

house

lizard

NAMES OF DAYS

These pictures from an Aztec codex show the 20 names for days from the farmers' calendar. These symbols were combined with a number from one to 13 to give the date, such as Three Vulture. The days were named after familiar creatures or everyday things, such as the lizard or water. Each day also had its own god. Children were often named after the day on which they were born, a custom that still continues in some parts of Mexico up to the present day.

serpent

death's head

deer

rabbit

water

dog

monkey

grass

Your finished Sun stone will not be as big as the original Aztec one. That measures 4m across and is the largest Aztec sculpture discovered so far.

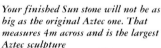

reed

jaguar

eagle

vulture

motion

flint knife

rain

flower

4 Roll out more clay and cut out some Sun's rays, a tongue and eyebrows. Glue them to the clay circle. Smooth the edges with water and leave to dry.

5 Copy the 20 Aztec symbols (*above*) for days on to squares of thin card. The card squares should be no more than 2cm x 2cm. Cut out. Paint brown.

6 Cover the clay circle with a thin coat of dark brown paint. Leave it to dry. Then add a thin coat of white paint to make the circle look like stone.

7 Glue the card symbols evenly around the edge of the clay circle, as shown. Paint the Sun stone with a thin layer of pva glue to seal and varnish it.

Practical Incas

Though the Incas were known for their fine work in precious metals, they also found practical solutions to more everyday needs. They built 24,000km of roads through the mountains of their empire.Their main buildings constructed from giant, many-sided blocks of stone all perfectly interlocking, were earthquake-proof.

Although there was no iron in the mountains, the Incas used many other materials for everyday items. Reeds were woven into baskets and mats from early prehistoric times. Bone, stone and wood were carved into small items such as bowls, pins, spoons and figures. Pottery was made in Peru from about 2000BC, rather later than in the lands to the north and east, and revolutionized the production, storage, transportation and cooking of food. South American potters did not use a wheel to shape their pots, but built them up in layers from coils of clay. The coils were smoothed out by hand or with tools, marked or painted, dried in the sun and then baked hard.

Many of the pre-Incan civilizations of the Andes produced beautifully patterned pottery.

POLISHED WOOD
This fine black *kero* (drinking vessel) was made by an Inca craftsman. It is of carved and polished wood. Timber was always scarce in the Inca Empire, but wood was widely used to make plates and cups. Rearing up over the rim of the beaker is a fierce-looking big cat, perhaps a puma or a jaguar.

MODELLED FROM CLAY
A fierce puma bares his teeth. He was made from pottery between AD500 and 800. The hole in his back was used to waft clouds of incense during religious ceremonies in the city of Tiwanaku, near Lake Titicaca.

A TIWANAKU POTTERY JAGUAR
You will need: chicken wire, wire-cutters, ruler, newspaper, scissors, pva glue, masking tape, flour, water, card, paint, water pot, paintbrush.

1 Cut a rectangle of chicken wire about 14cm long and 20cm wide. Carefully wrap it around to form a sausage shape. Close one end neatly.

2 Squeeze the other end of the sausage to form the jaguar's neck and head. Fold over the wire at the end to make a neat, round shape for his nose.

3 Make rolls of newspaper about 2.5cm long to form the jaguar's legs. Use strips of paper and glue to join them securely to the jaguar's body as shown.

PRETTY POLLY

This pottery jar, like many from Peru, comes with a handle and a spout. It is shaped and painted to look like a parrot and was made, perhaps 1,000 years before the Incas, by the Nazca potters of southern Peru.

shells   sand

clay

WATER OF LIFE

This Inca bottle is carved with a figure inside a tower collecting water. No community could survive very long without a good supply of fresh water. Many pots, bottles and beakers from the South American civilizations are decorated with light-hearted scenes of everyday activities. They give us a vivid idea of how people used to live.

The handle and spout design of your Tiwanaku jaguar is known as a stirrup pot, because the arrangement looks rather like the stirrup of a horse.

4 Mix the flour and water to a paste. Use it to glue a layer of newspaper strips all over the jaguar's body. Allow this layer to dry. You will need 3 layers.

5 Cut ears from card. Fix on with masking tape. Tape on rolls of newspaper to make the handle, spout and tail as in the finished pot above.

6 Leave the model in a warm and airy place to dry. Then paint it all over with reddish brown paint. Allow the paint to dry completely.

7 Use black paint and a fine brush to decorate the jaguar as shown in the picture. When the paint is dry, varnish with pva glue if you wish.

Inca Mining and Metalwork

THERE WERE RESOURCES OF gold and silver in the Andes mountains and the Inca peoples became expert at working these precious metals into fabulous vessels, jewellery and life-sized figures of animals. Copper was mined for weapons. Metalworkers were highly respected members of Inca communities. A stone bowl that was discovered in the Andahuaylas Valley was nearly 3,500 years old. It contained metalworking equipment and finely beaten gold foil.

The Incas often referred to gold as 'sweat of the Sun' and to silver as 'tears of the Moon'. These metals were sacred to the gods and also to the Inca emperor and empress. At the Temple of the Sun in the city of Cuzco, there was a whole garden made of gold and silver, with golden soil, golden stalks of maize and golden llamas. Copper was used by ordinary people. It was made into cheap jewellery, weapons and everyday tools. The Incas' love of gold and silver eventually led to their downfall, for it was rumours of their fabulous wealth that lured the Spanish to invade the region.

A SICAN LORD

This ceremonial knife with its crescent-shaped blade is called a *tumi*. Its gold handle is made in the shape of a nobleman or ruler. He wears an elaborate headdress and large discs in his ears. It was made between 1100 and 1300. The knife is in the style of the Sican civilization, which grew up after the decline of the Moche civilization in the AD700s.

A CHIMÚ DOVE

Chimú goldsmiths, the best in the Empire, made this plump dove. When the Incas conquered Chimor in 1470, they forced many thousands of skilled craftsmen from the city of Chan Chan to resettle in the Cuzco area and continue their work.

A TUMI KNIFE

You will need: card, ruler, pencil, scissors, self-drying clay, cutting board, rolling pin, modelling and cutting tools, pva glue, gold paint, paintbrush, water pot, blue metallic paper.

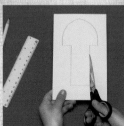

1 On card, draw a knife shape as shown and cut it out. The rectangular part should be 9cm x 3.5cm. The rounded part is 7cm across and 4.5cm high.

2 Roll out a slab of clay about 1cm thick. Draw a *tumi* shape on it as shown. It should be 12.5cm long and measure 9cm across the widest part at the top.

3 Use the cutting tool to cut around the shape you have drawn. Carefully take away the leftover clay. Make sure the edges are clean and smooth.

MINERAL WEALTH

To this day, the Andes are very rich in minerals. The Incas worked with gold, silver, platinum and copper. They knew how to make alloys, which are mixtures of different metals. Bronze was made by mixing copper and tin. However, unlike their Spanish conquerors, the Incas knew nothing of iron and steel. This put them at a disadvantage when fighting the Europeans.

copper   *silver*

gold

PANNING FOR GOLD

A boy labourer in modern Colombia pans for gold. Some Inca gold was mined, but large amounts also came from panning mountain rivers and streams in the Andes. The river bed was loosened with sticks, and then the water was sifted through shallow trays in search of any flecks of the precious metal that had been washed downstream.

INCA FIGURES

Small ritual figures of women and men from about 6cm high were often made in the Inca period. They were hammered from sheets of silver and gold and were dressed in miniature versions of adult clothing. They have been found on mountain-top shrine sites in the south-central Andes, in carved stone boxes in Lake Titicaca and at important temples.

The Chimú gold and turquoise tumi was used by priests at religious ceremonies. It may have been used to kill sacrifices.

4 Cut a slot into the bottom edge of the clay shape. Lifting it carefully, slide the knife blade into the slot. Use glue to make the joint secure.

5 Use a modelling tool to mark the details of the god on to the clay. Look at the finished knife above to see how to do this. Leave everything to dry.

6 When the clay has hardened, paint the whole knife with gold paint. Leave it to dry completely before painting the other side as well.

7 The original knife was decorated with turquoise. Glue small pieces of blue metallic paper on to the handle as shown in the picture above.

Inca Medicine and Magic

LIKE MOST PEOPLES in the world five hundred years ago, the Incas and their neighbours had some idea of science or medicine. However, curing people was believed to be chiefly a matter of religious rituals and magical spells. No doubt some of these did help people to feel better. Curing sick people was the job either of priests, or of the local healer or medicine man.

As in Europe at that time, Inca healers used fasting and blood-letting (allowing blood to flow from a cut) for many cures. They also tried blood transfusion (putting new blood into someone's body). They succeeded in this far earlier than doctors in other parts of the world, because peoples of the Andes shared the same blood group. The Incas could also set broken bones, amputate limbs, treat wounds and pull teeth. Medicines were made from herbs, roots, leaves and powders.

THE MEDICINE MAN
This Moche healer or priest, from about AD500, seems to be going into a trance and listening to the voices of spirits or gods. He may be trying to cure a sick patient, or he may be praying over the patient's dead body.

MAGIC DOLLS
Model figures like this one, made from cotton and reed, are often found in ancient graves in the Chancay River region. They are often called dolls, but it seems unlikely that they were ever used as toys. They were probably believed to have magical qualities. The Chancay people may have believed that the dolls helped the dead person in another world.

CARRYING COCA
Small bags like these were used for carrying medicines and herbs, especially coca. The leaves of the coca plant were widely used to stimulate the body and to kill pain. Coca is still widely grown in the Andes today. It is used to make the illegal drug cocaine.

MEDICINE BAG

You will need: scissors, cream calico fabric, pencil, ruler, paintbrush, water pot, acrylic or fabric paints, black, yellow, green and red wool, pva glue, needle and thread, masking tape.

1 Cut two 20cm squares of fabric. Draw a pattern of stripes and diamonds on the fabric and use acrylic or fabric paints to colour them.

2 For the tassels, cut about 10 pieces of wool 8cm long. Fold a piece of wool 15cm long in half. Loop it around each tassel as shown above.

3 Wind a matching piece of wool, 50cm long, around the end of the tassel. When you have finished, knot the wool and tuck the ends inside.

HERBAL REMEDIES

Drugs widely used in ancient Peru included the leaves of tobacco and coca plants. A yellow-flowered plant called calceolaria was used to cure infections. Cinchona bark produced quinine, a medicine we use today to treat malaria. That illness only arrived in South America after the Spanish conquest. However, quinine was used earlier to treat fevers. Suppliers of herbal medicines were known as *hampi kamayuq*.

cinchona tree   tobacco plant

SKULL SURGERY

Nazca surgeons were able to carry out an operation called trepanation. This involved drilling a hole in the patient's skull in an attempt to relieve pressure on the brain. The Incas believed this released evil spirits. A small silver plate was sometimes fitted over the hole as a protection.

Doctor on call! An Inca medicine chest took the form of a woven bag, carried on the shoulder.

A BAD OMEN

A comet shoots across the night sky. The Incas believed such sights would bring plague or disease in their wake. Other common causes of illness were believed to include witchcraft, evil spirits and a failure to please the gods. People tried to make themselves better by making offerings to the gods at *waq'as* (local shrines). Healers used charms or spells to keep their patients free from evil spirits.

4 Make nine tassels in all. Place them in groups of three along the bottom of the unpainted side of one of the pieces of fabric. Use glue to fix them in place.

5 Allow the glue to dry. Place the unpainted sides of the fabric pieces together. Sew around the edges as shown. Leave the top edge open.

6 Make a strap by plaiting together strands of wool as shown. Cross each outer strand in turn over the middle strand. Tape will help keep the work steady.

7 Knot the ends of the strap firmly. Attach them to both sides of the top of the bag with glue. Make sure the glue is dry before you pick the bag up.

Calculations Inca-style

INCA MATHEMATICIANS used a decimal system, counting in tens. To help with their arithmetic, people placed pebbles or grains of maize in counting frames. These had up to twenty sections. *Quipu* strings were also used to record numbers. Strings were knotted to represent units, tens, hundreds, thousands or even tens of thousands.

The Incas worked out calendars of twelve months by observing the Sun, Moon and stars as they moved across the sky. They knew that these movements marked regular changes in the seasons. They used the calendar to tell them when to plant crops. Inca priests set up stone pillars outside the city of Cuzco to measure the movements of the Sun.

As in Europe at that time, astronomy, the study of the stars, was confused with astrology, which is the belief that the stars and planets influence human lives. Incas saw the night sky as being lit up by gods and mythical characters.

FORTUNES FROM THE STARS AND PLANETS
An Inca astrologer observes the position of the Sun. The Incas believed that careful watching of the stars and planets revealed their influence on our lives. For example, the star pattern or constellation that we call the Lyre was known to the Incas as the Llama. It was believed that it influenced llamas and those who herded them.

THE SUN STONE
A stone pillar called *Inti Watana* (Tethering Post of the Sun) stood at the eastern edge of the great square in Machu Picchu. It was like a giant sundial and the shadows it cast confirmed the movements of the Sun across the sky – a matter of great practical and religious importance.

A QUIPU

You will need: scissors, rope and string of various thicknesses, a 90cm length of thick rope, paints, paintbrush, water pot.

1 Cut the rope and string into about 15 lengths measuring from 20cm to 80cm. Paint them in various bright colours. Leave them to dry completely.

2 To make the top part of the *quipu*, take a piece of thick rope, about 90cm long. Tie a knot in each end as shown in the picture above.

3 Next, take pieces of thinner rope or string of various lengths and colours. Tie them along the thicker rope, so that they all hang on the same side.

THE MILKY WAY

On dark nights, Inca priests looked for the band of stars that we call the Milky Way. They called it *Mayu* (Heavenly River) and used it to make calculations about seasons and weather conditions. In its darker spaces they saw the shadow of the Rain god Apu Illapu. The shape of the Milky Way was believed to mirror that of the Inca Empire.

KEEPERS OF THE QUIPU

Vast amounts of information could be stored on a *quipu*. A large one might have up to 2,000 cords. The *quipu* was rather like an Inca version of the computer, only the memory had to be provided by the operator's brain rather than a silicon chip. Learning the *quipu* code of colours, knots, and major and minor strings took many years. Expert operators were called *quipu-kamayuq*.

SUN WATCH

The *Inti Watana* (Tethering Post of the Sun) at Machu Picchu was one of many Sun stones across the Empire. *Sukana* (stone pillars) near Cuzco showed midsummer and midwinter sun positions. The Sun god, Inti, was believed to live in the north and go south each summer.

You have now designed a simple quipu. Can you imagine designing a system that would record the entire population of a town, their ages, the taxes they have paid and the taxes they owe? The Incas did just that!

4 Tie knots in the thinner ropes or strings. One knot you might like to try begins by making a loop of rope as shown in the picture above.

5 Pass one end of the rope through the loop. Pull the rope taut but don't let go of the loop. Repeat this step until you have a long knot. Pull it tight.

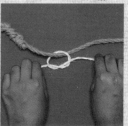

6 Make different sizes of knots on all the ropes or strings. Each knot could represent a family member, school lesson or other important detail.

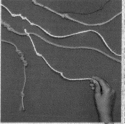

7 Add some more strings to the knotted strings. Your *quipu* may be seen by lots of people. Only you will know what the ropes, strings and knots mean!

Tribal Crafts in North America

NORTH AMERICAN INDIANS were expert craftsmen and women. Beautiful pots have been found dating back to around 1000BC. The people of the Southwest were renowned for their pottery. Black and white Mimbres bowls were known as burial pots because they were broken when their owner died and buried along with the body. Baskets and blankets were the other most important crafts. The ancient Anasazis were known as the basket-making culture because of the range of baskets they produced. Some were coiled so tightly they could hold water. The Apaches coiled large, flat baskets from willow and plant fibre, and the Paiutes made cone baskets, which were hung on their backs for collecting food. All North American Indians made use of the materials they had to hand such as wood, bark, shells, porcupine quills, feathers, bones, metals, hide and clay.

BASKET WEAVER
A native Arizona woman is creating a traditional coiled basket. It might be used for holding food or to wear on someone's head. Tlingit and Nootka tribes from the Northwest Coast were among those who wore cone-shaped basket hats.

POTTERY
Zuni people in the Southwest created beautiful pots such as this one. They used baskets as moulds for the clay or coiled thin rolls of clay around in a spiral. Afterwards, they smoothed out the surface with water. Birds and animals were favourite decorations.

DRILLING WALRUS TUSKS
An Inuit craftsman is working on a piece of ivory. He is using a drill to etch a pattern. The drill bit is kept firmly in place by his chin. This way, his hands are free to move the bow in a sawing action, pushing the drill point into the ivory.

MAKE A TANKARD

You will need: air-drying modelling clay, board, water in pot, pencil, ruler, cream or white and black poster paints or acrylic paints, fine and ordinary paintbrushes, non-toxic varnish.

1 Roll out a round slab of clay and press it into a flat circle with a diameter of about 10cm. Now, roll out two long sausage shapes of clay.

2 Slightly dampen the edges of the clay circle. Place one end of the clay sausage on the edge of the circle and coil it around. Carry on spiralling around.

3 Continue coiling with the other clay sausage. Then, use your dampened fingers to smooth the coils into a good tankard shape and smooth the outside.

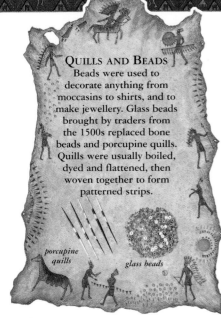

QUILLS AND BEADS

Beads were used to decorate anything from moccasins to shirts, and to make jewellery. Glass beads brought by traders from the 1500s replaced bone beads and porcupine quills. Quills were usually boiled, dyed and flattened, then woven together to form patterned strips.

porcupine quills

glass beads

TALKING BLANKET

It could take half a year for a Tlingit woman to make one of the famous Chilkat blankets. She wove cedar bark fibre and mountain goat wool with her fingers. The Tlingits said that if you knew how to listen, the blankets could talk.

FRUITS OF THE LOOM

Striped blankets were the speciality of Indians in the Southwest. This Hopi woman is using an upright loom made from poles. Pueblo people were the first North American Indians to weave like this.

Each tribe had its own pottery designs and colours. These geometric patterns were common in the Southwest.

4 Roll out another, small sausage shape of clay to make a handle. Dampen the ends and press it on to the clay pot in a handle shape. Leave to dry out.

5 Using a sharp pencil, mark out the design you want on your jug. You can follow the traditional indian pattern or make up your own.

6 Using poster paints or acrylic paints, colour in the pattern on the mug. Use a fine-tipped brush to create the tiny checked patterns and thin lines.

7 When the paint is dry, coat your mug in one or two layers of non-toxic varnish using an ordinary paintbrush. This will protect it.

Glossary

A

abacus A wooden frame with beads on rods, used for calculating.

acupuncture The treatment of the body with fine needles to relieve pain or cure illness.

alabaster A white stone used for making ornaments.

alloy A mixture of metals melted together to create a new metal that may be stronger or easier to work.

Althing An assembly of free men that passed laws in Iceland at the time of the Vikings.

amphitheatre An oval open-air arena surrounded by seats, used for public shows such as gladiator fights.

ancestor A member of the same family who died long ago.

Anno Domini (AD) A system used to calculate dates after the supposed year of Christ's birth. Anno Domini dates in this book are prefixed AD up to the year 1000 (e.g. AD521). After 1000 no prefixes are used (e.g. 1929).

anvil A heavy iron block on which metal objects can be hammered into shape.

aqueduct A channel for carrying water over long distances.

archaeologist Someone who studies ancient ruins and artefacts to learn about the past.

archaeology The scientific study of the past looking at the things people left behind, such as tools.

aristocracy A ruling class of wealthy, privileged people, or government by such people.

artefact An object that has been preserved from the past.

astrology The belief that stars, planets and other heavenly bodies shape our lives.

astronomy The scientific study of stars, planets and other heavenly bodies. In ancient times it was often mixed up with astrology.

auxiliaries Soldiers recruited from non-Roman citizens.

B

barbarians Wild, rough and uncivilized people. The word was invented in ancient Greece to describe foreign people, whose lifestyle was different to their own.

barter The exchange of goods, one for the other.

Before Christ (BC) The system used to calculate dates before the supposed year of Christ's birth. Dates are calculated in reverse (e.g. 2000BC is longer ago than 200BC). After 1000 no prefixes are used (e.g. 1929).

bellows A mechanism for pumping air into a fire or furnace.

Brahmin A high-status Hindu, often a priest.

brazier A metal stand for holding burning coals.

bronze A metal alloy, made by mixing copper with tin.

Buddhism World religion founded in ancient India by the Buddha in the 6th century BC.

burin A chisel-like flint tool.

C

campaign A series of battles fought by a ruler to bring an area under his control.

cartouche The oval border used in Egyptian hieroglyphs to show that the name it contains is a pharaoh or a god.

catapult A large wooden structure used during a siege to fire stones and iron bolts at the enemy.

causeway A raised walkway.

cavalry Soldiers on horseback.

century A unit of the Roman army, numbering from 80 to 100 soldiers.

chainmail Small rings of metal that are linked together to form a fine mesh, which is used to protect the body during battle.

circa (*c.*) Approximately. The symbol *c.* is used when the exact date of something is not known.

citizen A free person with the right to vote.

city-state A city and the area surrounding it which is controlled by one leader or government.

civil servant Official who carries out administrative duties for a government.

civilization A society that makes advances in arts, sciences, law, technology and government.

clan A group of people related to each other by ancestry or marriage.

cohort A division of the Roman army, at times numbering about 500 soldiers.

colonies Communities or groups of people who settle in another land, but still keep links with their own country.

colony A group of people who settle in another land, but still keep links with their own country.

Confucianism The Western name for the teachings of the philosopher Kong Fuzi (Confucius), which call for social order and respect for one's family and ancestors.

conscript Someone who is called up by the government to serve in the army.

conscription A term of service to the State, in which people have to work as labourers or soldiers.

consul One of two leaders of the Roman Republic elected each year.

coracle A small boat made of leather stretched over a wooden frame.

crossbow A mechanical bow that fires small arrows called bolts.

cubit A unit of measurement, the length of a forearm.

cuirass Armour that protects the upper part of the body.

cuneiform The first system of writing. It was invented by the Sumerians of Mesopotamia.

currency Form of exchange for goods such as money.

cylinder seal A small stone with a raised or sunken pattern. It could be rolled across soft clay to leave an impression. Seals identified the goods belonging to a person.

D

daimyo A Japanese noble or warlord.

Danegeld Money paid to Vikings by English or French rulers to prevent their lands being attacked.

democracy Government by the many, in which every citizen has the right to vote and hold public office.

descendant Person who is descended from an individual or group of people who lived earlier.

dictator A ruler with complete and unrestricted power.

distil The process of heating liquid to boiling point and collecting the condensed steam to make a purer liquid. Alcoholic spirits are made in this way.

druid A Celtic priest.

dugout canoe A canoe made by hollowing out a tree trunk.

dynasty A period of rule by the same royal family.

E

edict An order from a ruler or a government.

electrum A mixture of gold and silver, used for making coins.

emperor The ruler of an empire.

empire A group of lands ruled or governed by a single country.

enamel A hard, coloured glass-like substance, applied as a decorative or protective covering to metal or glass.

estate A large amount of land, houses and farms, usually owned by a single person or group.

evolution The changes that take place in a human, animal or plant species over millions of years, as it becomes more complex.

excavation A place where archaeologists are digging up the ground in order to discover more about the past.

F

federal Central government of a federation (a group).

feud A long-standing quarrel, especially between two families.

firing The process of baking clay or glass paste in a kiln to harden it and make it waterproof.

frontier A boundary between two countries.

G

galley A warship powered by oars.

garrison A band of soldiers living in a particular place.

geometric pattern A pattern made by lines, circles and triangles.

geometry A branch of mathematics concerning the measurements of lines, angles and surfaces.

gilding The process of applying a thin layer of gold, to metal or pottery.

gladiator A professional fighter, a slave or a criminal who in Rome, fought to death for entertainment.

government The way in which a country or state is ruled.

greaves Armour for the legs.

groma An instrument used by Roman surveyors to measure right angles and straight lines.

guilds Groups of skilled workers who check quality standards, train young people and look after old and sick members.

H

haft The handle of an axe.

harpoon A spear-like weapon with a detachable head that is tied to a line.

herbalism A method of healing people by using medicines made from plants.

hieroglyph A picture symbol used in writing.

hilt The handle of a sword.

Homo sapiens (wise man) The species to which all modern humans belong.

human sacrifice Killing people as an offering to the gods.

hunter-gatherer A person whose way of life involves hunting wild animals and gathering plant foods.

I

immigrants People who come to live in a land from other countries.

imperial Relating to the rule of an emperor or empress.

indigenous Native or originating from a country.

inlay To set or embed pieces of wood or metal in another material so that the surfaces are flat.

inscribed Lettering, pictures or patterns carved into stone or wood.

Inuit The native people of the North America Arctic and regions of Greenland, Alaska and Canada.

iron ore The rock that contains iron in its raw, natural form. The ore has to be crushed and then heated to release the metal.

irrigate To bring water to dry land.

irrigation The process of taking water to dry land for crops.

Islam The Muslim faith.

J

jade A highly prized smooth, green stone.

javelin A throwing spear.

junk A traditional Chinese sailing ship with square sails.

K

kaolin A fine white clay used in porcelain and paper making.

keel The long beam that supports the frame of a wooden ship, running along the base of the hull.

kiln Industrial oven in which clay or enamel, for example, are fired.

Koran Sacred book of Islam.

L

latitude Imaginary lines that run parallel to the Equator of the Earth. Navigators calculate latitude to know how far north or south they are.

legion A section of the Roman army made up only of Roman citizens.

legislation Making laws.

limestone A type of rock often used in building.

litter A portable bed or chair on which wealthy and privileged people were carried.

longitude A series of imaginary circles that pass around the Earth through the North and South poles. These are measured in degrees east and west of the Greenwich meridian. Navigators use longitude to know how far east or west they are.

loom A frame or machine used for weaving cloth.

M

magistrate An imperial officer of justice, similar to a local judge.

mercenary A soldier who fights in an army for money, not because it is the army of his own country.

merchant A person who buys and sells goods for a profit.

Mesopotamia The ancient name for the fertile region between the Tigris and Euphrates rivers.

metic A foreign resident in Athens, in ancient Greece.

midwife Someone who provides care and advice for women, before and after childbirth.

migration The movement of people, to other regions either permanently or at specific times of the year.

missionary A member of a religious organization who carries out charitable work and religious teaching.

mit'a Conscripted labour, owed to the Inca state as a form of tax.

monarchy Government by a king or queen.

monsoon Seasonal winds that blow in south Asia, bringing heavy rain.

N

nation Group of people who live in one territory and usually share the same language or history.

Near East The area comprising the countries of the eastern Mediterranean.

nobles People who are high in social rank.

nomad A member of a group that roams from place to place to find food or better land or to follow herds.

nomadic People who move from one area to another to find food, better land or to follow herds.

Normans Descendants of the Vikings who settled in a part of northern France (Normandy).

O

obelisk A pointed pillar, erected as a monument.

oligarchy Government by a group of rich and powerful people.

omen A sign of good or bad fortune in the future.

P

pack ice Floating sea ice.

papyrus A tall reed that is used to make a kind of paper.

parasite In Celtic times, the low-ranking follower of a chieftain.

Parthenon A temple in Athens.

peasant A poor country dweller.

pewter An alloy or mixture of metals, made from tin and lead.

phalanx A solid block of Greek hoplites (foot soldiers) in battle.

philosophy A Greek word meaning love of knowledge. Philosophy is the discipline of thinking about the meaning of life.

plate-armour Protective clothing made of overlapping plates of metal.

plebeian A member of the (free) common people of ancient Rome.

plumbline A weighted cord, held up to see if a wall or other construction is vertical.

plunder Stolen goods.

politics The art and science of government (from *polis*, city state).

porcelain The finest quality of pottery. It was made with kaolin and baked at a high temperature.

prehistoric Belonging to the time before written records were made.

priest An official who performs sacrifices and other religious rituals.

prospector A person who searches for valuable minerals such as gold.

prow The front end of a ship. Longship prows were often carved with dragon heads.

R

rampart A defensive mound of earth.

regent Someone who rules a country on behalf of another person.

relic Part of the body of a saint or martyr, or some object connected with them, preserved as an object of respect and honour.

relief A sculpture in which a design is carved from a flat surface such as a wall.

repoussé A metalworking technique that is used to create decorative raised patterns on a metal object.

republic A country that is not ruled by a king, queen or emperor but by representatives elected by citizens.

rigging The ropes used to support a ship's mast and sails.

rites Solemn procedures normally carried out for a religious purpose or as part of a ceremony.

ritual A procedure or series of actions that is often religious.

S

sacrifice The killing of a living thing in honour of the gods.

samurai Brave and highly trained Japanese warriors.

scabbard The container for a sword-blade. It is usually fixed to a belt.

seismoscope An instrument that reacts to earthquakes and tremors.

Senate The law-making assembly of the Roman Empire.

shaman A medicine man or woman believed to have powers to heal and contact spirits.

shield boss The metal plate that is fixed to the centre of a shield in order to protect the hand of the person holding the shield.

Silk Road The ancient trading route between China and Europe. This was the route by which Chinese silk reached Europe.

slaves People who were not free but were owned by their masters.

smelt To heat rock to a high temperature in order to melt and extract the metal within it.

society All the classes of people living in a particular community or country.

soldered Something that is joined together with pieces of melted metal.

spear-thrower A tool that acted as an extension of the arm, to give an extra leverage for throwing spears.

spindle A whirling tool used to make fibre, such as wool, into yarn for weaving.

standard A banner used by armies to rally their troops in battle or carry in parades.

status symbols Signs of wealth and power.

stela A tall stone pillar on which important records in words or pictures were inscribed.

stern The rear end of a ship.

stylus A pointed tool, such as the one used to scratch words on to a wax tablet.

surcoat A long, loose tunic worn over armour in Japan.

symbol A mark in a painting or on a stone that has a special meaning.

T

tachi The long sword that was carried by a samurai.

tapestry A cloth with a design sewn on to it.

tax Goods, money or services paid to a government.

temple A building used for worship or rituals. Such buildings were often specially designed for this purpose.

textile Any cloth that has been woven, such as silk or cotton.

Thing An assembly of free men that passed laws in Viking lands.

trading post General store where people from a wide area traded or swapped goods.

travois A platform for baggage formed by poles roped together. It was dragged by a person or tied to the back of a dog or horse.

treadwheel A wooden wheel turned by the feet of people, that was used to power mills or other machinery.

treaty Peace agreement.

tribe A group of people that shared a common language and way of life.

tribute Taxes paid in goods by conquered people.

tyranny Government by a cruel ruler.

U

umiak An Arctic rowing boat made from whalebone, covered with walrus hide and waterproofed with seal oil.

V

Venus figurine A small statue of a woman. She is usually shown with large hips, breasts and buttocks, and a full stomach. The figurines may have been worshipped as symbols of fertility or plenty, or carried as good luck charms.

W

warlord A man with a private army who controls a large region or territory by force.

woad A blue dye extracted from a plant that ancient Britons used to decorate their bodies.

Z

ziggurat A large temple with a broad, square base and stepped sides.

Index

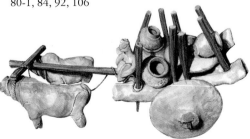

Acknowledgements

This edition is published by Hermes House

Hermes House is an imprint of Anness Publishing Ltd
Hermes House, 88–89 Blackfriars Road, London SE1 8HA
tel. 020 7401 2077; fax 020 7633 9499
info@anness.com

Published in the USA by Hermes House, Anness Publishing Inc.
27 West 20th Street, New York, NY 10011; fax 212 807 6813

A CIP catalogue record for this book is available from the British Library.

Publisher Joanna Lorenz
**Managing and Contributing
Editor** Gilly Cameron Cooper
Project Editor Rasha Elsaeed
Assistant Editor Sarah Uttridge
Editorial Reader Joy Wotton
Production Controller: Don
Campaniello
Authors Daud Ali, Jen Green,
Charlotte Hurdman, Fiona
Macdonald, Lorna Oakes,
Philip Steele, Michael Stotter,
Richard Tames
Consultants Cherry Alexander,
Nick Allen, Clara Bezanilla,
Felicity Cobbing, Penny Dransart,
Jenny Hall, Dr John Haywood,
Dr Robin Holgate, Michael
Johnson, Lloyd Laing, Jessie Lim,
Heidi Potter, Louise Schofield, Leslie Webster
Designers Simon Borrough, Matthew Cook, Joyce Mason, Caroline Reeves,
Margaret Sadler, Alison Walker, Stuart Watkinson at Ideas Into Print,
Sarah Williams
Special Photography John Freeman
Stylists Konika Shakar, Thomasina Smith, Melanie Williams

Printed and bound in China

Previously published as four separate volumes: *Tribes, Empires & Civilizations Through
the Ages*; *Politics, Society & Leadership Through the Ages*; *Travel, Conquest & Warfare
Through the Ages*; *Science, Crafts & Technology Through the Ages*.

10 9 8 7 6 5 4 3 2 1

Picture credits

b=bottom, t=top, c=centre, l=left, r=right

Ancient Art and Architecture Collection Ltd: cover main image

TRIBES, EMPIRES & CIVILIZATIONS
AKG: 16tl,20tl, 21cr, 33tr, 69r; Lesley and Roy Adkins:
47cr; Ancient Art and Architecture Collection: 22b, 27tc,
29ct, 40tr, 44cr,45br, 50b, 50l, 51tl, 51cl, 52cl,57tr, 57cr;
E.T Archive: 33c, 38l, 39tl, 39tr, 39bl, 63br; Bildarchiv
Preussischer Kulturbesitz: 21tr; Bridgeman Art Library:
28tr, 29tl, 41cr, 63tl; British Museum: 56tr; Macquitty
Collection: 35c; Corbis: 28cl, 64, 65br; James Davis: 35tr,
62br; C.M Dixon: 26tr, 26b, 27b, 40c, 44c, 45tr, 45cl, 65tl, 65tc,
65tr; Mary Evans Picture Library: 44tl, 45tl, 51bl, 51br; Robert
Harding: 17tr; Michael Holford: 17cr, 20tr, 21tl, 34tl, 47tr, 59c; Griffin Institute,
Ashmolean Museum: 22t; Link Photo Library: 29c; South American Picture Library:
58br, 59tl, 62tl, 63tl; Pierpont Morgan Library/Art source, New York: 13r; Peter
Newark: 68tl, 68tr, 69tl, 69tc; University of Oslo: 56cr; Ann and Bury Peerless: 33tl;
Tony Stone: 46-47; Visual Arts Library: 38r, 39br; Zefa: 26tl, 27tl, 27tr, 34c, 50r

POLITICS, SOCIETY & LEADERSHIP
AKG:78tl, 81tr, 82tr, 83c, 98tl, 121tl, 122tl, 127br; Lesley and Roy Adkins:
109t; The Ancient Art and Architecture Collection Ltd:84r, 84-85, 86br, 103tl,
107tl, 112t, 120cl, 121cl, 125tr; Japan Archive: 95tr, 95cr, 97tr, 98br, 99tl, 99tr
100bl, 101tr; The Bodleian Library: 119cl; The Bridgeman Art Library : 76bl,
77tr, 77br, 88cl, 89tr, 91c, 97tl, 104bl, 109b; The British Museum: 85t, 115b;
Bildarchiv Preussischer Kulturbesitz: 79bl, 80tl, 83tl; Bulloz: 79br; C M
Dixon:76tl, 86t, 94tl, 104br, 105tr, 105cl, 105br, 106l, 108bl, 110tl, 115t,
115cl, 116tl, 117bl, 117tr, 127bl; Musee Calvet, Avignon: 110br; Christies: 97bl;
Peter Clayton: 87t, 87b, 103bl; Corbis-Bettman: 126tr; Corbis: 88tl, 91tl, 95tl,
128tl, 128br, 129tr, 129cl, 129cr, 129b; Sylvia Corday: 77tl; E.T Archive (Art
Archive): 70-71, 89tl, 90tl, 93t, 93bl, 96br, 96bl, 116brx, 119tl; Mary Evans
Picture Library : 90c, 93br, 102tr, 106r; Werner Forman Archive: 83bl, 92bl,
94bl, 97cr, 111bl, 120tr, 123br, 124cl, 124tr; Robert Harding: 77bl, 80cr, 81cl;
David Hawkins: 79t; Michael Holford: 86bl, 95br, 108tr, 108br, 112cl, 117br,
118br; The Hutchison Library: 96rl, 101bl, 101br; Michael Nicholson: 102c,
103tr; National Museum of Wales: 111br; Peter Newark's Pictures: 126l, 127tl,
127tr; Andes Press Agency: 125tl; Mick Sharp: 112b, 113t, 115cl; South
American Photo Library: 118tl, 119tr, 121tr, 123tl, 123tr, 125cl; Still
Pictures:122b; Tony Stone: 91tr; TRIP:92br; University of Oslo: 114t; Visual
Arts Library: 116br; Victoria and Albert Museum: 89c; York University Trust:
113l; Zefa: 84l, 85b, 92tr, 114b

TRAVEL, CONQUEST & WARFARE
AKG: 144br, 155c, 170tl, 172tr, 177t, 184b, 186bl, 187tl, 179b, 188tl, 189tr;
Lesley and Roy Adkins: 165tl; B and C Alexander: 137tl, 151tl, 151cr; The Ancient
Art and Architecture Collection Ltd:138l, 139r, 142tl, 144br, 159b, 161tl, 162tr,
164tr, 166tl, 169tr, 173tl; Japan Archive: 159tr, 160tl; Bildarchiv Preussischer
Kulturbesitz: 154tl, 154cl; The Bridgeman Art Library: 145tr, 145bl, 145br, 157br,
174b, 175tr, 175cl, 183bl; The British Museum: 167b; Bruce Coleman: 153bl;
Bulloz: 154cr; Christies: 158bl, 158br, 159tl, 161bl; Corbis: 146bl, 151bl, 177b,
186tl; Corbis-Bettman: 176b, 176tl, 177bl, 186br, 188bl, 189bl; Sue Cunningham
Photographic: 182tr, 184cr; James Davis: 149c; C.M Dixon: 136tl, 143cl, 162cl,
163tr, 165tr, 165b, 166l, 167tr, 171tl, 171tr, 172tr, 174tr, 179c, 189tl; E.T Archive
(Art Archive): 140bl, 143cl, 145tr, 156tl, 156cr, 157t, 153r, 156tl, 156br, 157tr,
173tr, 173bl, 180br, 182tl, 184tl; Planet Earth pictures: 150bl; Mary Evans Picture
Library: 130-31, 149t, 151tr, 153tl, 163cl, 164br, 166t, 180tl, 185b; Fine Art
Photographic Library:168c; Werner Forman Archive: 137c, 141bl, 147cl, 171bl, 171c,
175tl, 183cl; Fortean Picture Library: 136r; Idemitsu Museum of Arts: 161cl; Images
Colour Library: 147tr; Robert Harding: 147tr, 148tl, 149c; Michael Holford: 146tl,
147t, 155t, 158tl, 160br, 164bl, 173br, 181; Radio Times Hulton Picture Library:
138r, 139r; Jenny Laing: 169tl, 169bl; MacQuitty Collection: 140tl, 141cl, 141br;
Peter Newark's Pictures: 187tr; Oxford Scientific Films: 150tl; Mick Sharp: 168tl,
175br; Skyscan: 169br; South American Picture Library: 178r, 181, 182c, 183t,
184tl, 185tr; Visual Arts Library: 141rtl, 142cl, 152c, 179r, 180bl; Zefa: 138r, 139l.

SCIENCE, CRAFTS & TECHNOLOGY
AKG: 230tl, 231bl, 231br, 233tr, 243bl, 247tl; The Ancient Art and Architecture
Collection Ltd: 199tr, 201tl, 214cl, 217bl, 219c, 228tl, 234cr, 243, 245tr; Ancient
Egypt Picture library: 209r, 209br; Japan Archive: 229tl; The Bridgeman Art Library:
202cl, 202cr, 203tr, 225bl, 227tl, 227cl, 242cl; Peter Clayton: 199cr, 213tr, 215tl,
215cl; Bruce Coleman: 199bl, 221tl; Corbis-Bettman: 246br; Corbis: 202tl, 203tl;
C M Dixon: 197tr, 197c, 198t, 198bl, 198br, 200l, 208l, 208r, 212cl, 212tr, 216l, 216r,
218cl, 218tr, 219bl, 228br, 230c, 231tl, 232tl, 246l, 247tr; Sue Cunningham
Photographic: 244l; E.T Archive (Art Archive): 190-91, 224bl, 226tr, 235tr, 239tl,
239cl, 241c; Mary Evans Picture Library: 199tl, 213cl, 214tl, 214cr; Werner Forman
Archive: 221bl, 221br, 232bl, 238cr, 240l, 245bl; Geoscience Features Picture
library: 217tr; Michael Holford: 217tl, 218bl, 218br, 240cr; The Hutchison
Library: 229tl; Images of India: 202cl; Jenny Laing: 233bl; Macquitty Collection:
224tr; Peter Newark's Pictures: 246tr; Andes Press Agency: 242tr; Science Photo
Library: 241cl; South American Photo Library: 236c, 238c, 243tl, 243tr, 244t;
Statens Historik Museum: 235c; Still Pictures: 241tr, 242cr, 237tl. Zefa: 220tl,
221tr, 225tr, 225br.

NOTES

NOTES

NOTES

NOTES

NOTES

NOTES

NOTES

NOTES